Bloom's Modern Critical Interpretations

Alice's Adventures in
  Wonderland
The Adventures of
  Huckleberry Finn
All Quiet on the
  Western Front
Animal Farm
As You Like It
The Ballad of the Sad
  Café
Beloved
Beowulf
Billy Budd, Benito
  Cereno, Bartleby the
  Scrivener, and Other
  Tales
Black Boy
The Bluest Eye
Brave New World
Cat on a Hot Tin
  Roof
The Catcher in the
  Rye
Catch-22
Cat's Cradle
The Color Purple
Crime and
  Punishment
The Crucible
Darkness at Noon
David Copperfield
Death of a Salesman
The Death of Artemio
  Cruz
The Divine Comedy
Don Quixote
Dracula
Dubliners
Emerson's Essays
Emma
Fahrenheit 451

A Farewell to Arms
Frankenstein
The General Prologue
  to the Canterbury
  Tales
The Grapes of
  Wrath
Great Expectations
The Great Gatsby
Gulliver's Travels
Hamlet
The Handmaid's Tale
Heart of Darkness
I Know Why the
  Caged Bird Sings
The Iliad
The Interpretation of
  Dreams
Invisible Man
Jane Eyre
The Joy Luck Club
Julius Caesar
The Jungle
King Lear
Long Day's Journey
  Into Night
Lord of the Flies
The Lord of the Rings
Love in the Time of
  Cholera
Macbeth
The Man Without
  Qualities
The Merchant of
  Venice
The Metamorphosis
A Midsummer Night's
  Dream
Miss Lonelyhearts
Moby-Dick
My Ántonia

Native Son
Night
1984
The Odyssey
Oedipus Rex
The Old Man and the
  Sea
On the Road
One Flew Over the
  Cuckoo's Nest
One Hundred Years of
  Solitude
Othello
Paradise Lost
The Pardoner's Tale
A Passage to India
Persuasion
Portnoy's Complaint
A Portrait of the Artist
  as a Young Man
Pride and Prejudice
Ragtime
The Red Badge of
  Courage
The Rime of the
  Ancient Mariner
Romeo & Juliet
The Rubáiyát of Omar
  Khayyám
The Scarlet Letter
A Scholarly Look at
  The Diary of Anne
  Frank
A Separate Peace
Silas Marner
Slaughterhouse-Five
Song of Myself
Song of Solomon
The Sonnets of
  William Shakespeare
Sophie's Choice

Bloom's Modern Critical Interpretations

The Sound and the Fury

The Stranger

A Streetcar Named Desire

Sula

The Sun Also Rises

The Tale of Genji

A Tale of Two Cities

The Tales of Poe

The Tempest

Tess of the D'Urbervilles

Their Eyes Were Watching God

Things Fall Apart

To Kill a Mockingbird

Ulysses

Waiting for Godot

Walden

The Waste Land

White Noise

Wuthering Heights

Young Goodman Brown

Bloom's Modern Critical Interpretations

Sophocles'
OEDIPUS REX
Updated Edition

Edited and with an introduction by
Harold Bloom
Sterling Professor of the Humanities
Yale University

CHELSEA HOUSE
PUBLISHERS
An imprint of Infobase Publishing

Bloom's Modern Critical Interpretations: Oedipus Rex, Updated Edition

©2007 Infobase Publishing

Introduction ©2007 by Harold Bloom

Chelsea House
An imprint of Infobase Publishing
132 West 31st Street
New York NY 10001

Library of Congress Cataloging-in-Publication Data
Sophocles' Oedipus Rex / Harold Bloom, editor. — Updated ed.
     p. cm.—(Bloom's modern critical interpretations)
  Includes bibliographical references and index.
  ISBN 0-7910-9309-3 (hardcover)
  1. Sophocles. Oedipus Rex. 2. Oedipus (Greek mythology) in
literature. I. Bloom, Harold. II. Title. III. Series.
PA4413.O7S66 2006
882'01—dc22   2006025276

Contributing Editor: Allison Stielau
Cover design by Keith Trego
Cover photo © Scala/Art Resource, NY

Printed in the United States of America
Bang EJB 10 9 8 7 6 5 4 3 2 1

This book is printed on acid-free paper.

Contents

Editor's Note   vii

Introduction   1
    Harold Bloom

Oedipus: Ritual and Play   5
    Francis Fergusson

On Misunderstanding the *Oedipus Rex*   17
    E.R. Dodds

The Innocence of Oedipus:
The Philosophers on *Oedipus the King, Part III*   31
    Thomas Gould

Introduction to *Oedipus the King*   71
    Bernard Knox

Speech and Silence: *Oedipus the King*   91
    Rebecca W. Bushnell

Oedipus and Teiresias   105
    Frederick Ahl

Introduction: What Is a Father?   141
    Pietro Pucci

The *Oedipus Rex* and the Ancient Unconscious   155
    Martha C. Nussbaum

Knowingness and Abandonment:
An Oedipus for Our Time   183
    Jonathan Lear

Life's Tragic Shape:
Plot, Design, and Destiny   205
    Charles Segal

Chronology   225

Contributors   227

Bibliography   231

Acknowledgments   235

Index   237

Editor's Note

My introduction emphasizes the guiltlessness of Oedipus and, by Sophoclean extension, of most of us. Thomas De Quincey said that the true answer to the riddle of the sphinx was not Man, but Oedipus himself.

Francis Fergusson sees Oedipus as a ritualistic scapegoat, but one who is more dramatic than theological, while E.R. Dodds urges us to understand an ultimate nihilism in the play, akin to the vision of Samuel Beckett.

Thomas Gould rightly insists that Oedipus is innocent, and thus allows the drama its cleansing function, after which Bernard Knox concludes that Oedipus had only one freedom: to choose the truth, by finding it out for himself.

In Rebecca W. Bushnell's interpretation, Oedipus attempts and fails (as we all must) to write his own story, while for Frederick Ahl the envious and hostile Tiresias nevertheless helps the hero to realize the truth.

Pietro Pucci, founding himself on the Post-Freudian convention that fatherhood itself is a fiction, calls into question also the possibility of truth, in the play or beyond.

The philosopher Martha C. Nussbaum suggests the pragmatic existence of an "ancient unconsciousness," and she calls for a confrontation between this archaic understanding and both Kleinian analysis and cognitive psychology.

In an intricate defense against "Freud-bashing," the Freudian philosopher Jonathan Lear shrewdly reminds us that the fantasies of Oedipus are not Oedipal, but concern his fear of lowly birth.

Charles Segal concludes this volume by judging the labyrinthine nature of Sophocles' tragedy to be endlessly paradoxical, because the unriddling hero confronts the truth and his own death as one fused entity.

HAROLD BLOOM

Introduction

Whether there is a "tragic flaw," a *hamartia*, in King Oedipus is uncertain, though I doubt it, as he is hardly a figure who shoots wide of the mark. Accuracy is implicit in his nature. We can be certain that he is free of that masterpiece of ambivalence—Freud's Oedipal complex. In the Age of Freud, we are uncertain what to do with a guiltless Oedipus, but that does appear to be the condition of Sophocles' hero. We cannot read *Oedipus the King* as we read the *Iliad* of Homer, where the gods matter enormously. And even more, we know it is absurd to read Oedipus as though it were written by Yahwist, or the authors of Jeremiah or Job, let alone of the Gospels. We can complete our obstacle course by warning ourselves not to compound Oedipus with *Hamlet* or *Lear*. Homer and the Bible, Shakespeare and Freud, teach us only how not to read Sophocles.

When I was younger, I was persuaded by Cedric Whitman's eloquent book on Sophocles to read Oedipus as a tragedy of "heroic humanism." I am not so persuaded now, not because I am less attracted by a humanistic heroism, but because I am uncertain how such a stance allows for tragedy. William Blake's humanism was more than heroic, being apocalyptic, but it too would not authorize tragedy. However the meaning of Oedipus is to be interpreted in our post–Nietzchean age, the play is surely tragedy, or the genre will lose coherence. E. R. Dodds, perhaps assimilating Sophocles to the *Iliad*, supposed that the tragedy of Oedipus honored the gods, without judging them to be benign or even just. Bernard Knox argues that the greatness of the gods and the greatness of Oedipus are irreconcilable, with tragedy the result of that schism. That reduces to the Hegelian view of tragedy as an agon between right and right, but Knox gives the preference to Oedipus, since the gods, being ever victorious, therefore cannot be heroic. A less Homeric reading than Dodds's, this seems to me too much our sense of heroism—Malraux perhaps, rather than Sophocles.

Freud charmingly attributed to Sophocles, as a precursor of psychoanalysis, the ability to have made possible a self–analysis for the playgoer. But then Freud called *Oedipus* an "immoral play," since the gods ordained incest and patricide. Oedipus therefore participates in our universal unconscious sense of guilt, but on this reading so do the gods. I sometimes wish that Freud had turned to Aeschylus instead, and given us the Prometheus complex rather than the Oedipus complex. Plato is Oedipal in regard to Homer, but Sophocles is not. I hardly think that Sophocles would have chastised Homer for impiety, but then, as I read it, the tragedy of Oedipus takes up no more skeptical stance than that of Plato, unless one interprets Plato as Montaigne wished to interpret him.

What does any discerning reader remember most vividly about *Oedipus the King*? Almost certainly, the answer must be the scene of the king's self–blinding, as narrated by the second messenger, here in David Grene's version:

> By her own hand. The worst of what was done
> you cannot know. You did not see the sight.
> Yet in so far as I remember it
> you'll hear the end of our unlucky queen.
> When she cam raging into the house she went
> straight to her marriage bed, tearing her hair
> with both her hands, and crying upon Laius
> long dead—Do you remember, Laius,
> that night long past which bred a child for us
> to send you to your death and leave
> a mother making children with her son?
> And then she groaned and cursed the bed in which
> she brought forth husband by her husband, children
> by her own child, an infamous double bond.
> How after that she died I do not know,—
> for Oedipus distracted us from seeing.
> He burst upon us shouting and we looked

to him as he paced frantically around,
begging us always: Give me a sword, I say,
to find this wife no wife, this mother's womb,
this field of double sowing whence I sprang
and where I sowed my children! As he raved
some god showed him the way—none of us there.
Bellowing terribly and led by some
invisible guide he rushed on the two doors, —
wrenching the hollow bolts out of their sockets,
he charges inside. There, there, we saw his wife
hanging, the twisted rope around her neck.
When he saw her, he cried out fearfully
and cut loose the dangling noose. Then, as she lay,
poor woman, on the ground, what happened after,
was terrible to see. He tore the brooches—
the gold chased brooches fastening her robe—
away from her and lifting them high
dashed them on his own eyeballs, shrieking out
such things as: they will never see the crime
I have committed or had done upon me!
Dark eyes, now on the days to come, look on
forbidden faces, do not recognize
those whom you long for—with such imprecations
he struck his eyes again and yet again
with the brooches. And the bleeding eyeballs gushed
and stained his beard—no sluggish oozing drops
but a black rain and bloody hail poured down.
So it has broken—and not on one head
but troubles mixed for husband and wife.
The fortune of the days gone by was true
good fortune—but today groans and destruction
and death and shame—of all ills can be named
not one is missing.
(1.1237–86)

The scene, too terrible for acting out, seems also too dreadful for
representation in language. Oedipus, desiring to put a sword in the womb of
Jocasta, is led by "some god" to where he can break through the two doors
(I shudder as I remember Walt Whitman's beautiful trope for watching a
woman in childbirth, "I recline by the sills of the exquisite flexible doors").

Fortunately finding Jocasta self–slain, lest he add the crime of matricide to patricide and incest, Oedipus, repeatedly stabbing his eyes with Jocasta's brooches, passes judgment not so much upon seeing as upon the seen, and so upon the light by which we see. I interpret this as his protest against Apollo, which brings both the light and the plague. The Freudian trope of blinding for castration seems to me less relevant here than the outcry against the god.

To protest Apollo is necessarily dialectical, since the pride and agility of the intellect of Oedipus, remorselessly searching out the truth, in some sense is also against the nature of truth. In this vision of reality, you shall know the truth, and the truth will make you mad. What would make Oedipus free? Nothing that happens in this play, must be the answer, nor does it seem that becoming an oracular god later on makes you free either. If you cannot be free of the gods, then you cannot be made free, and even acting as though your daemon is your destiny will not help you either.

The startling ignorance of Oedipus when the drama begins is the *given* of the play, and cannot be questioned or disallowed. Voltaire was scathing upon this, but the ignorance of the wise and the learned remains an ancient truth of psychology, and torments us every day. I surmise that this is the true force of Freud's Oedipus complex: not the unconscious sense of guilt, but the necessity of ignorance, lest the reality–principle destroy us. Nietzsche said it not in praise of art, but so as to indicate the essential limitation of art. Sophoclean irony is more eloquent yet:

> CREON: Do not seek to be master in everything, for the things you mastered did not follow you throughout your life.
> (*As Creon and Oedipus go out.*)

> CHORUS: You that live in my ancestral Thebes, behold this Oedipus, —him who knew the famous riddles and was a man most masterful; not a citizen who did not look with envy on his lot—see him now and see the breakers of misfortune swallow him! Look upon that last day always. Count no mortal happy till he has passed the final limit of his life secure from pain.

FRANCIS FERGUSSON

Oedipus: *Ritual and Play*

The Cambridge School of Classical Anthropologists has shown in great detail that the form of Greek tragedy follows the form of a very ancient ritual, that of the *Enniautos-Daimon*, or seasonal god.[1] This was one of the most influential discoveries of the last few generations, and it gives us new insights into *Oedipus* which I think are not yet completely explored. The clue to Sophocles' dramatizing of the myth of Oedipus is to be found in this ancient ritual, which had a similar form and meaning—that is, it also moved in the "tragic rhythm."[2]

Experts in classical anthropology, like experts in other fields, dispute innumerable questions of fact and of interpretation which the layman can only pass over in respectful silence. One of the thornier questions seems to be whether myth or ritual came first. Is the ancient ceremony merely an enactment of the Ur-Myth of the year-god—Attis, or Adonis, or Osiris, or the "Fisher-King"—in any case that Hero-King-Father-High-Priest who fights with his rival, is slain and dismembered, then rises anew with the spring season? Or did the innumerable myths of this kind arise to "explain" a ritual which was perhaps mimed or danced or sung to celebrate the annual change of season?

For the purpose of understanding the form and meaning of *Oedipus*, it is not necessary to worry about the answer to this question of historic fact.

From *The Idea of a Theater*, by Francis Fergusson, pp. 26–39. © 1949 by Princeton University Press.

The figure of Oedipus himself fulfills all the requirements of the scapegoat, the dismembered king or god-figure. The situation in which Thebes is presented at the beginning of the play—in peril of its life; its crops, its herds, its women mysteriously infertile, signs of a mortal disease of the City, and the disfavor of the gods—is like the withering which winter brings, and calls, in the same way, for struggle, dismemberment, death, and renewal. And this tragic sequence is the substance of the play. It is enough to know that myth and ritual are close together in their genesis, two direct imitations of the perennial experience of the race.

But when one considers *Oedipus* as a ritual one understands it in ways which one cannot by thinking of it merely as a dramatization of a story, even that story. Harrison has shown that the Festival of Dionysos, based ultimately upon the yearly vegetation ceremonies, included *rites de passage*, like that celebrating the assumption of adulthood—celebrations of the mystery of individual growth and development. At the same time, it was a prayer for the welfare of the whole City; and this welfare was understood not only as material prosperity, but also as the natural order of the family, the ancestors, the present members, and the generations still to come, and, by the same token, obedience to the gods who were jealous, each in his own province, of this natural and divinely sanctioned order and proportion.

We must suppose that Sophocles' audience (the whole population of the City) came early, prepared to spend the day in the bleachers. At their feet was the semicircular dancing-ground for the chorus, and the thrones for the priests, and the altar. Behind that was the raised platform for the principal actors, backed by the all-purpose, emblematic façade, which would presently be taken to represent Oedipus' palace in Thebes. The actors were not professionals in our sense, but citizens selected for a religious office, and Sophocles himself had trained them and the chorus.

This crowd must have had as much appetite for thrills and diversion as the crowds who assemble in our day for football games and musical comedies, and Sophocles certainly holds the attention with an exciting show. At the same time his audience must have been alert for the fine points of poetry and dramaturgy, for *Oedipus* is being offered in competition with other plays on the same bill. But the element which distinguishes this theater, giving it its unique directness and depth, is the *ritual expectancy* which Sophocles assumed in his audience. The nearest thing we have to this ritual sense of theater is, I suppose, to be found at an Easter performance of the *Mattias Passion*. We also can observe something similar in the dances and ritual mummery of the Pueblo Indians. Sophocles' audience must have been prepared, like the Indians standing around their plaza, to consider the playing, the make-believe it was about to see—the choral invocations, with dancing and chanting; the reasoned discourses and the terrible combats of the protagonists; the mourning, the rejoicing, and the contemplation of the final stage-picture or epiphany—as imitating and celebrating the mystery of human nature and destiny. And this mystery was at once that of individual growth and development, and that of the precarious life of the human City.

I have indicated how Sophocles presents the life of the mythic Oedipus in the tragic rhythm, the mysterious quest of life. Oedipus is shown seeking his own true being; but at the same time and by the same token, the welfare of the City. When one considers the ritual form of the whole play, it becomes evident that it presents the tragic but perennial, even normal, quest of the whole City for its well-being. In this larger action, Oedipus is only the protagonist, the first and most important champion. This tragic quest is realized by all the characters in their various ways; but in the development of the action as a whole if is the chorus alone that plays a part as important as that of Oedipus; its counterpart, in fact. The chorus holds the balance between Oedipus and his antagonists, marks the progress of their struggles, and restates the main theme, and its new variation, after each dialogue or agon. The ancient ritual was probably performed by a chorus alone without individual developments and variations, and the chorus, in *Oedipus*, is still the element that throws most light on the ritual form of the play as a whole.

The chorus consists of twelve or fifteen "Elders of Thebes." This group is not intended to represent literally all of the citizens either of Thebes or of Athens. The play opens with a large delegation of Theban citizens before Oedipus' palace, and the chorus proper does not enter until after the prologue. Nor does the chorus speak directly for the Athenian audience; we are asked throughout to make-believe that the theater is the agora at Thebes; and at the same time Sophocles' audience is witnessing a ritual. It would, I think, be more accurate to say that the chorus represents the point of view and the faith of Thebes as a whole, and, by analogy, of the Athenian audience. Their errand before Oedipus' palace is like that of Sophocles' audience in the theater: they are watching a sacred combat, in the issue of which they have an ail-important and official stake. Thus they represent the audience and the citizens in a particular way—not as a mob formed in response to some momentary feeling, but rather as an organ of a highly self-conscious community: something closer to the "conscience of the race" than to the overheated affectivity of a mob.

According to Aristotle, a Sophoclean chorus is a character that takes an important role in the action of the play, instead of merely making incidental music between the scenes, as in the plays of Euripides. The chorus may be described as a group personality, like an old Parliament. It has its own traditions, habits of thought and feeling, and mode of being. It exists, in a sense, as a living entity, but not with the sharp actuality of an individual. It perceives; but its perception is at once wider and vaguer than that of a single man. It shares, in its way, the seeking action of the play as a whole; but it cannot act in all the modes; it depends upon the chief agonists to invent and try out the detail of policy, just as a rather helpless but critical Parliament depends upon the Prime Minister to act but, in its less specific form of life, survives his destruction.

When the chorus enters after the prologue, with its questions, its invocation of the various gods, and its focus upon the hidden and jeopardized welfare of the City—Athens or Thebes—the list of essential *dramatis personae*, as well as the elements needed to celebrate the ritual, is complete, and the main action can begin. It is the function of the chorus to mark the stages of this action, and to perform the suffering and perceiving part of the tragic rhythm. The protagonist and his antagonists develop the "purpose" with which the tragic sequence begins; the chorus, with its less than individual being, broods over the agons, marks their stages with a word (like that of the chorus leader in the middle of the Tiresias scene), and (expressing its emotions and visions in song and dance) suffers the results, and the new perception at the end of the fight.

The choral odes are lyrics but they are not to be understood as poetry, the art of words, only, for they are intended also to be danced and sung. And though each chorus has its own shape, like that of a discrete lyric—its beginning, middle, and end—it represents also one passion or pathos in the changing action of the whole. This passion, like the other moments in the tragic rhythm, is felt at so general or, rather, so deep a level that it seems to contain both the mob ferocity that Nietzsche felt in it and, at the other extreme, the patience of prayer. It is informed by faith in the unseen order of nature and the gods, and moves through a sequence of modes of suffering. This may be illustrated from the chorus a have quoted at the end of the Tiresias scene.

It begins (close to the savage emotion of the end of the fight) with images suggesting that cruel "Bacchic frenzy" which is supposed to be the common root of tragedy and of the "old" comedy: "In panoply of fire and lightning / The son of Zeus now springs upon him." In the first antistrophe these images come together more clearly as we relish the chase; and the fleeing culprit, as we imagine him, begins to resemble Oedipus, who is lame, and always associated with the rough wilderness of Kitharon. But in the second strophe, as though appalled by its ambivalent feelings and the imagined possibilities, the chorus sinks back into a more dark and patient posture of suffering, "in awe," "hovering in hope." In the second antistrophe this is developed into something like the orthodox Christian attitude of prayer, based on faith, and assuming the possibility of a hitherto unimaginable truth and answer: "Zeus and Apollo are wise," etc. The whole chorus then ends with a new vision of Oedipus, of the culprit, and of the direction in which the welfare of the City is to be sought. This vision is still colored by the chorus's human love of Oedipus as Hero, for the chorus has still its own purgation to complete, cannot as yet accept completely either the suffering in store for it, or Oedipus as scapegoat. But it marks the end of the first complete "purpose-passion-perception" unit, and lays the basis for the new purpose which will begin the next unit.

It is also to be noted that the chorus changes the scene which we, as audience, are to imagine. During the agon between Oedipus and Tiresias, our attention is fixed upon their clash, and the scene is literal, close, and immediate: before Oedipus' palace. When the fighters depart and the choral music starts, the focus suddenly widens, as though we had been removed to a distance. We become aware of the interested City around the bright arena; and beyond that, still more dimly, of Nature, sacred to the hidden gods. Mr. Burke has expounded the fertile notion that human action may be understood in terms of the scene in which it occurs, and vice versa: the scene is defined by the mode of action. The chorus's action is not limited by the sharp, rationalized purposes of the protagonist; its mode of action, more patient, less sharply realized, is cognate with a wider, if less accurate, awareness of the scene of human life. But the chorus's action, as I have remarked, is not that of passion itself (Nietzsche's cosmic void of night) but suffering informed by the faith of the tribe in a human and a divinely sanctioned natural order: "If such deeds as these are honored," the chorus asks after Jocasta's impiety, "why should I dance and sing?" (lines 894, 895). Thus it is one of the most important functions of the chorus to reveal, in its widest and most mysterious extent, the theater of human life which the play, and indeed the whole Festival of Dionysos, assumed. Even when the chorus does not speak, but only watches, it maintains this theme and this perspective—ready to take the whole stage when the fighters depart.

If one thinks of the movement of the play, it appears that the tragic rhythm analyzes human action temporally into successive modes, as a crystal analyzes a white beam of light spatially into the colored bands of the spectrum. The chorus, always present, represents one of these modes, and at the recurrent moments when reasoned purpose is gone, it takes the stage with its faith-informed passion, moving through an ordered succession of modes of suffering, to a new perception of the immediate situation.

SOPHOCLES AND EURIPIDES, THE RATIONALIST

Oedipus Rex is a changing image of human life and action which could have been formed only in the mirror of the tragic theater of the Festival of Dionysos. The perspectives of the myth, of the rituals, and of the traditional *hodos*, the way of life of the City—"habits of thought and feeling" which constitute the traditional wisdom of the race—were all required to make this play possible. That is why we have to try to regain these perspectives if we are to understand the written play which has come down to us: the analysis of the play leads to an analysis of the theater in which it was formed.

But though the theater was there, everyone could not use it to the full: Sophocles was required. This becomes clear if one considers the very different use which Euripides, Sophocles' contemporary, makes of the tragic theater and its ritual forms.

Professor Gilbert Murray has explained in detail how the tragic form is derived from the ritual form; and he has demonstrated the ritual forms which are preserved in each of the extant Greek tragedies. In general, the ritual had its agon, or sacred combat, between the old King, or god or hero, and the new, corresponding to the agons in the tragedies, and the clear "purpose" moment of the tragic rhythm. It had its *Sparagmos*, in which the royal victim was literally or symbolically torn asunder, followed by the lamentation and/or rejoicing of the chorus: elements which correspond to the moments of "passion." The ritual had its messenger, its recognition scene, and its epiphany; various plot devices for representing the moment of "perception" which follows the "pathos." Professor Murray, in a word, studies the art of tragedy in the light of ritual forms, and thus, throws a really new light upon Aristotle's *Poetics*. The parts of the ritual would appear to correspond to parts of the plot, like recognitions and scenes of suffering, which Aristotle mentions, but, in the text which has come down to us, fails to expound completely. In this view, both the ritual and the more highly elaborated and individualized art of tragedy would be "imitating" action in the tragic rhythm; the parts of the ritual, and the parts of the plot, would both be devices for showing forth the three moments of this rhythm.

Professor Murray, however, does not make precisely these deductions. Unlike Aristotle, he takes the plays of Euripides, rather than Sophocles' *Oedipus*, as the patterns of the tragic form. That is because his attitude to the ritual forms is like Euripides' own: he responds to their purely theatrical effectiveness, but has no interest or belief in the pre-rational image of human nature and destiny which the ritual conveyed; which Sophocles felt as still alive and significant for his generation, and presented once more in *Oedipus*. Professor Murray shows that Euripides restored the literal ritual much more accurately than Sophocles—his epiphanies, for example, are usually the bodily showing-forth of a very human god, who cynically expounds his cruel part in the proceedings; while the "epiphany" in *Oedipus*, the final tableau of the blind old man with his incestuous brood, merely conveys the moral truth which underlay the action, and implies the anagoge: human dependence upon a mysterious and divine order of nature. Perhaps these distinctions may be summarized as follows: Professor Murray is interested in the ritual forms in abstraction from all content; Sophocles saw also the spiritual content of the old forms: understood them at a level deeper than the literal, as imitations of an action still "true" to life in his sophisticated age.

Though Euripides and Sophocles wrote at the same time and for the same theater, one cannot understand either the form or the meaning of Euripides' plays on the basis of Sophocles' dramaturgy. The beautiful lyrics sung by Euripides' choruses are, as I have said, incidental music rather than organic parts of the action; they are not based upon the feeling that all have a stake in the common way of life and therefore in the issue of the present action. Euripides' individualistic heroes find no light in their suffering, and bring no renewal to the moral life of the community: they are at war with the very clear, human, and malicious gods, and what they suffer, they suffer unjustly and to no good end. Where Sophocles' celebrated irony seems to envisage the *condition humaine* itself—the plight of the psyche in a world which is ultimately mysterious to it—Euripides' ironies are all aimed at the incredible "gods" and at the superstitions of those who believe in them. In short, if these two writers both used the tragic theater, they did so in very different ways.

Verral's *Euripides the Rationalist* shows very clearly what the basis of Euripides' dramaturgy is. His use of myth and ritual is like that which Cocteau or, still more exactly, Sartre makes of them—for parody or satirical exposition, but without any belief in their meaning. If Euripides presents the plight of Electra in realistic detail, it is because he wants us to feel the suffering of the individual without benefit of any objective moral or cosmic order—with an almost sensational immediacy: he does not see the myth, as a whole, as significant as such. If he brings Apollo, in the flesh, before us, it is not because he "believes" in Apollo, but because he disbelieves in him, and wishes to reveal this figment of the Greek imagination as, literally, incredible. He depends as much as Sophocles upon the common heritage of ritual and myth: but he "reduces" its form and images to the uses of parody and metaphorical illustration, in the manner of Ovid and of the French Neoclassic tradition. And the human action he reveals is the extremely modern one of the psyche caught in the categories its reason invents, responding with unmitigated sharpness to the feeling of the moment, but cut off from the deepest level of experience, where the mysterious world is yet felt as real and prior to our inventions, demands, and criticisms.

Though Sophocles was not using the myths and ritual forms of the tragic theater for parody and to satirize their tradition, it does not appear that he had any more naïve belief in their literal validity than Euripides did. He would not, for his purpose, have had to ask himself whether the myth of Oedipus conveyed any historic facts. He would not have had to believe that the performance of *Oedipus*, or even the Festival of Dionysos itself, would assure the Athenians a good crop of children and olives. On the contrary he must have felt that the tragic rhythm of action which he discerned in the myth, which he felt as underlying the forms of the ritual, and which he realized in so many ways in his play, was a deeper version of human life than any particular manifestation of it, or any conceptual understanding of it, whether scientific and rationalistic, of theological; yet potentially including them all. If one takes Mr. Troy's suggestion, one might say, using the Medieval notion of fourfold symbolism, that Sophocles might well have taken myth and ritual as literally "fictions," yet still have accepted their deeper meanings—trope, allegory, and anagoge—as valid.

Oedipus: The Imitation of an Action

The general notion we used to compare the forms and spiritual content of tragedy and of ancient ritual was the "imitation of action." Ritual imitates action in one way, tragedy in another; and Sophocles' use of ritual forms indicates that he sensed the tragic rhythm common to both.

But the language, plot, characters of the play may also be understood in more detail and in relation to each other as imitations, in their various media, of the one action. I have already quoted Coleridge on the unity of action: "not properly a rule," he calls it, "but in itself the great end, not only of the drama, but of the epic, lyric, even to the candle-flame cone of an epigram—not only of poetry, but of poesy in general, as the proper generic term inclusive of all the fine arts, as its species."[3] Probably the influence of Coleridge partly accounts for the revival of this notion of action which underlies the recent studies of poetry which I have mentioned. Mr. Burke's phrase, "language as symbolic action," expresses the idea, and so does his dictum: "The poet spontaneously knows that 'beauty is as beauty *does*' (that the 'state' must be embodied in an 'actualization')." (*Four Tropes*.)

This idea of action, and of the play as the imitation of an action, is ultimately derived from the Poetics. This derivation is explained in the Appendix. At this point I wish to show how the complex form of *Oedipus*—

its plot, characters, and discourse—may be understood as the imitation of a certain action.

The action of the play is the quest for Laius' slayer. That is the overall aim which informs it "to find the culprit in order to purify human life," as it may be put. Sophocles must have seen this seeking action as the real life of the Oedipus myth, discerning it through the personages and events as one discerns "life in a plant through the green leaves." Moreover, he must have seen this particular action as a type, or crucial instance, of human life in general; and hence he was able to present it in the form of the ancient ritual which also presents and celebrates the perennial mystery of human life and action. Thus by "action" I do not mean the events of the story but the focus or aim of psychic life from which the events, in that situation, result.

If Sophocles was imitating action in this sense, one may schematically imagine his work of composition in three stages, three mimetic acts: 1. He makes the plot: i.e., arranges the events of the story in such a way as to reveal the seeking action from which they come. 2. He develops the characters of the story as individualized forms of "quest." 3. He expresses or realizes their actions by means of the words they utter in the various situations of the plot. This scheme, of course, has nothing to do with the temporal order which the poet may really have followed in elaborating his composition, nor to the order we follow in becoming acquainted with it; we start with the words, the "green leaves." The scheme refers to the "hierarchy of actualizations" which we may eventually learn to see in the completed work.

1. The first act of imitation consists in making the plot or arrangement of incidents. Aristotle says that the tragic poet is primarily a maker of plots, for the plot is the "soul of a tragedy," its formal cause. The arrangement which Sophocles made of the events of the story—starting near the end, and rehearsing the past in relation to what is happening now—already to some degree actualizes the tragic quest he wishes to show, even before we sense the characters as individuals or hear them speak and sing.

(The reader must be warned that this conception of the plot is rather unfamiliar to us. Usually we do not distinguish between the plot as the form of the play and the plot as producing a certain effect upon the audience—excitement, "interest," suspense, and the like. Aristotle also uses "plot" in this second sense. The mimicry of art has a further purpose, or final—as distinguished from its formal—cause, i.e., to reach the audience. Thinking of the Athenian theater, he describes the plot as intended to show the "universal," or to rouse and purge the emotions of pity and terror. These two meanings of the word—the form of the action, and the device for reaching the audience—are also further explained in the Appendix. At this point I am using the word *plot* in the first sense: as the form, the first actualization, of the tragic action.)

2. The characters, or agents, are the second actualization of the action. According to Aristotle, "the agents are imitated mainly with a view to the action"—i.e., the soul of the tragedy is there already in the order of events, the tragic rhythm of the life of Oedipus and Thebes; but this action may be more sharply realized and more elaborately shown forth by developing individual variations upon it. It was with this principle in mind that Ibsen wrote to his publisher, after two years' of work on *The Wild Duck*, that the play was nearly complete, and he could now proceed to "the more energetic individuation of the characters."

If one considers the Oedipus–Tiresias scene which I have quoted, one can see how the characters serve to realize the action of the whole. They reveal, at any moment, a "spectrum of action" like that which the tragic rhythm spread before us in temporal succession, at the same time offering concrete instances of almost photographic sharpness. Thus Tiresias "suffers" in the darkness of his blindness while Oedipus pursues his reasoned "purpose"; and then Tiresias effectuates his "purpose" of serving his mantic vision of the truth, while Oedipus "suffers" a blinding passion of fear and anger. The agents also serve to move the action ahead, develop it in time, through their conflicts. The chorus meanwhile, in some respects between, in others deeper, than the antagonists, represents the interests of that resolution, that final chord of feeling, in which the end of the action, seen ironically and sympathetically as one, will be realized.

3. The third actualization is in the words of the play. The seeking action which is the substance of the play is imitated first in the plot, second in the characters, and third in the words, concepts, and forms of discourse wherein the characters "actualize" their psychic life in its shifting forms, in response to the ever-changing situations of the play. If one thinks of, plotting, characterization, and poetry as successive "acts of imitation" by the author, one may also say that they constitute, in the completed work, a hierarchy of forms; and that the words of the play are its "highest individuation." They are the "green leaves" which we actually perceive; the product and the sign of the one "life of the plant" which, by an imaginative effort, one may divine behind them all.

At this point one encounters again Mr. Burke's theory of "language as symbolic action," and the many contemporary studies of the arts of poetry which have been made from this point of view. It would be appropriate to offer a detailed study of Sophocles', language, using the modern tools of analysis, to substantiate my main point. But this would require the kind of knowledge of Greek which a Jebb spent his life to acquire; and I must be content to try to show, in very general terms, that the varied forms of the poetry of *Oedipus* can only be understood on a histrionic basis: i.e., as coming out of a direct sense of the tragic rhythm of action.

In the Oedipus–Tiresias scene, there is a "spectrum of the forms of discourse" corresponding to the "spectrum of action" which I have described. It extends from Oedipus' opening speech—a reasoned exposition not, of course, without feeling but based essentially upon clear ideas and a logical order—to the choral chant, based upon sensuous imagery and the "logic of feeling." Thus it employs, in the beginning, the principle of composition which Mr. Burke calls "syllogistic progression," and, at the other end of the spectrum, Mr. Burke's "progression by association and contrast." When the Neoclassic and rationalistic critics of the seventeenth century read *Oedipus*, they saw only the order of reason; they did not know what to make of the chorus. Hence Racine's drama of "Action as Rational": a drama of static situations, of clear concepts and merely illustrative images. Nietzsche, on the other hand, saw only the passion of the chorus; for his insight was based on *Tristan*, which is composed essentially in sensuous images, and moves by association and contrast according to the logic of feeling: the drama which takes "action as passion." Neither point of view enables one to see how the scene, as a whole, hangs together.

If the speeches of the characters and the songs of the chorus are only the foliage of the plant, this is as much as to say that the life and meaning of the whole is never literally and completely present in any one formulation. It takes all of the elements—the shifting situation, the changing and developing characters, and their reasoned or lyric utterances, to indicate, in the round, the action Sophocles wishes to convey. Because this action takes the form of reason as well as passion, and of contemplation by way of symbols; because it is essentially moving (in the tragic rhythm); and because it is shared in different ways by all the characters, the play has neither literal unity nor the rational unity of the truly abstract idea, or "univocal concept." Its parts and its moments are one only "by analogy"; and just as the Saints warn us that we must believe in order to understand, so we must "make believe," by a sympathetic and imitative act of the histrionic sensibility, in order to get what Sophocles intended by his play.

It is the histrionic basis of Sophocles' art which makes it mysterious to us, with our demands for conceptual clarity, or for the luxury of yielding to a stream of feeling and subjective imagery. But it is this also which makes it so crucial an instance of the art of the theater in its completeness, as though the author understood "song, spectacle, thought, and diction" in their primitive and subtle roots. And it is the histrionic basis of drama which "undercuts theology and science."

Notes

1. See especially Jane Ellen Harrison's *Ancient Art and Ritual*, and her *Themis* which contains an "Excursus on the ritual forms preserved in Greek Tragedy" by Professor Gilbert Murray.

2. A phrase Fergusson has defined as the movement that shapes the play as it progresses episode by episode.

3. The essay on *Othello*.

E. R. DODDS

On Misunderstanding the Oedipus Rex[1]

On the last occasion when I had the misfortune to examine in Honour Moderations at Oxford I set a question on the *Oedipus Rex*, which was among the books prescribed for general reading. My question was 'In what sense, if in any, does the *Oedipus Rex* attempt to justify the ways of God to man?' It was an optional question; there were plenty of alternatives. But the candidates evidently considered it a gift: nearly all of them attempted it. When I came to sort out the answers I found that they fell into three groups.

The first and biggest group held that the play justifies the gods by showing—or, as many of them said, 'proving'—that we get what we deserve. The arguments of this group turned upon the character of Oedipus. Some considered that Oedipus was a bad man: look how he treated Creon— naturally the gods punished him. Others said 'No, not altogether bad, even in some ways rather noble; but he had one of those fatal ἁμαρτίαι that all tragic heroes have, as we know from Aristotle. And since he had a ἁμαρτία he could of course expect no mercy: the gods had read the *Poetics*.' Well over half the candidates held views of this general type.

A second substantial group held that the *Oedipus Rex* is 'a tragedy of destiny'. What the play 'proves', they said, is that man has no free will but is a puppet in the hands of the gods who pull the strings that make him dance. Whether Sophocles thought the gods justified in treating their puppet as

From *Greece & Rome*, 2nd Ser., vol. 13, no. 1 (April 1966), pp. 37–49. © 1966 by Cambridge University Press.

they did was not always clear from their answers. Most of those who took this view evidently disliked the play; some of them were honest enough to say so.

The third group was much smaller, but included some of the more thoughtful candidates. In their opinion Sophocles was 'a pure artist' and was therefore not interested in justifying the gods. He took the story of Oedipus as he found it, and used it to make an exciting play. The gods are simply part of the machinery of the plot.

Ninety per cent of the answers fell into one or the other of these three groups. The remaining ten per cent had either failed to make up their minds or failed to express themselves intelligibly.

It was a shock to me to discover that all these young persons, supposedly trained in the study of classical literature, could read this great and moving play and so completely miss the point. For all the views I have just summarized are in fact demonstrably false (though some of them, and some ways of stating them, are more crudely and vulgarly false than others). It is true that each of them has been defended by some scholars in the past, but I had hoped that all of them were by now dead and buried. Wilamowitz thought he had killed the lot in an article published in *Hermes* (34 [1899], 55 ff.) more than half a century ago; and they have repeatedly been killed since. Yet their unquiet ghosts still haunt the examination-rooms of universities— and also, I would add, the pages of popular handbooks on the history of European drama. Surely that means that we have somehow failed in our duty as teachers?

It was this sense of failure which prompted me to attempt once more to clear up some of these ancient confusions. If the reader feels—as he very well may—that in this paper I am flogging a dead horse, I can only reply that on the evidence I have quoted the animal is unaccountably still alive.

I

I shall take Aristotle as my starting point, since he is claimed as the primary witness for the first of the views I have described. From the thirteenth chapter of the *Poetics* we learn that the best sort of tragic hero is a man highly esteemed and prosperous who falls into misfortune because of some serious (μεγάλη) ἁμαρτία: examples, Oedipus and Thyestes. In Aristotle's view, then, Oedipus' misfortune was directly occasioned by some serious ἁμαρτία; and since Aristotle was known to be infallible, Victorian critics proceeded at once to look for this ἁμαρτία. And so, it appears, do the majority of present-day undergraduates.

What do they find? It depends on what they expect to find. As we all know, the word ἁμαρτία is ambiguous: in ordinary usage it is sometimes applied to false moral judgments, sometimes to purely intellectual error—the average Greek did not make our sharp distinction between the two. Since *Poetics* 13 is in general concerned with the moral character of the tragic hero, many scholars have thought in the past (and many undergraduates still think) that the ἁμαρτία of Oedipus must in Aristotle's view be a moral fault. They have accordingly gone over the play with a microscope looking for moral faults in Oedipus, and have duly found them—for neither here nor anywhere else did Sophocles portray that insipid and unlikely character, the man of perfect virtue. Oedipus, they point out, is proud and over-confident; he harbours unjustified suspicions against Teiresias and Creon; in one place (lines 964 ff.) he goes so far as to express some uncertainty about the truth of oracles. One may doubt whether this adds up to what Aristotle would consider μεγάλη ἁμαρτία. But even if it did, it would have no direct relevance to the question at issue. Years before the action of the play begins, Oedipus was already an incestuous parricide; if that was a punishment for his unkind treatment of Creon, then the punishment preceded the crime—which is surely an odd kind of justice.

'Ah,' says the traditionalist critic, 'but Oedipus' behaviour on the stage reveals the man he always was: he was punished for his basically unsound character.' In that case, however, someone on the stage ought to tell us so: Oedipus should repent, as Creon repents in the *Antigone*; or else another speaker should draw the moral. To ask about a character in fiction 'Was he a good man?' is to ask a strictly meaningless question: since Oedipus never lived we can answer neither 'Yes' nor 'No'. The legitimate question is 'Did Sophocles intend us to think of Oedipus as a good man?' This *can* be answered—not by applying some ethical yardstick of our own, but by looking at what the characters in the play say about him. And by that test the answer is 'Yes'. In the eyes of the Priest in the opening scene he is the greatest and noblest of men, the saviour of Thebes who with divine aid rescued the city from the Sphinx. The Chorus has the same view of him: he has proved his wisdom, he is the darling of the city, and never will they believe ill of him (504 ff.). And when the catastrophe comes, no one turns round and remarks 'Well, but it was your own fault: it must have been; Aristotle says so.'

In my opinion, and in that of nearly all Aristotelian scholars since Bywater, Aristotle does *not* say so; it is only the perversity of moralizing critics that has misrepresented him as saying so. It is almost certain that Aristotle was using ἁμαρτία here as he uses ἁμάρτημα in the *Nicomachean Ethics* (1135ᵇ12) and in the *Rhetoric* (1374ᵇ6), to mean an offence committed in ignorance of some material fact and therefore free from πονηρία√a or κακία.[2] These parallels seem decisive; and they are confirmed by Aristotle's second example—Thyestes, the man who ate the flesh of his own children in the belief that it was butcher's meat, and who subsequently begat a child on his own daughter, not knowing who she was. His story has clearly much in common with that of Oedipus, and Plato as well as Aristotle couples the two names as examples of the gravest ἁμαρτία (*Laws* 838c). Thyestes and Oedipus are both of them men who violated the most sacred of Nature's laws and thus incurred the most horrible of all pollutions; but they both did so without πονηρία, for they knew not what they did—in Aristotle's quasi-legal terminology, it was a ἁμάρτημα, not an ἀδίκημα. That is why they were in his view especially suitable subjects for tragedy. Had they acted knowingly, they would have been inhuman monsters, and we could not have felt for them that pity which tragedy ought to produce. As it is, we feel both pity, for the fragile estate of man, and terror, for a world whose laws we do not understand. The ἁμαρτία of Oedipus did not lie in losing his temper with Teiresias; it lay quite simply in parricide and incest—a μεγάλη ἁμαρτία indeed, the greatest a man can commit.

The theory that the tragic hero must have a grave moral flaw, and its mistaken ascription to Aristotle, has had a long and disastrous history. It was gratifying to Victorian critics, since it appeared to fit certain plays of Shakespeare. But it goes back much further, to the seventeenth-century French critic Dacier, who influenced the practice of the French classical dramatists, especially Corneille, and was himself influenced by the still older nonsense about 'poetic justice'—the notion that the poet has a moral duty to represent the world as a place where the good are always rewarded and the bad are always punished. I need not say that this puerile idea is completely foreign to Aristotle and to the practice of the Greek dramatists; I only mention it because on the evidence of those Honour Mods. papers it would appear that it still lingers on in some youthful minds like a cobweb in an unswept room.

To return to the *Oedipus Rex*, the moralist has still one last card to play. Could not Oedipus, he asks, have escaped his doom if he had been more careful? Knowing that he was in danger of committing parricide and incest, would not a really prudent man have avoided quarrelling, even in self-defence, with men older than himself, and also love-relations with women older than himself? Would he not, in Waldock's ironic phrase, have compiled a handlist of all the things he must not do? In real life I suppose he might. But we are not entitled to blame Oedipus either for carelessness in failing to compile a handlist or for lack of self-control in failing to obey its injunctions. For no such possibilities are mentioned in the play, or even hinted at; and it is an essential critical principle that *what is not mentioned in the play does not exist*. These considerations would be in place if we were examining the conduct of a real person. But we are not: we are examining the intentions of a dramatist, and we are not entitled to ask questions that the dramatist did not intend us to ask. There is only one branch of literature where we *are* entitled to ask such questions about τὰ ἐκτὸς τοῦ δράματος, namely the modern detective story. And despite certain similarities the *Oedipus Rex* is not a detective story but a dramatized folktale. If we insist on reading it as if it were a law report we must expect to miss the point.[3]

In any case, Sophocles has provided a conclusive answer to those who suggest that Oedipus could, and therefore should, have avoided his fate. The oracle was *unconditional* (line 790): it did not say 'If you do so-and-so you will kill your father'; it simply said 'You will kill your father, you will sleep with your mother.' And what an oracle predicts is bound to happen. Oedipus does what he can to evade his destiny: he resolves never to see his supposed parents again. But it is quite certain from the first that his best efforts will be unavailing. Equally unconditional was the original oracle given to Laius (711 ff.): Apollo said that he *must* (χρῆναι) die at the hands of Jocasta's child; there is no saving clause. Here there is a significant difference between Sophocles and Aeschylus. Of Aeschylus' trilogy on the House of Laius only the last play, the *Septem*, survives. Little is known of the others, but we do know, from *Septem* 742 ff., that according to Aeschylus the oracle given to Laius *was* conditional: 'Do not beget a child; for *if* you do, that child will kill you.' In Aeschylus the disaster *could* have been avoided, but Laius sinfully disobeyed and his sin brought ruin to his descendants. In Aeschylus the story was, like the *Oresteia*, a tale of crime and punishment; but Sophocles chose otherwise—that is why he altered the form of the oracle. There is no suggestion in the *Oedipus Rex* that Laius sinned or that Oedipus was the victim of an hereditary curse, and the critic must not assume what the poet has abstained from suggesting. Nor should we leap to the conclusion that Sophocles left out the hereditary curse because he thought the doctrine immoral; apparently he did not think so, since he used it both in the *Antigone* (583 ff.) and in the *Oedipus at Colonus* (964 ff.). What his motive may have been for ignoring it in the *Oedipus Rex* we shall see in a moment.

I hope I have now disposed of the moralizing interpretation, which has been rightly abandoned by the great majority of contemporary scholars. To mention only recent works in English, the books of Whitman, Waldock, Letters, Ehrenberg, Knox, and Kirkwood, however much they differ on other points, all agree about the essential moral innocence of Oedipus.

II

But what is the alternative? If Oedipus is the innocent victim of a doom which he cannot avoid, does this not reduce him to a mere puppet? Is not the whole play a 'tragedy of destiny' which denies human freedom? This is the second of the heresies which I set out to refute. Many readers have fallen into it, Sigmund Freud among them;[4] and you can find it confidently asserted in various popular handbooks, some of which even extend the assertion to Greek tragedy in general—thus providing themselves with a convenient label for distinguishing Greek from 'Christian' tragedy. But the whole notion is in fact anachronistic. The modern reader slips into it easily because we think of two clear-cut alternative views—either we believe in free will or else we are determinists. But fifth-century Greeks did not think in these terms any more than Homer did: the debate about determinism is a creation of Hellenistic thought. Homeric heroes have their predetermined 'portion of life' (μοῖρα); they must die on their 'appointed day' (αἴσιμον ἦμαρ); but it never occurs to the poet or his audience that this prevents them from being free agents. Nor did Sophocles intend that it should occur to readers of the *Oedipus Rex*. Neither in Homer nor in Sophocles does divine foreknowledge of certain events imply that all human actions are predetermined. If explicit confirmation of this is required, we have only to turn to lines 1230 f., where the Messenger emphatically distinguishes Oedipus' self-blinding as 'voluntary' and 'self-chosen' from the 'involuntary' parricide and incest. Certain of Oedipus' past actions were fate-bound; but everything that he does on the stage from first to last he does as a free agent.

Even in calling the parricide and the incest 'fate-bound' I have perhaps implied more than the average Athenian of Sophocles' day would have recognized. As A. W. Gomme put it, 'the gods know the future, but they do not order it: they know who will win the next Scotland and England football match, but that does not alter the fact that the victory will depend on the skill, the determination, the fitness of the players, and a little on luck'.[5] That may not satisfy the analytical philosopher, but it seems to have satisfied the ordinary man at all periods. Bernard Knox aptly quotes the prophecy of Jesus to St. Peter, 'Before the cock crow, thou shalt deny me thrice.' The Evangelists clearly did not intend to imply that Peter's subsequent action was 'fate-bound' in the sense that he could not have chosen otherwise; Peter fulfilled the prediction, but he did so by an act of free choice.[6]

In any case I cannot understand Sir Maurice Bowra's[7] idea that the gods *force* on Oedipus the knowledge of what he has done. They do nothing of the kind; on the contrary, what fascinates us is the spectacle of a man freely choosing, from the highest motives, a series of actions which lead to his own ruin. Oedipus might have left the plague to take its course; but pity for the sufferings of his people compelled him to consult Delphi. When Apollo's word came back, he might still have left the murder of Laius uninvestigated; but piety and justice required him to act. He need not have forced the truth from the reluctant Theban herdsman; but because he cannot rest content with a lie, he must tear away the last veil from the illusion in which he has lived so long. Teiresias, Jocasta, the herdsman, each in turn tries to stop him, but in vain: he must read the last riddle, the riddle of his own life. The immediate cause of Oedipus' ruin is not 'Fate' or 'the gods'—no oracle said that he must discover the truth—and still less does it lie in his own weakness; what causes his ruin is his own strength and courage, his loyalty to Thebes, and his loyalty to the truth. In all this we are to see him as a free agent: hence the suppression of the hereditary curse. And his self-mutilation and self-banishment are equally free acts of choice.

Why does Oedipus blind himself? He tells us the reason (1369 ff.): he has done it in order to cut himself off from all contact with humanity; if he could choke the channels of his other senses he would do so. Suicide would not serve his purpose: in the next world he would have to meet his dead parents. Oedipus mutilates himself because he can face neither the living nor the dead. But why, if he is morally innocent? Once again, we must look at the play through Greek eyes. The doctrine that nothing matters except the agent's intention is a peculiarity of Christian and especially of post-Kantian thought. It is true that the Athenian law courts took account of intention: they distinguished as ours do between murder and accidental homicide or homicide committed in the course of self-defence. If Oedipus had been tried before an Athenian court he would have been acquitted—of murdering his father. But no human court could acquit him of pollution; for pollution inhered in the act itself, irrespective of motive. Of that burden Thebes could not acquit Oedipus, and least of all could its bearer acquit himself.

The nearest parallel to the situation of Oedipus is in the tale which Herodotus tells about Adrastus, son of Gordies. Adrastus was the involuntary slayer of his own brother, and then of Atys, the son of his benefactor Croesus; the latter act, like the killing of Laius, fulfilled an oracle. Croesus forgave Adrastus because the killing was unintended (ἀέκων), and because the oracle showed that it was the will of 'some god'. But Adrastus did not forgive himself: he committed suicide, 'conscious' says Herodotus, 'that of all men known to him he bore the heaviest burden of disaster'.[8] It is for the same reason that Oedipus blinds himself. Morally innocent though he is and knows himself to be, the objective horror of his actions remains with him and he feels that he has no longer any place in human society. Is that simply archaic superstition? I think it is something more. Suppose a motorist runs down a man and kills him, I think he ought to feel that he has done a terrible thing, even if the accident is no fault of his: he has destroyed a human life, which nothing can restore. In the objective order it is acts that count, not intentions. A man who has violated that order may well feel a sense of guilt, however blameless his driving.

But my analogy is very imperfect, and even the case of Adrastus is not fully comparable. Oedipus is no ordinary homicide: he has committed the two crimes which above all others fill us with instinctive horror. Sophocles had not read Freud, but he knew how people *feel* about these things—better than some of his critics appear to do. And in the strongly patriarchal society of ancient Greece the revulsion would be even more intense than it is in our own. We have only to read Plato's prescription for the treatment to be given to parricides (*Laws* 872 c ff.). For this deed, he says, there can be no purification: the parricide shall be killed, his body shall be laid naked at a cross-roads outside the city, each officer of the State shall cast a stone upon it and curse it, and then the bloody remnant shall be flung outside the city's territory and left unburied. In all this he is probably following actual Greek practice. And if that is how Greek justice treated parricides, is it surprising that Oedipus treats himself as he does, when the great king, 'the first of men', the man whose intuitive genius had saved Thebes, is suddenly revealed to himself as a thing so unclean that 'neither the earth can receive it, nor the holy rain nor the sunshine endure its presence' (1426)?

III

At this point I am brought back to the original question I asked the undergraduates: does Sophocles in this play attempt to justify the ways of God to man? If 'to justify' means 'to explain in terms of *human* justice', the answer is surely 'No'. If human justice is the standard, then, as Waldock bluntly expressed it, 'Nothing can excuse the gods, and Sophocles knew it perfectly well.' Waldock does not, however, suggest that the poet intended any attack on the gods. He goes on to say that it is futile to look for any 'message' or 'meaning' in this play: 'there is no meaning', he tells us, 'in the *Oedipus Rex*; there is merely the terror of coincidence'.[9] Kirkwood seems to take a rather similar line: 'Sophocles', he says, 'has no theological pronouncements to make and no points of criticism to score.'[10] These opinions come rather close to, if they do not actually involve, the view adopted by my third and last group of undergraduates—the view that the gods are merely agents in a traditional story which Sophocles, a 'pure artist', exploits for dramatic purposes without raising the religious issue or drawing any moral whatever.

This account seems to me insufficient; but I have more sympathy with it than I have with either of the other heresies. It reflects a healthy reaction against the old moralizing school of critics; and the text of the play appears at first sight to support it. It is a striking fact that after the catastrophe no one on the stage says a word either in justification of the gods or in criticism of them. Oedipus says 'These things were Apollo'—and that is all. If the poet has charged him with a 'message' about divine justice or injustice, he fails to deliver it. And I fully agree that there is no reason at all why we should require a dramatist—even a Greek dramatist—to be for ever running about delivering banal 'messages'. It is true that when a Greek dramatic poet had something he passionately wanted to say to his fellow citizens he felt entitled to say it. Aeschylus in the *Oresteia*, Aristophanes in the *Frogs*, had something to say to their people and used the opportunity of saying it on the stage. But these are exceptional cases—both these works were produced at a time of grave crisis in public affairs—and even here the 'message' appears to me to be incidental to the true function of the artist, which I should be disposed to define, with Dr. Johnson, as 'the enlargement of our sensibility'. It is unwise to generalize from special cases. (And, incidentally, I wish undergraduates would stop writing essays which begin with the words 'This play *proves* that...'. Surely no work of art can ever 'prove' anything: what value could there be in a 'proof' whose premises are manufactured by the artist?)

Nevertheless, I cannot accept the view that the *Oedipus Rex* conveys *no* intelligible meaning and that Sophocles' plays tell us nothing of his opinions concerning the gods. Certainly it is always dangerous to use dramatic works as evidence of their author's opinions, and especially of their religious convictions: we can legitimately discuss religion *in* Shakespeare, but do we know anything at all about the religion of Shakespeare? Still, I think I should venture to assert two things about Sophocles' opinions:

First, he did not believe (or did not always believe) that the gods are in any human sense 'just';

Secondly, he did always believe that the gods exist and that man should revere them.

The first of these propositions is supported not only by the implicit evidence of the *Oedipus Rex* but by the explicit evidence of another play which is generally thought to be close in date to it. The closing lines of the *Trachiniae* contain a denunciation in violent terms of divine injustice. No one answers it. I can only suppose that the poet had no answer to give.

For the second of my two propositions we have quite strong *external* evidence—which is important, since it is independent of our subjective impressions. We know that Sophocles held various priesthoods; that when the cult of Asclepius was introduced to Athens he acted as the god's host and wrote a hymn in his honour; and that he was himself worshipped as a 'hero' after his death, which seems to imply that he accepted the religion of the State and was accepted by it. But the external evidence does not stand alone:

it is strongly supported by at least one passage in the *Oedipus Rex*. The celebrated choral ode about the decline of prophecy and the threat to religion (lines 863–910) was of course suggested by the scene with Creon which precedes it; but it contains generalizations which have little apparent relevance either to Oedipus or to Creon. Is the piety of this ode purely conventional, as Whitman maintained in a vigorous but sometimes perverse book?[11] One phrase in particular seems to forbid this interpretation. If men are to lose all respect for the gods, in that case, the Chorus asks, τί δεῖ με χορεύειν (895). If by this they mean merely 'Why should I, a Theban elder, dance?', the question is irrelevant and even slightly ludicrous; the meaning is surely 'Why should I, an Athenian citizen, continue to serve in a chorus?' In speaking of themselves as a chorus they step out of the play into the contemporary world, as Aristophanes' choruses do in the *parabasis*. And in effect the question they are asking seems to be this: 'If Athens loses faith in religion, if the views of the Enlightenment prevail, what significance is there in tragic drama, which exists as part of the service of the gods?' To that question the rapid decay of tragedy in the fourth century may be said to have provided an answer.

In saying this, I am not suggesting with Ehrenberg that the character of Oedipus reflects that of Pericles,[12] or with Knox that he is intended to be a symbol of Athens:[13] allegory of that sort seems to me wholly alien to Greek tragedy. I am only claiming that at one point in this play Sophocles took occasion to say to his fellow citizens something which he felt to be important. And it was important, particularly in the period of the Archidamian War, to which the *Oedipus Rex* probably belongs. Delphi was known to be pro-Spartan: that is why Euripides was given a free hand to criticize Apollo. But if Delphi could not be trusted, the whole fabric of traditional belief was threatened with collapse. In our society religious faith is no longer tied up with belief in prophecy; but for the ancient world, both pagan and Christian, it was. And in the years of the Archidamian War belief in prophecy was at a low ebb; Thucydides is our witness to that.

I take it, then, as reasonably certain that while Sophocles did not pretend that the gods are in any human sense just he nevertheless held that they are entitled to our worship. Are these two opinions incompatible? Here once more we cannot hope to understand Greek literature if we persist in looking at it through Christian spectacles. To the Christian it is a necessary part of piety to believe that God is just. And so it was to Plato and to the Stoics. But the older world saw no such necessity. If you doubt this, take down the *Iliad* and read Achilles' opinion of what divine justice amounts to (xxiv. 525–33); or take down the Bible and read the Book of Job. Disbelief in divine justice as measured by human yardsticks can perfectly well be associated with deep religious feeling. 'Men', said Heraclitus, 'find some things unjust, other things just; but in the eyes of God all things are beautiful and good and just.'[14] I think that Sophocles would have agreed. For him, as for Heraclitus, there is an objective world-order which man must respect, but which he cannot hope fully to understand.

IV

Some readers of the *Oedipus Rex* have told me that they find its atmosphere stifling and oppressive: they miss the tragic exaltation that one gets from the *Antigone* or the *Prometheus Vinctus*. And I fear that what I have said here has done nothing to remove that feeling. Yet it is not a feeling which I share myself. Certainly the *Oedipus Rex* is a play about the blindness of man and the desperate insecurity of the human condition: in a sense every man must grope in the dark as Oedipus gropes, not knowing who he is or what he has to suffer; we all live in a world of appearance which hides from us who-knows-what dreadful reality. But surely the *Oedipus Rex* is also a play about human greatness. Oedipus is great, not in virtue of a great worldly position—for his worldly position is an illusion which will vanish like a dream—but in virtue of his inner strength: strength to pursue the truth at whatever personal cost, and strength to accept and endure it when found. 'This horror is mine,' he cries, 'and none but I is *strong* enough to bear it' (1414)—Oedipus is great because he accepts the responsibility for *all* his acts, including those which are objectively most horrible, though subjectively innocent.

To me personally Oedipus is a kind of symbol of the human intelligence which cannot rest until it has solved all the riddles—even the last riddle, to which the answer is that human happiness is built on an illusion. I do not know how far Sophocles intended that. But certainly in the last lines of the play (which I firmly believe to be genuine) he does generalize the case, does appear to suggest that in some sense Oedipus is every man and every man is potentially Oedipus. Freud felt this (he was not insensitive to poetry), but as we all know he understood it in a specific psychological sense. 'Oedipus' fate', he says, 'moves us only because it might have been our own, because the oracle laid upon us before birth the very curse which rested upon him. It may be that we were all destined to direct our first sexual impulses towards our mothers, and our first impulses of hatred and violence towards our fathers; our dreams convince us that we were.'[15] Perhaps they do; but Freud did not ascribe his interpretation of the myth to Sophocles, and it is not the interpretation I have in mind. Is there not in the poet's view a much wider sense in which every man is Oedipus? If every man could tear away the last veils of illusion, if he could see human life as time and the gods see it, would he not see that against that tremendous background all the generations of men are as if they had not been, ἴσα καὶ τὸ μηδὲν ζώσας (1187)? That was how Odysseus saw it when he had conversed with Athena, the embodiment of divine wisdom. 'In Ajax' condition', he says, 'I recognize my own: I perceive that all men living are but appearance or unsubstantial shadow.'

ὁρῶ γὰρ ἡμᾶς οὐδὲν ὄντας ἄλλο πλὴν
εἴδωλ, ὁσοιπερ ζῶμεν, ἢ κούφην οκιάν.[16]

So far as I can judge, on this matter Sophocles' deepest feelings did not change. The same view of the human condition which is made explicit in his earliest extant play is implicit not only in the *Oedipus Rex* but in the *Oedipus Coloneus*, in the great speech where Oedipus draws the bitter conclusion from his life's experience and in the famous ode on old age.[17] Whether this vision of man's estate is true or false I do not know, but it ought to be comprehensible to a generation which relishes the plays of Samuel Beckett. I do not wish to describe it as a 'message'. But I find in it an enlargement of sensibility. And that is all I ask of any dramatist.

NOTES

1. A paper read at a 'refresher course' for teachers, London Institute of Education, 24 July 1964.

2. For the full evidence see O. Hey's exhaustive examination of the usage of these words, *Philol.* 83 (1927), 1–17; 137–63. Cf. also K. von Fritz, *Antike und Moderne Tragödie* (Berlin, 1962), 1 ff.

3. The danger is exemplified by Mr. P. H. Vellacott's article, 'The Guilt of Oedipus', which appeared in this journal (vol. xi [1964], 137–48) shortly after my talk was delivered. By treating Oedipus as an historical personage and examining his career from the 'common-sense' standpoint of a prosecuting counsel Mr. Vellacott has no difficulty in showing that Oedipus must have guessed the true story of his birth long before the point at which the play opens—and guiltily done nothing about it. Sophocles, according to Mr. Vellacott, realized this, but unfortunately could not present the situation in these terms because 'such a conception was impossible to express in the conventional forms of tragedy'; so for most of the time he reluctantly fell back on 'the popular concept of an innocent Oedipus lured by Fate into a disastrous trap'. We are left to conclude either that the play is a botched compromise or else that the common sense of the law-courts is not after all the best yardstick by which to measure myth.

4. Sigmund Freud, *The Interpretation of Dreams* (London, Modern Library, 1938), 108.

5. A. W. Gomme, *More Essays in Greek History and Literature* (Oxford, 1962), 211.

6. B. M. W. Knox, *Oedipus at Thebes* (Yale, 1957), 39.

7. C. M. Bowra, *Sophoclean Tragedy* (Oxford, 1944), ch. v.

8. Herodotus 1.45. Cf. H. Funke, *Die sogenannte tragische Schuld* (Diss. Köln, 1963).

9. A. J. A. Waldock, *Sophocles the Dramatist* (Cambridge, 1950, 158, 168.

10. G. M. Kirkwood, *A Study of Sophoclean Drama* (Ithaca, 1958), 271.

11. C. H. Whitman, *Sophocles* (Cambridge, Mass., 1951), 133–5.

12. V. Ehrenberg, *Sophocles and Pericles* (Oxford, 1954). 141 ff.

13. B. M. W. Knox, op. cit., ch. ii.

14. Heraclitus, fragm. 102.

15. Sigmund Freud, op. cit. 109.

16. *Ajax* 124–6.

17. *O.C.* 607–15: 1211–49.

THOMAS GOULD

The Innocence of Oedipus:
The Philosophers on Oedipus the King, Part III[1]

E. R. Dodds has complained recently that the undergraduates at Oxford still read *Oedipus the King*, and Greek tragedy in general, in ignorance of the new enlightened thinking that they could have found in almost any scholarly work on the subject today.[2] They drearily repeat, he says, the very misconceptions that Wilamowitz thought he had put an end to seventy years ago. He finds the idea still depressingly common, for instance, that Greek tragedies always show men coming to bad ends because of "tragic flaws" in their character. The students could have been disabused of this notion, Dodds points out, by reading any one of quite a number of excellent books or articles. Two of Dodds' complaints may not be as justified as this one, however. On two important counts the undergraduates seem to have been right and their examiner wrong. And since Dodds, quite correctly, implies that his views represent those of the majority among recent scholars, it is worth looking at these two points.

First, there is the general agreement among modern critics that the greatest of the Greek tragedies were never tragedies of fate, that, whatever the reader thinks who comes fresh to the text without the benefit of scholarly and critical works, the finest tragedies never show good men being crushed by destinies that they could not have avoided. To believe in tragedies of fate,

---

From *Arion* 5, no. 4 (Winter 1966), pp. 478–525). © 1966 by *Arion*.

according to Dodds and to many others, is worse even than to believe in a "tragic flaw."

The second point concerns Aristotle on the "tragic flaw." Did he or did he not assert that in a play in which the protagonist is shown coming to grief the catastrophe must be felt to be due, at least in part, to some avoidable error on the part of the protagonist? Since Bywater's time, as Dodds says, more and more scholars have come to the conclusion that Aristotle required only that there be an unavoidable mistake in the facts. This is now the orthodox position. Yet ordinary readers, ignorant of the works of these critics, still tend to assume that Aristotle demanded a flaw in the protagonist's character or intellect.

I would like to champion the judgment of the naive reader on both of these questions.

1

There is a line of reasoning that goes something like this. If the *Oedipus* is a tragedy of fate, the story of a man who is ruined by forces he cannot be expected to have understood or influenced, then the protagonist of the story was obviously not responsible for his misery in any way. But if he was not responsible for what happened to him, he is a mere puppet and his story is sad, but not "tragic"; it cannot engage our moral sensibility and it cannot, therefore, be profound or moving. But the *Oedipus* is profound and moving. Therefore it is not a tragedy of fate.

If we ask someone who feels this way about the play just why he wants Oedipus to be "responsible," we usually get a rather complicated answer. First of all it will be vigorously denied, more than likely, that what is wanted is that our playwrights show us punishments fitting crimes—a world where the good are always rewarded and the bad made to pay for their failings. If we admitted this we would be admitting that Aristotle's theory of the "tragic flaw" (interpreted in the old-fashioned way) was really right after all. Whatever is meant by "responsible" in this context, it is usually not the same as criminal guilt. What is wanted, apparently, is "free will" or "free choice" in the protagonist's actions. "What fascinates us," Dodds suggests, "is the spectacle of a man freely choosing from the highest motives a series of actions which lead to his own ruin." Oedipus must be innocent of harboring any culpable desires, then; and yet it must be he, acting freely, who brought on the catastrophe, not the gods, not fate.

There is a muddle here somewhere, surely. Oedipus' intentions were good, but the results of his actions were bad; and the explanation for this is that he did not have certain important pieces of information. One would have thought that we were reduced to one of two possibilities. Either Oedipus could not have come into possession of the important facts however much he had improved his intelligence or character, which would mean that something else must have been at fault for his catastrophe—chance, the world, fate, or the gods. Or Oedipus brought his misery upon himself and nothing external is to be blamed, in which case it must be true that Oedipus would have been able to avoid his catastrophe had he been a better man or at least a better thinker. Yet, according to the theory we are considering, neither of these is the case: it is denied that Oedipus is brought down by things external to him, but it is also denied that his uncompelled moves were bad or foolish in any way.

There are two favorite ways of coping with this difficulty. Sometimes it is suggested that Oedipus would not have avoided his misery by having been a better man, but he *could* have remained prosperous and happy if he had been a *less* good man. I shall examine this strange theory in Section 3 below. The other way out is to point to the fact that the Greeks before the Stoics had not yet conceived of the will as we do and so did not see fate and free will as exclusive alternatives. That is, if we think away "our" notion of the will and accept Sophocles' idea of it, we will be able to see that Oedipus acted freely and was responsible for what happened even though the whole sequence of events is repeatedly said to be the work of the gods.

Our first task, then, is to examine the difference between the ancient and the modern notions of the will.

Neither the poets nor the philosophers of classical Greece had any difficulty in distinguishing between voluntary and involuntary actions; between situations where a man could act as he saw fit and situations where, because of nature, the gods or other men, a man could not so act; between human acts in which the character of the actor could be read (and praised or blamed accordingly) and acts where nothing could be justly inferred about the character of the men involved, and so on. They also knew full well, of course, that some men were decisive, energetic and able to make their characters felt by the world, whereas others either lacked energy or opportunity or for some other reason did not so often or so effectively impress their unique personalities on the events in which they were involved. What, then, is meant by the complaint that the ancients did not have "our" notion of the will? Usually what is meant is that it rarely, if ever, occurred to the Greeks (before the Stoics and Epicureans) that in the act of making a decision a man is introducing a surge of energy (or a twist, or a focus) that could not be accounted for by the sum total of all antecedent events. The ancients tended to think that the crucial distinction was that between a man who is allowed to act according to his character and a man who is given no such opportunity; but they also thought that the character was probably determined by all of the things that had happened in his past (his habits, education, reading, accidental encounters, even the experiences in his previous lives, according to Plato, and certainly the experiences of his society even in the years before he was born). Modern readers, on the other hand, are very often made uncomfortable by this formulation. Unless the will can break the chains of efficient causes which are governed by unalterable mechanical laws, it is argued, we are not "free," and we cannot blame anyone for anything: a man's character would be made for him, not by him, and his every act would already be determined before he was born. In such an idea, it is feared, we have an intellectualized version of fatalism.

From Homer to Aristotle both poets and philosophers tended to ask not "was he free?" as we might do, but "is he responsible (*aitios*)?" The questions are the same in that they both are attempts to identify the extent to which events were in our power, so that we will be able to assign praise and blame with justice. They are different questions, however, in that the latter, the ancient question, is answered in the affirmative if it can be shown that the men involved acted according to their characters; the modern question, on the other hand, can on occasion be a request for something else in addition to this. It can also express a desire to know whether there Were men involved in the events in question to whose inner tendencies or thoughts we can trace at least some of the real causes of the events—"causes" now being used, not in a practical sense (was he brought up well? should he be re-educated? must we try to change his character by persuasion or punishment?), but in a metaphysical sense (were there new beginnings at the moments of decision-making which cannot be restated as effects of antecedent events?).

The ambiguity in the English word "responsible" is the cause of many misunderstandings. There are at least three things that we could mean when we ask to what extent a man is "responsible" for what he did. The word can mean 1) that the man so described acted in accordance with his own character, saying nothing about what determined that character, 2) that in addition to being "responsible" in this way, the man's character might have been different had he developed different habits in his past, saying nothing about what things would have had to be different in order that he should develop different habits, or 3) that in addition to these two requirements, somehow, either at the moment we are concentrating on or in the past when his character was being formed, there was within him somewhere a new beginning, a turn or an impulse that cannot be entirely accounted for by antecedent events.

Although the Greek word *aitios* was capable of the same ambiguities (cf. *Nic.Eth.* 3.5), in the period before the Stoics and Epicureans, as I have said, it *almost* always meant the first, or the first combined with the second; the third possibility did not seem vital or appropriate. This restriction may have been, not a weakness, however, but the strength of the Greek moralists. With this meaning of "responsibility" they were able to distinguish clearly enough between moral and immoral actions; between the man who put a high value on looking ahead, calculating, moving with due forethought, etc., and the man who saw no value in such planning; between the man who hated the desires within his own psyche that were capable of leading him to self-defeating goals (the man of conscience, the man who could feel guilt) and the man who was too willing to look for purely external sources for his failures, and so on. By having nothing to do with the third sense of "responsibility," they could then concentrate on the circumstances that were responsible for a man's character's being what it was, in hopes always of finding something that could be changed in order to improve men's characters in the future.

The main difficulty, as the earlier Greeks saw it, was not in the nature of the will, but the consequences of the power and the intentions of the gods. Were the gods humane? all of them or merely some? could you choose your own divinity or did it choose you? was divinity all-powerful or not? did it care whether human beings were happy? were the rules that the gods themselves were subject to comforting or appalling things? One's tests for human "responsibility" necessarily varied according to the way one answered questions like these. And yet, because they also asked about the character of the man and whether or not he was acting gladly, the Greeks of the classical period stayed remarkably clear of the maze of puzzles that such questions could lead to; and they usually stayed clear of the worst features of oriental fatalism also, even when their answers to these questions about the gods were most bitter and pessimistic.

The *Iliad* already shows us a whole range of subtly different attitudes toward the presence of the power of divinity. Paris was thought by Hector and others to have drawn annoyingly incorrect conclusions from the fact that human destinies are in the laps of the gods. Once, when he is scolded by Helen, he tells her to stop criticizing him: Menelaus had won this time, with the help of his god; he, Paris, would win on some other occasions with the help of *his* god (3.438ff, again at 6.339). But Hector had an even more appalling vision of the power of the gods or fate and of the helplessness of men than Paris had (and Homer makes us feel that Hector was not only perceptive but pious, too, and knew what he was talking about), yet his fatalism did not tend to make him craven or self-indulgent at all. Indeed, it made his criticism of his brother all the sharper. In one breath Hector says that Zeus obviously sent Paris to be a bane to his countrymen; in the next he wishes Paris would die swiftly; then he goes off to see him in order to upbraid him and to change his ways (6.280–5). Helen constantly criticizes *herself*, although she believes, or says she believes, that the gods willed her disastrous yielding to Paris (6.349; at 6.357–8 Helen makes a conjecture as to what the purpose of the gods might have been). Helen struggles against her *daimôn*, in marked contrast to Paris, who, when he is favored by the same goddess, yields willingly and takes pride in the fact (3.65). Although Helen blames herself—or rather *because* she blames herself—neither Hector nor Priam do blame her. I do not hold you responsible (*aitiē*), says Priam. The gods are responsible in my eyes. The elders agree, though they wish she would go away nevertheless.

In the fifth century Gorgias composed a defense of Helen in which everything *but* character is given as a cause. The results are startling. She could not be blamed, he says, because she must have gone with Paris for one of four reasons (*aitiai*): either 1) because of the plans of fortune and the premeditations of the gods, or 2) because she was seized by force, or 3) because she was won over by reason, or 4) because she was captured by desire (fr. B 11, 6). Euripides gives Helen a similar, though even more elaborate, defense in the *Trojan Women*; but he then has Hecuba refute these reasons one by one. Hecuba's main weapon is to translate Helen's observations back into terms of the personal character implied. Thus Helen says that Aphrodite could not be resisted by a mortal; Hecuba retorts that "Aphrodite" is a misleading name for a certain well-known kind of weakness (988–9).

As Aeschylus tells the story, both Clytemnestra and Orestes committed crimes because the curse of the house of Atreus had to be worked out. Yet Aeschylus obviously disapproves of Clytemnestra, even though he portrays Orestes as entirely blameless. Clytemnestra can apparently be held responsible, despite the existence of the divine plan, because she was, nevertheless, acting willingly, according to her character—she saw the course of action open to her as one that fitted well with her vision of how she would like things to be. (Aegisthus was attractive and it was convenient that Agamemnon should be got out of the way.) The case was otherwise with Orestes: he was truly horrified by the demands of heaven. Apollo had repeatedly to impress on the young man that the consequences of not killing his mother would be even more revolting than the polluting crime itself. And so Orestes is thought admirable, Clytemnestra not.

A belief in fate or the ultimate triumph of divine will does not always make judgments of human excellence impossible or nonsensical. There are different ways of judging men implied in different conceptions of the divine will. According to the Stoics, for instance, the wise man is the man who, as he does what the rulers of the universe will have him do, finds that it is exactly what he would have wanted to do anyhow. ("Ducunt volentem fata, nolentem trahunt," attributed by Seneca to Cleanthes, *SVF* 1.119.) On this theory, it is Clytemnestra, not Orestes, who acted well—if we can accept the curse as the plan of Providence. The Stoics, of course, denied that divinities could have conflicting desires or that different divinities were triumphant at different moments in history. For them, therefore, the discovery that someone did gladly what divinity would have him do was a sufficient test of that person's moral excellence. Aeschylus assumed that divinity could want for a man what a man ought not to want for himself; the Stoics were certain that doing the god's will—living according to nature—is invariably the shortest path to happiness, also to a feeling of freedom and to true goodness. Neither the Stoics nor Aeschylus, then, allowed their belief in the inevitable triumph of divine plans to deprive them of a way to distinguish good men from bad men. Indeed, their different conceptions of divinity helped define their different schemes for praise and blame.

But perhaps it is wrong to speak of the need to distinguish better men from worse men as though this were a secondary consideration. It is obviously primary. A society that deprived itself of the means to influence the character and desires of its members just could not last very long. And the most important means that it has to effect changes of this sort is to make its disapproval felt by a wrongdoer or potential wrongdoer and so make that person hate the part of himself that harbors the destructive desire. If we let a man who has acted regrettably speak blandly of forces external to his character, when the circumstances are the same once more he is likely to make the same disastrous move all over again. This is why Hector and Helen cannot allow Paris to lessen his disgrace by pointing to the role of the gods in his defeat, and why the Achaean princes cannot change their feelings toward Agamemnon even if they half accept his conjecture that it must have been a god who took his wits away the day that he alienated Achilles. Paris and Agamemnon are judged "responsible" in the sense that they acted according to their character; regrettable events were traced to regrettable tendencies in these men, and these tendencies were thought to be capable of being improved by the instillation of shame or guilt. They saw no inconsistency between this attitude and a belief in powerful and frequent divine interventions.

On the other hand, this does not mean that Homer or the tragedians thought that men were *never* able to lessen their responsibility for a crime or disastrous act by pointing to the role of the gods. We accept Patroclus' plea (*Il.* 16.845) that he was not disgraced because Apollo and Zeus were really his killers, not Hector. And we accept Orestes' plea that Apollo forced him to kill his mother. It is entirely possible, therefore, that Sophocles meant us to accept Oedipus' plea that the gods, not he himself, are responsible for his wretchedness. If Sophocles were a Platonist or a Stoic or a Christian, then we would be right to insist that divine action alone could not be responsible for Oedipus' misery; but Sophocles was none of these things. Sophocles seems to have honored the gods and thought them wonderful and believed them to be on the side of excellence and justice in the long run; but so did Homer and Aeschylus. He seems also to have accepted, with Homer and Aeschylus, the possibility that the gods could ruin the lives of excellent and well-intentioned men.

Sophocles could believe, then, that Oedipus was undone by external things and that Oedipus was in no way responsible for his misery; and yet this would not make him a universal fatalist. Nor would it make his Oedipus a puppet without character or excellence. There is nothing to prevent us from seeing what kind of man the protagonist of the story is—complicated, unique, conscientious, impetuous, brilliant—even if his major goals are hideously frustrated in the end. Sophocles no doubt assumed that many, perhaps most, men, good and bad, were given frequent opportunities to act according to their characters. It is evidently only very special men, in his belief, who are systematically prevented by divinity from pursuing their own goals. This is a vision of things that may baffle us or disappoint us (even while we are moved by the play itself), but the baffling or disappointing part is not the notion of the will that is implied; it is the conception of divinity. At least there is no obvious way that we can think away "our" notion of will and accept an older notion and so make Oedipus responsible for his own miseries again.

2

So far we have considered only the significance of fatalism in the *Oedipus*, Sophocles' assumptions about destiny and the plans of the gods. There is another, related problem, however—the question of determinism. The two positions might be distinguished one from the other as follows: If you believe that there is a superhuman force or being that sometimes (or regularly or always) overrides men's desires and intentions, canceling them out, making them ineffectual, in order to fulfill its own primeval designs, then you are a fatalist; but if you believe, that complete knowledge of a man's character plus his circumstances would tell you why he had to do what he did, even during those moments when he felt he was free—when he says that he could have done something else—you should be called not a fatalist, but a determinist.[3] Sometimes when modern critics conceive a desire to show that Oedipus was free and responsible for at least some of the things that happen to him, what they seem to fear is not fatalism so much as the supposed consequences of determinism.

When these interpreters point to the fact that the ancients did not have "our" notion of the will, what they appear to mean is that since "our" notion of the will is the true one, whereas the ancient conception does not allow for true freedom or moral responsibility, and since the *Oedipus* nevertheless engages our sympathies profoundly when we read it or witness a performance today, we must be justified in assuming that Sophocles had an instinctive understanding of the human will that transcended the theories put forward by his countrymen. Before the Epicureans, it is pointed out, the Greeks rarely if ever doubted that men's varying characters, visions and desires were caused by what they were born with plus all that had happened to them up to the moment of their varying "decisions," yet they were rarely troubled by the implications of this assumption. In particular they did not see that if this were true all sensations of free choice would be illusory and all praise and blame unrealistic. It is implied that if the ancients had seen these supposed consequences, they would have stopped talking the way they did about the external factors responsible for men's acts. Therefore, if we are to put ourselves in the right frame of mind to enjoy the *Oedipus*, to be deeply moved by its plot, we must simply think away or discount all such "deterministic" talk.

It is the oracles that cause the trouble, of course. If we accept the assumption that a god can really predict infallibly what a man will do before he is even born, then we must either assume a fatalism, at least in this one man's life, or, if not that, we must accept the assumption that the causes for our every act were in existence even before we were born. We might say that Oedipus was "fated" to do what he did if the gods had a purpose that could only be effected by selecting Oedipus for a role he did not choose for himself, "determined" if the god did not interfere but merely saw correctly the nexus of causes and effects that resulted inevitably in his "doing" what he did—just as the same god might predict what any man ever "did."

Unlike Aeschylus (*Seven Against Thebes* 742ff) and Euripides (*Phoenician Women* 18ff), Sophocles presents the oracle to Laius as unconditional and therefore purposeless (or at least not illuminating any purpose). Delphi told Laius, according to Jocasta, that his doom would be to die by the hand of his son. That is all. In *Oedipus at Colonus*, too, Sophocles has Oedipus defend his innocence (in response to Creon's taunts) by saying that the gods were responsible—and the plea is all the more effective because no moral purpose is discerned in the gods' moves. There were versions of the Oedipus legend in which Oedipus was "fated" to do what he did; that is, a moral plan could be discerned in all the wretchedness suffered by the various members of his family. Sophocles consistently mutes this feature of the story, however. The absence of any mention of a crime committed by Laius is in fact unique and quite remarkable.

According to one versions Laius, while enjoying the hospitality of Pelops, fell in love with, and then carried off, his host's youngest son. It was this that made it right that Laius die by the hand of his own son. The punishment fitted the crime. In the versions in which this earlier history is not stressed, the god nevertheless gives Laius a *choice*: either so to conduct himself that he cannot have a son or to engender a son and then be killed by him. Even if we assume that the god knew which Laius would do, his prediction still points to some fault in Laius as the cause of subsequent suffering.[4] There is not a word of any of this in any surviving play by Sophocles. When, in the *Antigone*, Ismene and Antigone fear the working of a family curse, it is the consequences of the accidental marriage between Oedipus and Jocasta that they fear, not any old remembered crime of Laius'. In the *Oedipus at Colonus* (964ff) Oedipus says of his unwitting patricide and incest: this is the way the gods wanted it, *perhaps* because they had some ill will for my family from of old. Then he adds that he knows this *because* in him himself there was no flaw to upbraid in payment for which he had done these things against his parents and himself. And then he adds a second proof. If an oracle is given to a father that his son will kill him, he asks—if that oracle is given before the son is born—how could one blame the son?

Undergraduates reading these plays without the benefit of the scholars are almost always troubled by the oracles. What *does* follow from the fact that the god knew before the birth of Oedipus exactly what he would do? If these students were to turn to the new orthodoxy for help, however, they would find, alas, not a solution so much as an aphorism. Oedipus' acts were "not predestined," suggests Bernard Knox, "merely predicted, an essential distinction."[5] "The Olympians have not willed [Oedipus'] fall," says Cedric Whitman, "they have foretold it. To say that the gods are responsible, as Oedipus does [*O.T.* 1329f], means at most that they permit life to be as it turns out to be."[6] "In [Sophocles'] plays," says Gordon Kirkwood, "events do not take place because the oracles say that events will; on the contrary, the oracles say that events will take place because they are going to. There is no fatalism involved in the oracular utterance itself; the oracles need not say why the events will take place, and they may come about because of human character, though it may also involve divine will."[7] In other words, we can think away the oracles and judge the responsibility of Oedipus and others as though oracles did not exist.

This is really a radical way out, however, because Oedipus certainly and Sophocles almost certainly would not have agreed. In both plays Oedipus is shown banking heavily on the significance of the fact that everything that he had done had been foretold exactly.

The proof that there is such a thing as exact foreknowledge does not necessarily imply that the being who has this knowledge is himself the one who has set the events in motion. On this point Knox and the rest are certainly right. The existence of an infallible foreknower does seem to imply, however, that one of the following things must be true. Either 1) there is some force in the universe that wishes things to turn out in a certain way, however men will feel about it. (If this force has the power to override men's wills when the time comes, it does not matter whether it knows what their desires will be or not. The force in question may or may not be identical with—or in league with—the source of the prediction.) Or 2) there is nothing indeterminate in the world—the nexus of efficient causes is not interrupted by the wills of the men and gods involved; a god need only know what is true now, therefore, in order to have certain knowledge of the future. Or 3) there is at least one god who is so unlimited in his power that he can actually have foreknowledge even of yet undetermined things. Men are free and will be held responsible for what they do. Divinity knows what they will do neither because it itself will bring these things about nor because the causes determining the men's moves are already in existence; divinity knows merely because it can see into the future. There is no kind of knowledge that it does not have.

Sometimes when modern readers are able to convince themselves that the oracles do not limit Oedipus' freedom, they may have this third possibility in mind. Unfortunately it is the one of the three that Sophocles is least likely to have entertained. It is probably a late idea that grew out of a desperate attempt to acquit an omnipotent deity of any responsibility for those of men's decisions that he would rather had been otherwise. Epicurus set the challenge for the Stoics (according to Lactantius, in *The Anger of God* ch. 13). God either wants to remove evils but cannot, he argued, or he can but does not want to, or he can and wants to, or he neither can nor wants to. If he wants to but cannot, he is weak—which is not a quality of god; if he can but does not want to, he is ungenerous—which is also unlike god; if he neither can nor wants to, he is both weak and ungenerous—that is, he cannot be god; but if he can and wants to, which is what one would expect of god, where does evil come from and why does not god remove it? This argument was especially embarrassing for the Stoics because they accepted god's foreknowledge and insisted that there were accurate oracles. If god can see when a man is about to do a foolish or destructive thing but does not interfere, surely that means he either cannot or does not want to stop the sinner. One Stoic solution, that god could have foreknowledge and yet the sinner, not god, will still be responsible for the sin, depends on the idea that the act of "choice" introduces a new motion not caused by antecedent events. This idea may have originated in the Epicurean theory of the indeterminate atomic "swerve" at the moment of decision making, or it may come from a non-philosophic way of thinking, but it cannot be found for certain very far back into the fourth century. The Stoic ideas of will and foreknowledge were later taken up by the Christians (e.g., Augustine's *De libero arbitrio*, Bk. 3), and that, presumably, is why this approach seems to many people today to be such a natural and inevitable solution. It is very unlikely that this was Sophocles' solution, however.

Making abstract pronouncements about the significance of oracles, then, is a hazardous procedure. We would do better to stick close to the text and see what Sophocles has Oedipus say about these things.

Throughout both *Oedipus the King* and *Oedipus at Colonus*, the problem is worried over in these terms: was Oedipus a willing or unwilling perpetrator of the crimes? Was he an agent at all, or only a victim? and was the *daimôn* that was responsible for his misery (*kakodaimonia*) his own *daimôn*, in the sense of his intelligence and character, or was it an independent being for whose actions he need take no blame?

These things are all considered to be exactly equivalent: he is the one who really did it; he acted willingly and knowingly; from the consequences one may justly infer his character. Pollution, horror, even self-loathing followed from Oedipus' acts; his life is ruined, all his good works undone. But like job, Oedipus insists that the explanation must be sought for not in his character but in divinity. That is, not only do the consequences bear no resemblance to the goal he was motivated by; the consequences could not have been altered had he been a better man, a man motivated by worthier goals. He concludes that he was really a victim, not an actor. Do not be afraid of me, says the aged, mutilated outcast (*O.C.* 266f), because these things were done to me, not by me. My nature is not evil.

You have suffered, says the chorus later on (*O.C.* 537). Yes, Oedipus replies, things horrible to bear. You did things, says the chorus; *no*, I "did" nothing. (The verb ἔρδειν can mean either "to act" or "to do harm to someone.") Very similar language is used in *Oedipus the King*; in the crucial scene just after the self-mutilation (1297ff)

In both plays the involuntary nature of Oedipus' crimes is insisted on and underlined. The messenger stepping forward to describe Jocasta's death and Oedipus' blinding (*O.T.* 1230) says that these events, unlike the patricide and incest which were involuntary things, were voluntary, they were miseries deliberately chosen as such; that is, this time, *un*like the times before, the actors knew what the consequences would be.

When Creon, in the later play, speaks of the patricide and incest in tones that suggest that Oedipus, because of these crimes, is not only polluted (*O.C.* 945) but also a man without dignity or rights, Oedipus replies in fury that he bore these things against his will, (964). "One thing I know," he says (985ff); "*your* attack against me and my mother is a wilful act, whereas I married her unwillingly, nor is it by my will that I am speaking of her now." The truth of the matter is, he says, that "I shall not be deemed a bad man, either in that marriage or that killing of my father which you always hurl at me with bitter words."

What makes these acts involuntary, according to Oedipus, is the absence of the crucial information (983); as a consequence of their being involuntary in this sense, they fall into a special class, he insists—crimes that do not stem from a criminal's act (967–8).

The point that we are made to concentrate on, then, is Oedipus' "will" defined very strictly as "moves toward goals thought to be desirable." The question, worried over in both plays, is this: if a man enters into an action with his own consent and the action has appalling consequences, how automatically does it follow that he is a bad man (*O.C.* 270)?

The trouble is, when Oedipus' claim to innocence is spelled out on this level and in these terms, it seems much too simple. There is no room for doubt: he is not responsible for the evils. But then why is Oedipus in such agony? Oedipus is profoundly disturbed by what he has not "done." Why should he be, we may ask, if he really believes what he says about his own innocence? This is the source of the greatest trouble for some interpreters.

The puzzling thing is that Oedipus seems to harbor two seemingly contradictory feelings about himself at one and the same time: he is brilliantly clear and quite consistent about one consequence of his having committed these horrible crimes involuntarily—namely, that it means he is not to be thought of as a bad man; but it never occurs to him that he is freed by this fact from the uncleanness of the guilty man. His first thought after the discovery is that it means that he is not protected by any god and that he is unholy, a product of unholy parents (*O.T.* 1360). At line 1131 of the *Oedipus at Colonus* the blind old man forgets for just an instant and asks Theseus to give him his hand, that he might touch it and even kiss it, if that is lawful. Suddenly he rears back: "How could I, reduced to utter wretchedness, desire that you touch me, me with whom all stains of evil live?" Yet Oedipus says that he "did" no evil. In the modern world this would be a slightly odd, perhaps neurotic, frame of mind. It is not so odd, however, in the setting of the Greek notions of pollution. Innocence could be established quickly and decisively, but cleanliness, it seems, was won more slowly.

At the beginning of the *Oedipus at Colonus*, Oedipus, in his ignorance, blindness and helplessness, accidentally commits yet one more impiety: he trespasses unintentionally, like Philoctetes, on holy ground. To the alarmed inhabitants he announces that this time, for all his frightening appearance, he has a right to ask for sanctuary. "For I have come as one who is holy," he says (*O.C.* 287), "pious, and one who brings benefits to these citizens." He is holy because he is suppliant to the Furies (44), pious because he has come in obedience to Apollo (102). His claim to these qualities is really proleptic, however. That is, as he has said in his prayer to the Furies earlier on (86ff), he has reason to believe that his uncleanness is *almost* over. When Apollo had decreed those many woes, he spoke of this place as the end, he says, a rest after so many years. There he would make the last turn in this wretched life, and Apollo had also said that to those who would accept him, he would be a source of benefits; to those who drove him away as a pariah, he would bring disaster. In other words, the people who understood enough to realize that, terrible as he was, he ought at the last to be welcomed, protected and allowed to stay, these people would be blessed by the presence of his grave.

Even Orestes, whose innocence is much clearer than that of Oedipus, could not be automatically declared clean after the heaven-fated matricide. It took time. His pollution (*Eum.* 281) was ritually cleansed at Delphi when it was fresh, but still the Furies pursued him. The bloodstain is "sleepy" and is "dying away," pleads Orestes. As evidence he points out that he had met many people who were not harmed by being with him. "Time, as it grows old," he says, "undoes all things alike."[8] And yet more anguish awaited him.

The idea of pollution continued into the fourth century at least. Plato speaks with quite unqualified approval of the old notions concerning the blood guilt that was thought to cling even to involuntary killers (*Laws* 9.865), The tragedians are right, he says (*Laws* 8.838), when they show us Oedipus as unholy, hated of the gods and longing for death. Plato specifically includes among polluted men a man who has actually perpetrated a violation with his own hand even if he did what he did entirely involuntarily (865b). Some importance seems to have been put on the accomplishment of the act by one's own hand. By Athenian law, even an involuntary homicide, if the accused is supposed to have done it with his hand, was tried at the august Areopagos, whereas even a voluntary homicide, if the accused is only thought to have planned or commissioned it, was tried by a lesser court, the Palladion. The attitude implied in this distinction explains, perhaps, the stress which Sophocles puts on the fact that Oedipus killed Laius with his own hand (*O.T.* 107, 139–40, 266, 810, 821, 1331, etc.). Like Orestes, or like any Athenian who had committed a lawful homicide (such as killing a highwayman who had struck first, cf. Demosthenes 23.53, Aeschines 1.91,

Antiphon 4d,3), Oedipus might expect eventually to be welcomed back into the community; but this was never achieved without time and difficulty. According to Demosthenes (23.72) an involuntary killer went into exile for a while (like Oedipus), and, even after he was allowed to return, had to perform sacrifices and undergo cleansing.

A man who was the carrier of a pollution (*miaros*) may sometimes have felt the uncleanness as something terrible. At least that is the impression we get from *Oedipus at Colonus* 1131ff, quoted above. And the special nature of Oedipus' involuntary violations would in any case have made his stain no ordinary one. Perhaps most men would have considered him beyond cleansing. Still, the suffering of Oedipus in these two plays cannot really be explained in terms of peculiarly Greek rules concerning pollutions. We, who have no such feelings about ritual pollution, nevertheless respond to this long dead way of talking almost as though it were our own. What are we really responding to?

It is just common sense, one might have thought, not to feel badly about a violation, however terrible, if the deed was truly involuntary and could not have been avoided by having been a better person. Yet that is not the way it works, at least in many cases. After Deianeira unwittingly destroys her husband, the chorus tries to comfort her: Whenever we trip up not of our own volition, the anger felt is tempered, and so it should be now with you (*The Women of Trachis* 727ff). But Deianeira answers: He will never talk like this who has a share in the wrong; only he who has no burden of his own. In other words, attempts to cope rationally with feelings of self-hatred, especially in cases involving accidental harm done to those we love, are not always very easy. This problem is still with us, surely. We might put it slightly differently from the Greeks, that is all. It is often the feeling of guilt that most puzzles us: is it the beginning of wisdom and morality or is it an illness of which we should be cured? We sometimes suspect that self-hatred such as Deianeira felt probably indicates the presence of a culpable desire, at least on an unconscious level; on the other hand, we are also impressed by the harm that men do, to their own lives and to others', as the result of exaggerated or unjustified self-loathing.

Also involved in this talk of pollution is the ability of a society to treat an individual rationally, especially its ability to temper its fear and anger at a violator when it is plain that the person had not done what he did because his character was bad. Toward those who have harmed us we can be forgiving if, and only if, the harm was not intended, says Cleon (Thucydides 3.40). But the Athenians failed to be impressed by Cleon's argument on this occasion—the revolt of Mytilene—and voted, out of humanity, a punishment that would have been appropriate, according to Cleon, only if the Mytileneans had betrayed Athens involuntarily. As the war continued, this kind of confusion was repeated many times, but the results were ever less frequently humane. Again and again Thucydides describes men treating with utterly unreasonable resentment those who could not have been expected to act otherwise. He saw this as one of the chief horrors of the war. Consider the prominence he gives to the Spartan condemnation of the Plataeans and to the Athenian slaughter of the Melians.

This problem, too, is still very much with us. Should we treat criminals as ill? enemies as deprived and unenlightened? How much do a man's intentions count for? What are the fair criteria for "reduced responsibility" or "mitigating circumstances"? Should we try to replace hatred with pity? loathing with tolerance and love?

Many of these questions can be—and often are—translated into terms of the single problem: what if anything in human action is truly voluntary? This is true of the ancient debate as well. Somebody in Sophocles' *Tyro* (fr. 665, Pearson: the play concerns a mortal woman who was seduced by Poseidon) expresses the sentiment we have seen elsewhere in his dramas: No man is evil if he did wrong unwillingly. We may contrast this with Socrates' famous dictum, no one is evil *willingly*. As usual, Sophocles' idea would have seemed more normal to the average Greek than Socrates'. It is universally agreed upon by lawmakers, Plato complains, that there is a clear and vital difference between voluntary and involuntary wrongdoing (*Laws* 9.860); but this is not the right procedure, he says. The right distinction, he insists (862), is that between harmful acts and harmful acts that are traceable to a human being of bad character. If it can be determined that we have an example of the latter sort, then, in addition to compensating for the wrong done, we must correct the character or intelligence of the agent. The reason why it is useless to ask whether the deed was done willingly or unwillingly is that all men in fact pursue their own true, unillusory well-being, and all bad men are bad only because they are pursuing a false vision of their good under the impression that it is the true notion. Punishment then, or persuasion or education or whatever the appropriate measure is, will benefit not only the punisher, but the punished as well. It will cure the reason and restore the moral sense that alone can lead to happiness. The original and distinctive premises in Socratic thinking are two: 1) that happiness depends on the establishment of the correct power structure within each man's psyche, i.e., there is one and only one part of the psyche that would lead each man to true victory for the whole person in the fulness of his existence, and 2) that the part of the psyche of which this is true—and this part only—will, if given command over the other parts, lead a man not only to happiness, but also to the life that is most rewarding and helpful for his fellow men.

The sentiments of Sophocles and Socrates are not contradictory; both define a punishable action as one that stems from a badly motivated human move. The two ideas differ very sharply indeed, however, as Plato saw clearly enough, in what they imply about the natural (and divinely guaranteed) consequences in this life of having a good character and pursuing the right goals. Do happiness and goodness invariably go hand in hand? Socrates said yes; Sophocles, no. Socrates and Plato beg us to start with the awareness of wretchedness or happiness and infer from that whether we are pursuing illusory or genuinely valuable ends. If you are wretched, they say, then you may assume that there are hateful drives within your soul carrying you to false visions. Sophocles, on the other hand, asks us to accept involuntary unhappiness as not only possible, but in certain cases a significant and moving phenomenon.

And so the modern reader of the *Oedipus* who is puzzled by the fact that Oedipus did not allow the knowledge of the involuntary nature of his crimes to soften his own wretchedness, if he then infers that Oedipus really did "will" the acts in some sense, must first be led through the evidence for Sophocles' assumptions about pollution and involuntary wrongdoing. Next it might be suggested that his inference may stem from a failure to appreciate the difficulty that we ourselves still have in coping rationally with such things—especially with our feelings of responsibility for whatever happens to those nearest to us. Perhaps their belief in pollution gave some Greeks a ritual way to deal with problems and temptations which we find all the more troublesome for having left behind that way of thinking. As Freud points out in a famous passage in *The Interpretation of Dreams* (standard Eng. ed. of complete works, 4.267f), the *Oedipus* is not merely the story of a man crushed by overpowering forces that he could not influence, it is the story of a man trapped by such forces into doing very special things: "His destiny moves us only because it might have been ours—because the oracle laid the same curse upon us before our birth as upon him. We shrink back from him with the whole force of the repression by which the wishes have ... been held down within us. Like Oedipus, we live in ignorance of these wishes, repugnant to morality, which have been forced upon us by Nature."

Freud, like Plato, argued that we knew of these desires from our dreams. If this is so, then Sophocles is playing a very dangerous game indeed when he has Jocasta try to comfort Oedipus by telling him (980ff): Do not worry about marrying your mother; many a man before this has slept with his mother in dreams, too. On the surface this means only that a prophecy to the effect that we will sleep with our mother need not upset us, inasmuch as many men have been given such prophetic warnings, in their dreams as well as by oracles, but none actually went through with it. (The καί just might be read as concessive, also: many have lain with their mothers, although only in their dreams.) But the effect is to remind us that complacency about having such desires only, without fulfilling them, is not easily won. Here is a man who is no more criminal in his wishes than we are, but who was tricked by the gods into living them in his waking life.

Throughout the *Oedipus* Sophocles takes great care that we can separate our thinking about ourselves from our concern for Oedipus. He does this, among other ways, by using what has been called, since Bishop Thirlwall's time, dramatic or Sophoclean "irony";[9] that is, by having a character say something that has one meaning for himself, another for us— giving us "proof" that we are not watching our own story, but his. If we down here in the audience know something that he up there on the stage does not know, then our separate identities have been proved and it cannot be ourselves whose tragedy we are witnessing. But in this passage (as elsewhere also), Sophocles compels us to come close to facing our own predicament even while he lets us think that we are excited for Oedipus, not for ourselves.

But another, even more important effect of this constant, almost heavy-handed, use of "irony" in the *Oedipus* is to give us a sense of predestination. Something far larger than Oedipus seems to be mocking him by making him say things again and again that he will look back on later with bitterness. And this brings us back to our earlier question, whether the uncanny correctness of the oracle which was given before Oedipus was born implies a fatalism or some kind of determinism.

Sophocles' description of the role of the gods in the lives of men is, as we noted earlier, without any very clear sense that there is purpose or justice in their actions. Lives of intelligent and well-intentioned men are wasted right and left, and "there is nothing in all this," as the chorus says at the end of *The Woman of Trachis*, "that is not Zeus." But Zeus seems almost to be a name for unavoidable unhappiness, no more. A reader who did not believe in fate or divinity might well be moved by the thought that Oedipus was undone by the same destiny that could undo us all, as Freud suggested, meaning by "destiny" no more than the bitter realities of life, Cocteau's infernal machine. Oedipus' complaint, therefore, that Delphi had predicted what he would do before he was conceived, could be understood, not as a complaint against the malice or heartlessness of real gods, but merely as a demonstration that intelligence and good intentions are never enough to protect one even from the most horrible errors. The treatment of the oracles by Knox and the rest seems to suggest that something of this sort is the case.

The evidence is in favor of the other assumption, however—that is, that Sophocles, for all his freedom from the usual Greek assumptions about the aid that good men could expect from gods, did nevertheless think of divinity as alive and wonderful in some mysterious way. He would be more accurately described as a fatalist than a determinist. Oedipus is not Everyman; he is, as he says even in the earlier play, selected for a very special fate (*O.T.* 1455–8). True, he calls this doom a "marvelous evil" and he is horrified, not overjoyed; but he need not mean that divinity's moves were evil from its own point of view. He may well mean only that the way in which he has been marked off from all other men obviously involves misery for himself to a previously unheard-of extent. Sophocles' picture of his death in the *Oedipus at Colonus* is not really inconsistent with this. Oedipus is cleansed, finally—he had been unwilling to let Theseus touch him just a few minutes earlier, but at the very end he asks Theseus to give him his hand, 1632—and he goes with steadiness and strength, not in despair, when summoned by the thunder and the supernatural voice; nevertheless his suffering is not wiped off the record by his final transfiguration—any more than Christ's is. We do not envy Oedipus. Yet a purpose of sorts has been discerned at last: because his suffering was truly fearful and because it was not given in punishment for anything he had done, therefore out of a terrible evil a terrible beauty is born. The grave of Oedipus will be a blessing to the land.

The messenger reminds the chorus (*O.C.* 1587ff) how the blind old man, rose up and walked into the sacred grove as though he saw: none of his friends was leading him. Surely we are being invited to remember the messenger's speech in *Oedipus the King* (1258) where Oedipus is said to have let out a terrible cry and gone to the bedroom where he would find the dead Jocasta, "as though someone were leading him, for it was none of us who stood by him." The *daimôn* who ruined Oedipus' life now returns at the end in order to complete his obscure design. The design may not be as comprehensible or comforting as more conventional religious visions, but we cannot call it unreligious, unless we are willing to condemn the voice from the whirlwind in *Job* as unreligious too.

3

Some modern readers take comfort from the fact that what the gods made Oedipus do—kill his father and take his father's place with his mother—happened years before the action of the play begins; these fated incidents are "outside" the play, therefore, as Aristotle says all illogicalities should be. The plot that grips us, it is felt, concerns these horrible memories incidentally only. The essential plot is one of wilful self-discovery. Here is how Dodds sums it up, for instance:

> Oedipus might have left the plague to take its course; but pity for the suffering of his people compelled him to consult Delphi. When Apollo's word came back, he might still have left the murder of Laius uninvestigated; but pity and justice require him to act. He need not have forced the truth from the reluctant Theban herdsman; but because he cannot rest content with a lie, he must tear away the last veil from the illusion in which he has lived so long. Teiresias, Jocasta, the herdsman, each in turn tries to stop him, but in vain: he must read the last riddle, the riddle of his own life. The immediate cause of Oedipus' ruin is not "Fate" or "the gods"—no oracle said that he must discover the truth— and still less does it lie in his own weakness; what causes his ruin is his own strength and courage, his loyalty to Thebes, and his loyalty to the truth. In all this we are to see him as a free agent, hence the suppression of the hereditary curse. (*op. cit.* 43)

There are two things that make this theory attractive in the eyes of many readers. First, by declaring the patricide and incest to be incidental to the action, we can avoid the most distressing consequences of the Freudian and Platonic suggestion according to which our excitement at a play must be explained in terms of our own secret involvement. (It is much nicer to think of ourselves as bravely hunting for our true identities than as trying to cope with ancient sexual troubles.) And second, of course, the theory seems to solve the problem raised by our conviction that a play about a man who was not a "free agent" could not move us.

There is an essential distinction, then, according to this theory, between what Oedipus did those many years ago when he committed patricide, then incest, and the things he does within the course of the plot itself. The former may have been fated; but in each move that we see him make on stage he has a choice, there is a decision he must come to. Here is Bernard Knox's version (italics mine):

> The hero is faced with a *choice* between possible (or certain) disaster and a compromise which if *accepted* would betray the hero's own conception of himself, his rights, his duties. The hero *decides* against compromise, and that *decision* is then assailed, by friendly advice, by threats, by actual force. But he *refuses* to yield; he *remains true to himself*, to his physis, that "nature" which he

inherited from his parents and which is his identity. From this *resolution* stems the dramatic tension ... from the *stubborn insistence* of Oedipus at Thebes on knowing the full truth, first about Laius' murder and then about himself, and from old Oedipus' *resolve* to be buried in Attic soil. In each play the hero is subjected to pressure from all sides ... Oedipus tyrannos runs into Tiresias' majestic refusal to speak, the compromising advice of Jocasta and her final desperate appeal, the agonized supplication of the herdsman at the last moment. Later at Colonus he faces the strong disapproval of Theseus, the revulsion of the chorus, the arguments, threats, and violence of Creon, and the appeal of his son .... The Sophoclean hero and his situation are best described in that marvelous image which in the last play of all compares the blind old man to "some sea cape in the North, with storm waves beating against it from every quarter" ... [*O.C.* 1240–1]. Like the cape, the hero *rides out the buffeting* of the storm and *remains unmoved.*

(*The Heroic Temper* [Berkeley and Los Angeles 1964] 8–9)

Nobody would want to deny that there is much truth in this manner of summing up what is stirring and admirable about the typical Sophoclean hero. It can surely be overdone, however. The refusal to yield or compromise is also a characteristic of a number of non-heroic figures in Sophocles' plays, most spectacularly Creon in the *Antigone*. (Creon does yield in the end, of course, after the gods make clear where they stand; but the same is true of Philoctetes too, after all.) Refusing to take the prudent course in order to remain true to one's nature is admirable only if one's nature is itself admirable.

What we usually mean when we say that one man remained true to his nature, whereas another did not, is that the first man, unlike the second, eschewed mere survival or security, or perhaps a short-lived or wicked power or pleasure, because he was motivated by a remoter and nobler vision of what is truly worth preserving or pursuing. Thus Knox speaks of Oedipus' remaining "true to himself, to his *physis*, that 'nature' which he inherited from his parents and which is his identity." (Notice that there is no room here for the Stoic and Christian theory of a decision as an original surge of energy. A "decision" is taken to be a move toward one alternative because that appears to the agent to fit better than other possible courses do with his vision of how he would like things to be. This is still the most practical assumption unless we are wrestling with problems of evil and the concept of a god who is invariably benign.) But good men and bad men alike can act according to their characters, their essential natures, if they are given an opportunity—that is, if they are put in a situation where at least one course open to them has calculable consequences that fit with the thing they value most. If there were no such moments, we would never be sure what a man's character was. And the admirableness or despicableness of his character is most clearly seen when the price for taking the right path is very high. The real difference between the "decisions" that resulted in Oedipus' committing patricide and incest and the "decisions" that led him to discover what he had done is that the latter, unlike the former, are so set up that we can see by the alternative to which he was attracted that his character was admirable. And even that should not be overstressed: which of us in his place would have let Thebes languish in the plague or have failed to pursue the hunt for the killer of Laius or for the identity of his parents in response to Tiresias' absurd-sounding accusations or Jocasta's sudden, inexplicable plea? Even at the last moment, when Oedipus knows in his heart what he will hear in a minute from the reluctant herdsman, is Oedipus' persistence really a feat that none of us would be capable of?

It would seem to take two things to make a dilemma "tragic": a protagonist who is an excellent man—one whose vision of life makes him act well even when compromise or prudence would have prolonged his existence (or his power or comfort or reputation); and a universe in which a good action can sometimes lead to bitter unhappiness, whereas less good actions would have been rewarded with things rightly prized as worth pursuing. If you have the former only, a man who chooses rightly, then you can conclude, like Socrates, that the things this good man gives up were not really worth the having. In that case an unjust death, for instance, will be like the execution of Socrates, no occasion for tears at all if it is correctly understood. On the other hand, the introduction of the second factor, a world where the most worthwhile things can only be got by being the kind of man whom we should not admire, brings with it a fresh problem. The goodness of the good man who, in order to be true to his nature, turns down these truly worthwhile things, needs some explanation, some further justification; otherwise he will appear quixotic or just foolish. That is, as Socrates and Plato were not slow to point out, tragedians tend to imply that the reason why one ought to be good is apparently not that being good brings us the most rewarding experiences possible in human life. But that thesis can be maintained, the philosophers argued, only if we assume that the gods do not in fact ensure that good men get good things, bad men bad things. If you are a humanist through and through, if, in other words, you believe that you can defend your notion of human excellence on, rational grounds, introducing no irrational or inscrutable divinities—or no divinities who act otherwise than to reinforce the "humane" conduct of affairs—then Sophoclean tragedy is absurd. And so it would seem that fate and divine causation are a necessity for a play like the *Oedipus*: if it were not for the presence of this supernatural and essentially incomprehensible force we should have to conclude either 1) that it was all just a very sad accident, and Oedipus ought not to feel too badly, or 2) that Oedipus should not be so sure that his suffering was not a payment for some genuine fault, or 3) that Oedipus was undoubtedly rewarded in the end if he was truly good.

It is often presented as self-evident, indeed blazingly clear, that Sophocles chose to dramatize Oedipus' discovery of his old crimes, not the actual commission of those crimes, because the former are self-willed, whereas the latter were not. Only in this way, it is asserted, could he play down the traditional role of fate in the legend and make of it a moving play, one about a free agent acting on his own. But it is just as possible to explain his choice with the observation that at the time when Oedipus was actually committing the crimes he *thought* he was the master of his own life—he thought that gods merely reinforced the law that men of good intention tended to be rewarded for their efforts—whereas on that terrible day when he was made to see what he had done, he could see how wrong he had been, how horrible and unpredictable the hand of fate had been all along. "Let my lot move where it will," he concludes (*O.T.* 1458). And even the self-revelation is not really self-caused. The god sent the plague, then directed Oedipus to find the killer of Laius; and perhaps the god sent the messenger from Corinth as well—at least that is the feeling we are given when the Corinthian arrives with his fateful information just as Jocasta sacrifices to Apollo, "because you are the nearest *daimôn*" (919). Oedipus accepts the title "perpetrator" (1331) only for the self-blinding. That alone strikes the others on stage as something that Oedipus should be held responsible for. But Oedipus points out that he had been reduced to so wretched a position by the gods that, horrible as the consequences of the blinding were, they were nevertheless less horrible than the alternatives—to kill himself and so look on his parents, or live seeing and so look on his children.

4

The ancients talked of the power to do what one wants (or what seems best, or what really is best) and responsibility (the justice with which one could infer from an act whether or not the man was good) more often than they spoke of freedom. Nevertheless, their notions could easily be translated into terms of freedom—and sometimes were, as in *Republic* 8 and 9. They too, just like ourselves, assumed that freedom was a very desirable thing.

They could imagine a man as being free, however, even if it were assumed that the causes for his actions could ultimately be traced to things outside himself. A man is free, they thought, if at least one of the possibilities presented to him is among those he could imagine with pleasure. If none appeals to him, he is under constraint, not free. They might also insist, as the Socratics did for instance, that if freedom is really a good thing, then an additional factor must be present: the thing that the man imagines with pleasure must be *correctly* imagined, i.e., if he gets what he wishes he will not be disappointed. His character must be such that when given a chance to act according to it, according to his own vision of what is worth pursuing, he will move toward the highest possible happiness. After all, the most obvious reason for calling a man's habits or his notion of what is valuable bad or foolish is that we think he is pursuing self-destructive goals. And a self-destructive goal is one which will eventually result in the disappearance of his freedom; he will find himself blocked, disheartened, frustrated, or actually restricted by society.

It will be noticed that this conception of the problem leaves plenty of room for "free" actions even if it is assumed, as it usually was in antiquity, that chance, nature, the gods, and the society that educated us were among them the real causes of men's characters being what they were. It did not occur to them—nor should it have—that just because the causes for our behavior can always be traced to things outside us in this manner, therefore there is no point in trying to change society, influence politics, sharpen the criteria for assigning praise and blame, revolutionize education, please the gods, and so on. If A moves to interfere with B's pursuit of what he thinks valuable (by calling B bad or foolish, or educating him, or having him arrested, or whatever) the appropriate question to ask is not did As desire to interfere come into being ultimately as the result of causes outside of A, but will the results of the interference be good or bad? for A and B both or only for A? etc. The "lazy argument," as the Stoics called it (see von Arnim, *SVF* 2.277–79), the conclusion that, because a man's recovery from an illness must be determined by things already in existence, therefore he will recover whether he calls a doctor or not, is fallacious. (See also Gilbert Ryle, *Dilemmas* [Cambridge 1954] ch. 2, "It was to Be.") One of the most crucial of the causes determining his recovery is the existence (or future existence, depending on how far back we go) of a conviction in his head that a doctor's presence would be desirable.

There are several reasons why modern readers find distasteful or inadequate this idea that one ought not to look at the causes of a man's character to find out if he is acting "freely"—the idea that freedom means only the opportunity to act according to one's character (or the opportunity so to act if one's character is good, if we follow the Socratic line). One reason is that, like the Hellenistic and Christian philosophers, we have a habit of looking not for those points in a chain of causes that are of greatest practical importance, but for ultimate origins. The philosophers of the classical period avoided much confusion, however, because they thought of a man's character primarily in terms of the vision of what is valuable that motivates him. Socrates catalogued men according to the thing they cherished most: wine, honor, wisdom, etc. (*Republic* 5.475). If we cling to that as what we most want to know when we ask what a man's character is, then, when we entertain the possibility that an observer might, with certain knowledge of our character and our situation, predict infallibly what we will do, even during those moments when we feel most free, the thought will just no longer disturb us. The causes of our characters will be sought in a practical spirit: if our vision of life has led us to unrewarding things, we shall look for those factors in our past—our education, our reading, and the values cherished by our society, for instance—that might profitably be *changed*.

But for many people this is not the end of the problem either. The difficulty that some find with the classical notion of the will is that it seems to them to be empty of everything that they mean when they say that they want to be "free." According to Plato a man is free if and only if he is motivated by a set of values that will not lead him into a trap; the man who is best equipped for life, as Aristotle puts it, is the person for whom what appears to be most worth pursuing and what really is worth pursuing are one and the same (*Nic.Eth.* 3.4). To do what you think to be to your benefit is useless, Socrates points out (*Gorgias* 466ff), unless you are right that it will benefit you. The highest freedom, therefore, will be achieved if you are absolutely certain about the true good. In one sense, then, you have no choice at all when you are really free. Only one course of action is open to the truly free man, the one that he *knows* will lead to happiness.

There are in fact two main difficulties with this formulation of complete freedom, both felt already by the ancients themselves. First, it seems to violate our need to feel that we are each unique. If perfection in the art of living must be bought at the price of pursuing only what divinity and all other men want us to pursue, we would prefer (in some moods, anyhow) to remain imperfect; we cherish the right to make our own mistakes. Plato points out (*Republic* 9.590d–e) that all societies, without exception, must hold their young in check. They do not let them do what appears to them to be to their good, and they only liberate them and call them adult and responsible when they think that the young will want just what their elders want them to want. They assume that the children would not have been free if they had been let go while they still had immature desires. And in fact, Plato says, the truth can only make a few men free; the rest are so ill-equipped to understand the important things even in their mature years that their nearest approach to true freedom will be to be made by the laws to do what they would have wanted to do had they been as perspicacious as the framers of those laws. That the ancients were perfectly capable of being made uncomfortable by this thought is clear from Plato's vigorous parody of the Democratic Man. Not that there is a clear way out of Plato's conclusion, however. Even the most eloquent defenders of the freedom to make mistakes (e.g., John Stuart Mill and Isaiah Berlin) have had to build their arguments largely on practical considerations. The issue is still very much alive, in any case, and is part of the quarrel between Catholics and Protestants, and that between Socialists and Capitalists (the Communist Party and the Catholic Church finding themselves bedfellows not for the first time).

The second difficulty with the notion that complete freedom is equivalent to having a perfect character is more serious. It involves the existence, power and benevolence of divinity. God's will is my freedom, says Epictetus. If we can learn to value what divinity (or Nature or Reason)[10] would want us to value, then we will be free in the sense that 1) everything we want will be in our power and 2) there will be nothing more rewarding that we could have been pursuing instead. And yet, if one believes, as the Fathers of the Church were bound to do, for instance, that divinity could do anything it wanted to do and what it wanted for all of us was that we achieve this most rewarding of all possible kinds of freedom, then a new difficulty arises. How are we going to account for God's refusal to make himself manifest in all his glory so that we *must* choose him, or at least to have arranged things so that we never failed to do things his way in the end, to our own supreme benefit? If freedom in the highest sense is certainty about what it would be best for us to devote ourselves to, and God could give us this certainty any time he wished, why has he so far refused to do so? The Christian answer,[11] of course, is to say that this is *not* freedom in the highest sense; freedom in the highest sense is the ability to make decisions, in uncertainty. This is the other side of the notion that the best freedom is freedom to make our own mistakes. To be unerringly disposed, whether by passion or by intellect, toward Our true well-being, plus living in a favorable time and place, then, is thought to be less desirable than to be allowed to do what merely appears to be for our own good, even when we know full well that we might be making a disastrous error; to be set alternatives one of which is demonstrably better than the other is thought to be less valuable than to be set alternatives neither one of which can be shown without a doubt to be preferable to the other. And so valuable is this freedom, it is believed, that God gives it to us knowing that it will mean that most of us will in our ignorance "choose" damnation.

No wonder, then, that we quite often get a complicated and rather muddy answer when we ask a modern reader of the *Oedipus* just what he means when he insists that the protagonist must have been "free." Inappropriate ideas—some charged with great emotion—are likely to crowd into our heads and prevent us from getting straight what actually happens in the course of the play.

We must first think away the Stoic and Christian contributions to the debate about "freedom," and then try to recover the excitement and confusion of the quarrel that involved sophists, poets and philosophers in Sophocles' Athens.

In *Republic* 2.380a, Socrates quotes from a lost play by Aeschylus[12] where it is said that "god plants criminal responsibility in men," whenever he wishes to destroy a family utterly. Socrates is horrified. Divinity is not responsible (*aitios*) for all things good and bad, "as the many think"; it is responsible only for a few things in men's lives, Socrates insists (379c). "For the good things nothing else should be held responsible (*aitiateon*), but for evils other things, *not* god, must be sought as the cause (*aitia*)." The gods ruled the universe, Socrates and Plato thought, to the extent that the men of the most excellent character could be guaranteed to win the best things life has to offer. But the existence—indeed, predominance (*Republic* 2.379c4–5; *Laws* 9.906a)—of self-destructive energy in the world and in human moves proves that divinity is not able to do what would be best of all, to free everyone by giving them only true desires. Freedom is possible only for the wise, according to Socrates, and for those of the foolish who are lucky enough to be trained and governed by the wise. Although the gods presumably want us all to be happy and can guarantee that all who are truly perceptive will be so, they cannot obliterate those features of incarnate existence that make men less than perfectly perceptive.

The philosophers were right when they insisted that the tragedians did not see things in this light. Sophocles represents the gods as invariably getting their way, although at the expense of the happiness of many a good man. He regularly shows the gods as operating on a scale of values that cuts across the strivings of some of the best of men; their highest intention is something other than to reward all men who are good, and a man who finds his plans frustrated by divinity need not conclude that his goals were therefore impious or immoral in addition to being contrary to divine plans. Sophocles represented the final victory of the gods as beautiful and ultimately to man's best interests; the benefits of the divine interventions, however, are usually remote and obscure. Above all, there is no obvious benefit in this life for the god's innocent victim himself. Troy needs the innocent suffering of Philoctetes, Salamis that of Ajax, Athens that of Oedipus, we need the heroes, and the martyrs are memorable and thrilling to watch. We are thankful for the innocent suffering of these heroes in some obscure way. But we cannot actually learn anything from them as to why we should be good. Or at least we cannot learn what some of Sophocles' contemporaries thought was the first premise of any moral system, that the reason why one should be truly excellent is that only then can one be truly free.

The Stoics had every reason to call Socrates their most important predecessor, at least in one respect. Socrates was the first to argue that complete freedom in the classical sense was really quite possible to achieve if one were intelligent enough. That is, the gods are humane in their demands and nature is benign, so a man who does the wisest of the things possible for him to do at every turn will in fact inevitably achieve lasting happiness, no matter how ill-advised and unjust the actions of other men toward him might be. But Socrates' was only the most startling and influential suggestion in what was really a prolonged and articulate debate. It may be that there never had been, and never has been since, a crisis in morality that was so brilliantly and so variously talked about by those living through it. Sometimes the debate centered on the scale of values received from society (was conventional morality a trap to take away your freedom? could you be free only if you were a *tyrannos*? will a shrewd man always circumvent the demands of his society?), sometimes on the role of the gods (are men's laws divinely inspired and administered or is there a superhuman code that cuts across men's laws? is this superhuman code liberating and really more humane than laws framed by mortals or is it something impossible for men to live by and be happy?).

Hard as it is to extract any logical argument from the plays of Sophocles (far harder than in the case of Aeschylus or Euripides), some things can be inferred about his stand in the debate about freedom: 1) The gods use the excellence of some men to bring benefits to mankind, or to certain cities or families, anyhow. 2) The most beneficial of human lives are not those which are enriched with happiness, but those full of innocent suffering. 3) The innocent suffering is contrived not by unjust men, but by the gods themselves; and the pious onlooker, the one who stands to benefit from the catastrophe, is he who realizes the godsent, involuntary nature of the pollution incurred by the sufferer. 4) The gods need not be thought of as bringing about involuntary pollution by ordering a good man to do something contrary to his nature, as Aeschylus thought; they sometimes allow him to act voluntarily on good motives and then make a mockery of the voluntary nature of what he had done by showing that he had not had some crucial piece of information. 5) Freedom can be, won, therefore, neither in Socrates' nor the sophists' way, or at least this freedom is not guaranteed by the gods; they choose good men, not bad, to be the martyrs for the world.

What Oedipus is shown doing on the stage, hunting the killer of Laius, attempting to find out the identity of his parents, and so on: even this has an element of the involuntary in it. That is, the gods know, but he does not, that the outcome of his efforts is going to be stupefyingly different from what he could possibly guess. We hardly think about that, however; what occupies us most is Oedipus' discovery of what he had done involuntarily in the past, to his parents and to himself. We are watching a man come to the realization that he was, and had been for many years, although he did not know it, one of the chosen of the gods. By dramatizing the discovery instead of the innocent acts themselves, Sophocles has sharpened to an incredible degree the bitterness of being such a chosen one, the folly of supposing that a man can be free by being good. We may well ask why such a vision stirs us rather than depressing us or disgusting us as it did some of the Socratics, but we ought not to deny that this is the implication of the action we are watching.

Instead of saying that since the *Oedipus* moves us, therefore Oedipus must be a free agent, we should do better to say that since the *Oedipus* moves us, and he is obviously *not* free, the assumption that only the actions of a free agent could engage our deepest sympathies and interest ought to be looked at again. We should at least not close the debate before it is begun.

5

There is another common argument that runs as follows: Greek tragedies do not in fact show us stories of men suffering catastrophes because of faults in their character or intellect. Aristotle understood Greek tragedy. Therefore Aristotle, when he said that, the best kind of protagonist is one whose fall is caused by a major *hamartia*, cannot have meant by *hamartia* a mistake that indicates a flaw in the protagonist's character or intellect. As Professor Page puts it, "since [Aristotle] illustrates his theme with the example of *Oedipus* (among others), it is clear that he is thinking of involuntary *hamartia*" (ed. of *Agamemnon* xxix n.2).

That the word *hamartia* in *Poetics* 13 means an unavoidable mistake in the facts is confidently believed by the majority of critics today. The passages in Aristotle which are most often quoted in support of this idea are *Nicomachean Ethics* 5.8 and *Rhetoric* 1.1374b5ff. The scholars most often cited as having "demonstrated" this interpretation are O. Hey (*Philologus* 83 [1927] 1–17 and 137–63), P. W. Harsh (*TAPA* 76 [1945] 47–58), and Bywater and

Else in their commentaries *ad loc*. Now there is no doubt that the word, taken in isolation, might mean "mistake in fact," that *hamartêma* does mean that, both in key passages in Aristotle's own writing and also in interesting passages in the tragedies themselves. But it is also true that the word *can* mean a catastrophic error for which one can blame oneself morally, and this use, too, can be found both in Aristotle (e.g. *Nic.Eth.* 3.110b28ff) and in tragedy (e.g., *Antigone* 126ff). It is simply not possible to find a conclusive answer to the puzzle of *Poetics* 13 by studying the various uses of the word *hamartia* and adding to that only our own understanding of what in fact does happen in the tragedies.

Before Aristotle gives his description of the best kind of protagonist, he eliminates all of the kinds that would fail to serve the natural function of tragedy, the pleasurable production of pity and fear in the audience. Heading the list and very roundly condemned indeed is the truly admirable and excellently equipped man, for if he is seen to fall from good fortune to bad fortune, the experience for the audience will be *miaron*, "unclean," polluted and therefore polluting. (From other parts of the *Poetics* we can infer that such a man could, without bad effects, be shown going from bad to good fortune, but such a plot would be considered by Aristotle to produce a pleasure other than that appropriate for tragedy, e.g., 1453a35.) But neither do we want a wicked or depraved man, whether falling into misery or triumphant. "What is left is someone between these extremes, a man who does not stand out for his excellence or justice, nor yet does he fall into misfortune because of wickedness or vice."

At this point nobody could deny that Aristotle is asking for a protagonist who has some imperfections in his character. If he had not gone on to use the word *hamartia* there would be no doubt about it: not only is it better that the man be less than spectacular with regard to human excellence and justice, if the plot fails to show him to be flawed in these qualities the spectacle of his downfall will be "unclean." Aristotle cannot be merely eliminating an insipidly perfect, saintly man; he cannot be saying merely that audiences are more sympathetic to "human" figures than to impossibly good men. The word *miaron* is too strong to allow that interpretation. He is saying that unless the audience sees that the protagonist has a flawed character, they will have an appalling, defiling experience instead of the appropriate pleasure.

Nor is it possible to assert confidently that Aristotle did not want this imperfection of character to be the cause, or a cause, of the protagonist's fall into misfortune. Although he says that pity can only be aroused by the spectacle of one coming to a misfortune that he did not deserve (1453a4), and although he uses for the act that brings the man down a word (*hamartia*) of neutral coloring, a word that might well include non-culpable mistakes, the rhetoric of these sentences seems nevertheless to imply that the mistaken move is *proof* that the protagonist, though he is not a wicked man, is not a man of outstanding virtue, either. Both times that the protagonist's catastrophic *hamartia* is spoken of it is in explanation of the requirement that he be in between the outstandingly good man and the outstandingly bad man. He should fall not through wickedness or vice but through a *hamartia* (1453a10); "he should be a man either such as we have described or better rather than worse, falling from good to bad fortune through a great *hamartia*" (a16).

Among the most famous and admired passages in the *Poetics* are those concerned with the requirement that there be a necessary connection between the character of the protagonist and the plot. When we find Aristotle discussing the various possible kinds of plot (1452b23) in terms of these same two things, therefore, i.e., whether the movement is toward unhappiness or away from it, and whether the protagonist is good or bad, we should surely expect him, in describing the best of all plots, to do so in terms of the *relation* between the moral excellence of the protagonist and his passage from or to misfortune. One thing that would certainly disturb Aristotle about the fall of an excellent man is that the connection between this good man's character and his fall would seem to be necessarily a tenuous one. The catastrophe should occur to a man sufficiently excellent (and highly placed and successful) so that we feel that such a thing ought not to have happened to such a man; but if the man did *nothing*, he ought not to have done, there would appear to be no connection between character and plot at all. Or so Aristotle may well have supposed.

But Aristotle is saying much more than this. It is not only an artistic blunder to show perfectly blameless suffering; the spectacle is a polluting one, *miaron*, he says. This is an unusual, perhaps even a unique, use of the word *miaron*. Applied to an act, it nearly always means (in the fourth and fifth centuries, anyhow) that the event brings a *miasma* or pollution. Applied to a person it means that he has done, or is the kind of man who might do, something that makes him a carrier of a pollution and therefore one who will pollute everyone who comes into contact with him.[13] The opposite of *miaros* is *katharos*, *hagnos* or *hosios*, "cleansed," or "pure" (e.g., Plato, *Laws* 9.865ff, Antiphon 2a10, Andocides 1.96 *SEG* 12.81.11, *O.T.* 823, 1383, *O.C.* 945). Although this is hard to prove, it seems that it was especially appropriate to call a person *miaros* if he had violated, or was thought capable of violating, a close family tie.[14]

The word occurs again in the next chapter of the *Poetics*. There Aristotle argues that the best plots are those in which the suffering results from deeds done (or intended) within the family, "as when the murder or whatever is carried out or intended by brother against brother, son against father, mother against son, or son against mother" (1453b19–22). That is why tragedians keep returning to the houses of Alcmeon, Oedipus, Orestes, Meleager, Thyestes, Telephus and a few others, he says (1453a20–1). The worst variation on this theme, he goes on to say, is the story of a person intending such a deed in full knowledge of what he is doing, who then does not do it after all. "For it both has the *miaron*, and in addition (because there is no suffering) it is not tragic" (1543b39). Better is the situation where the person goes through with such a deed not knowing what he is doing, and then discovers afterward what he has done. "For the *miaron* is not present, and the effect of the discovery is shattering" (1454a4). (Such, he had said earlier [1453b31], is the situation in Sophocles' *Oedipus*.) Best of all, however, is the story of someone about to commit such an act in ignorance, who then finds out the truth and so does not go through with it. We have to fill in the reasons why Aristotle preferred this last situation. First, there is "suffering," because a deed of the right sort is intended by a man who would not have wanted to do such a thing knowingly. (Aristotle has already said that an intended violation of a family tie is enough to cause "suffering"; it need not be carried out. Aristotle is obviously thinking of the perpetrator's "suffering," not the victim's—which is just what we should expect if his models are stories like those of Oedipus and Thyestes. In the worst kind of plot, where the deed is also intended but not carried out, the would-be perpetrator undertakes the deed voluntarily, with full knowledge of the identity of the victim; that apparently is why it is appropriate to say that there is no "suffering" in his story.) Secondly, since in the best version the deed, which would have been free of *miaria* anyhow, is not even carried out, the situation is as free of *miaria* as a story of such a violation could be. Also, it is possible that Aristotle considered the "discovery" to be best of all in this version. Because it comes in time to prevent the dreaded act, it is thrilling but *not* shattering.

So anxious was Aristotle to show that in the best plays *miaria* was minimized, he appears to have been driven to a conclusion in chapter 14 that is hard, if not impossible, to reconcile with his preference in the chapter before for an unhappy, rather than a happy, ending.

The word *miaron* in chapter 14, then, seems to have been chosen because of its common connection with a violation of family ties. And that fact makes it difficult to avoid the conclusion that this was also the case in chapter 13 when Aristotle called the spectacle of innocent suffering *miaron*. There must be some difference in the two uses, however. He says in chapter 14 that Oedipus committed his violation in ignorance and that in such situations. there is suffering, but "*miaria* is not present." In chapter 13 the story of Oedipus is also singled out as one that is not *miaron*, but for a different reason altogether: Oedipus and Thyestes are mentioned (1453a11) as examples of the very best kind of protagonist, in that. they are not pre-eminently good, yet do not fall because of vice, either; they fall because of some *hamartia*, and belong to the class of men who, in the beginning at least, are highly thought of, very successful and famous. There are two different things, therefore, that would have made the story of Oedipus *miaron*—if Oedipus had known what he was doing, *or* if he had been a thoroughly excellent man instead of one of the intermediate kind. His act had to have two qualities that are by no means easy to reconcile one with the other: it had to be done in ignorance, and it had nevertheless to stem from an imperfection in his character. The failure to have either one would have heightened the *miaria* to an intolerable degree, Aristotle insists.

Why it should be thought that there would be pollution if Oedipus were to be portrayed as knowing full well what he was about to do is easy enough to see. Show a violation too horribly criminal and there is a *miaria* right there in the theater involving even the audience itself. But why this should also be the result of showing a violation which is done in ignorance of the victim's identity, but which in addition to that is done because of no fault at all in the protagonist's character—that is much harder to see. For this idea we must go not to the tragedies themselves or to archaic ideas of pollution, but back once more to the Socratic revolution and the quarrel between Socrates and the poets. According to Socrates and his descendants, as we have seen, the universe is so arranged that it is in fact impossible (or at least extremely unlikely, according to Aristotle's version) that a man who has all the virtues will do something that will cast him into genuine unhappiness. The man who is pre-eminent in excellence and justice is the man who has the necessary conditions for success. Indeed, Socrates even said that such a man had the *sufficient* conditions for happiness, and Plato and Aristotle each modified this notion only a little. To present a story, then, of a man who had what were believed to be necessary and sufficient conditions for happiness but who nevertheless did the kind of thing that all men hoped that they would never do, would be to present a picture of the universe that is false in the most dangerous and corrupting way possible. Socrates and Plato looked at Aeschylus, Sophocles and Euripides and saw that this was exactly what they did do. Again and again good men were either forced directly to do something of the most polluting kind or they were kept in ignorance and then shown later what they had done—forced[15] or tricked by the gods themselves. No wonder that the censorship of the tragedies was so large a part of Plato's ethics: to be present at a tragedy and be profoundly moved by it was just about the most dangerous kind of defilement that a man could be exposed to.

Now Aristotle, for rather complicated philosophical reasons, came to the conclusion that writing tragedies and attending them must be a natural and therefore good-directed activity. Witnessing violations within the family must ultimately be an aid, not a hindrance, to the philosophic life, he seems to have concluded. But he had Plato's arguments to overcome before he could get anybody to believe this. If he had agreed with Plato that the vision implied in tragedies was indeed contrary to what men must come to believe if they were to win happiness, then it would have been necessary to conclude that tragedies were either ludicrous or dangerous. But he could accept neither of these alternatives if he supposed that tragedies were "rational," a help to the good life. And yet Aristotle did not wish to contend that the Socratic view of life was basically incorrect, either. He took the only remaining way out. He concluded that Plato had read the plays incorrectly. *If* tragedies did indeed imply that a man who had achieved the necessary and sufficient conditions for happiness could nevertheless be forced or tricked by the gods to do what no good man should ever want to do—one of the things we all hope most passionately that we shall never do—then watching and enjoying these tragedies would clearly be a dangerously misleading experience in the eyes of Socrates, Plato *or* Aristotle. But the best tragedies, Aristotle argued, do not *really* imply any such thing, for they have protagonists who do, what they do, in part at least, because they are not perfectly good men.

From the fact that most of the key words in the *Poetics* seem to be echoes of Plato's arguments against the poets, we ought probably to conclude that the treatise was aimed mainly at those of Plato's followers who still clung to the master's decision about tragedy. The appearance of a surprising and uncharacteristic word like *miaron*, then, might well be explained as a result of this aspect of the work. That is, it may have been a word that would not have occurred to Aristotle had not one of his opponents used it first. And indeed we find that this whole cluster of words, μίασμα, μιαρός, μιάστωρ, μιαίνειν, μιαιφονεῖν, μιαιφόνος, μιαρία, so common and crucial in the tragedies, is also found frequently in Plato, but is simply not part of Aristotle's vocabulary at all. Plato was still vitally interested in pollutions, as we have seen, although he had some new ideas about them. But Aristotle just did not think in terms of pollution. (No wonder he was unwilling to admit, what tragedies show all the time, that a man could do something through no fault of his own and yet feel unclean for what he had done!) The explanation for his choice of *miaron* in *Poetics* 13, then, must surely be sought in the usage of Plato or of Plato's more orthodox supporters in the Academy.

Plato called the lowest part of the psyche, "*miaron* to an extreme degree" (*Republic* 9.589e4). And at the very close of the *Republic*, Socrates implies that if that lowest part gets command of the whole person, the result is a *miasma* that the psyche takes with it even into the next world. (If we live well—according to intelligence—we shall cross Lethe safely, he says, and "we shall not be polluted with regard to our psyche," [10.621c2, cf. *Phaedo* 81b].) Of course, when the lowest part finds its desires frustrated by intelligence, it calls the restrictions put on it by the higher part *miaroi* (*Republic* 8.5624); but the truth is just the other way around: it is the yearnings at the lowest part that are really *miaroi*. (We might be reminded of the scene in the *Antigone* where Creon and his son quarrel as to which of the two is really *miaros*, which of the two is violating the more sacred ties in pursuing his desires [744ff].) Plato often used strong words indeed to indicate the unholiness of our basest desires. The lowest part of the psyche is entirely without god, he says (*Republic* 9.589e4), and to judge from its Sprees in our dreams, there is nothing it will not do. It will commit 1) incest 2) *miaiphonein*, "*miasma*-causing murders," stopping at nothing in the choice of a victim (571d2) and 3), eat what must not be eaten (a reference to crimes like that of Thyestes?). And *this* is the part of the psyche, Plato argues, that is awakened, fed and made strong; by watching tragedies!

The word *miaron* and the verbs and nouns related to it are, as I have said, not found in Aristotle. There are in fact only five exceptions, the three appearances of *miaron* in the *Poetics* and two appearances of *miaiphonos*, a rare compound meaning "guilty of having committed a *miasma*-causing murder." This is, of course, just the adjectival form of the verb used by Plato in the passage on unholy dreams quoted above, *miaiphonein*. Once in the *Nicomachean Ethics* (1177b10) Aristotle is reaching out for an absurdly strong word: a man would have to be completely *miaiphonos*, he says, to want to turn his own people into enemies merely in order to have someone against whom he could wage war. But the other occurrence of this word *is* more interesting, because it comes in a discussion of "pity" and "fear." If we are pained at the unmerited suffering of others, he says (*Rhetoric* 2.1386b28), we shall take delight, or at least not be pained, by the deserved punishment of a *miaiphonos* or one who strikes his own father (πατραλοίας, another Platonic word appearing only here in Aristotle; cf. *Republic* 596b6). Evidently, then, the notion of pollution occurred to Aristotle only in connection with tragedy and the question why we should enjoy it.

In the *Laws*, when Plato goes into the question of *miasmata*, he decides, as we have seen, that the old belief, according to which even involuntary violators of family ties should be held to be *miaroi*, is correct. He says that playwrights, therefore, who bring on stage "Oedipus, Thyestes, or

Macareus" are right to show them, once these heroes realize what they have done, horrified to the point of wanting to kill themselves (8.838). The stories of Oedipus and Thyestes are also the ones most obviously suggested in the catalogue of wicked dreams in the *Republic*, as we have just noticed. When, therefore, we find Aristotle choosing once more these same two heroes as the best examples of the ideal protagonist (*Poetics* 13.1453a11), we may begin to guess that these figures had become stock examples in the discussion of tragedy in the Academy. And we may also guess that the supposed *miaria* of their acts is what made them such suitable examples for the Platonists. That is surely how we should explain the fact that Aristotle talks of *miaria* only in connection with tragedy.

To Plato it seemed clear that Oedipus was *miaros*, and that anyone who allowed himself to get sympathetically excited by his crimes was risking that most dangerous of *miasmata*, the surrender to the part of his psyche that is just as *miaros* as Oedipus. But Aristotle turned the tables on Plato. Because Oedipus did not know the identity of his victim, he is not really *miaiphonos*, he argued. And anyhow, the only really *miaron* experience would be the spectacle of completely innocent suffering, for that would be a violation of all that the Socratics held most dear. Any Platonist would have to admit that this was a clever reversal of the master's argument. He could console himself, however, with the observation that it rests on an impossible reading of Attic tragedy.

The opposite to the incurrence of *miaria* is *katharsis*. Did Aristotle first hit upon that name for the thing that good tragedies did for us because of his anxiety to deny the charge that there was *miaria* in such experiences? Or did he first think of it in its medical use (which is certainly uppermost in his discussion in *Politics* 8), in response to Plato's notion of tragedy as "filling," "stuffing" or "satisfying" the lowest part of the psyche (*Republic* 10.606a4,5,6; cf. 9.57c6,7)?

Aristotle did not believe that there was a part of our psyche that was naturally *miaros*, a part that loved Oedipus' doing what he did. For him an irrational passion was only an inefficient passion, one of a pair that had to be steered between; what it wanted was always a real good in itself. When he found that he enjoyed tragedy, therefore, he could not but conclude that it must somehow be a rational enjoyment. He could hardly deny that tragedies regularly violated the very important assumption that excellence is recognized by success in the achievement of real happiness in this life; dreadful things were always happening in tragedies to people to whom such things ought not to happen. But he found a minor good to be achieved even by that upsetting spectacle: we were cleansed or emptied of our exaggerated tendencies toward pity and fear, he suggested. And he did deny that the philosophers' assumption was *completely* contradicted by good tragedies. He could not conceive of himself liking such a plot; that would be truly *miaron*, he says. But all one needed to convert an experience that would be *miaron* into an experience of the opposite sort, a *katharsis*, was to introduce a modicum of justice: the protagonist must be assumed to have made at least one great mistake, however excellent he may have been in all other ways. A factual mistake that was not his fault is not enough. The *hamartia* must be evidence of some imperfection in the protagonist's character or intellect.

6

Aristotle should be ignored, therefore, and the *Oedipus* read as a tragedy of fate. But we are still left with the problem why a tragedy of fate should be so stirring, so seemingly profound. We surely cannot just leave it, as Goethe did, for instance, that the sublimest form of tragedy is in fact that which shows a man crushed by an insoluble problem or by an unavoidable necessity. It may be true; but why is it true?

Plato offered an explanation for the attractiveness of such a spectacle, but we do not want to go all the way with him, either. We cannot imagine ourselves coming to the conclusion that Greek tragedy should not be shown to those who have not been given the "antidote" of Socratic philosophy. Still, Plato's opposition to the tragedians was based on two considerations, each of which contains an interesting observation, even if neither need be taken quite as Plato took it.

First, there is the suggestion that *if* we believed the Socratic vision of life, then tragedies must either look nonsensical to us or they must get their power by satisfying a latent longing within us not to believe the truth. This much is surely correct. It is Plato, not Aristotle, who read the plays correctly. *If* we accepted Socrates' assumption that the universe is so constructed that no good man can be deprived of anything truly valuable, then tragedies must, if they move us, appeal to something in us that works on a false notion of life. But few of us are willing to subscribe to the Socratic vision of life without reservations. We might agree, for instance, that the human qualities that we admire ought to be those that do in fact lead to true happiness; but we might still suspect that personal happiness and social happiness must each be compromised for the sake of the other, and that either can be undone by chance or natural forces at any time. We could then conclude that tragedies need not be banned on the supposition that they imply false things about morality and life. Yet we should still be left with the valuable observation that tragedies do in fact tend regularly to emphasize something which is, in a way, the reverse of what philosophers and other moral teachers often want to emphasize. Moral philosophers, anxious always to improve things, try to get us to look within for the true causes of our failures. They want us always to be fearful of the possibility that we might be pursuing false goods and harboring hateful desires that cannot lead to happiness. Tragedies, on the other hand, show men coming to bad ends even when their goals were rational and their desires not the sort that they should be ashamed of or regret at all.

Philosophers want us to replace resentment with guilt. They want us to assume the burden for our own failures. Indeed, our parents and teachers have told us much the same thing as long as we can remember. Perhaps we can learn this lesson too well, however. Taken full strength, this is a comforting lesson only if a man is already strong and deeply satisfied with himself and life, day after day, every hour of every day. The vast majority of us would welcome some relief from the feeling of guilt and regret, at least from time to time. We would like to be able to feel that what we have missed *had* to be missed, that we could not have got it however wise we had been or less subject to base yearnings. just to be allowed to resent something outside ourselves would help. That is much less painful than guilt. Better yet would be a vision that would make it alright in the end, a vision implying that there is a divine beauty to be discerned even in our failings. Maybe we did not really fail at all if our unhappiness is part of a divine scheme.

Plato's second complaint is that the part of us that enjoys all those polluting crimes portrayed by the tragedians is the part that actually yearns to commit those very crimes, even though we are not conscious in our waking hours of harboring any such yearnings or resentments. This suggestion too, though it seems to be reinforced by modern studies of dreams and the unconscious, need not be taken without modifications. Above all, Plato was surely wrong in conceiving a fear of art because of this connection it would seem to have with the unconscious.

We are not necessarily "reducing" great literature to something dangerous, or silly, or base when we say that—in addition to containing harmless delights and to stimulating conscious perceptions of things human—it sometimes also taps unconscious fantasies which are upsettingly primitive. When we are young and incapable of better things, what we hunger for is stories that have heroes or heroines with whom we can identify consciously, just as in a daydream. Such stories are aids to daydreams, really. When we "grow out" of a certain kind of story we often do so for the same reasons that might lead us to abandon a daydream—either we become painfully aware that it is "unrealistic," i.e., the dreamed—of goal is just too improbable, if not downright impossible; or the achievement no longer seems an attractive and satisfying thing to go after. Then, if the whole class of stories in which we identify with the protagonist more or less consciously no longer seems to touch anything very important in our lives—they do not let us dream the dreams we really must or want to dream—we are ready to graduate to serious literature. Here our sympathies and parallel fantasies go underground. One sign that we have reached this step is that we find unhappy endings sometimes just as good as happy endings. And certainly things happen to the protagonists—death, failure and the most appalling accidents—that rarely, if ever, figure in our conscious desires. But this takes great art: our unconscious lives are unconscious precisely because we have found that waking life is tolerable only if we refuse to own up to them. To say of a tragedy, then, that it allows us to live through things that we have long kept from our conscious awareness, is to say that the skill and art of the writer must have been extraordinary.

Plato's two observations (thus modified) have this in common: both point to the possibility that tragedy can, among other things, allow us to cope with fear, impossible desires, a sense of loss and irrational self-hatred, some of which date back to our earliest childhood. If this, is what Aristotle had meant by his suggestion that tragedy provides a *katharsis* of pity and fear, we should have to conclude that he was right. Unfortunately, Aristotle spoiled the idea by insisting that the protagonist be not completely innocent. If it were not for the innocence of the protagonist and the clear presence of a power that he could not have been expected to understand or overcome, living through his crimes and failures would be very painful, not cleansing and exhilarating at all.

NOTES

1. Part I appeared in *Arion* 4.3, Part II in *Arion* 4.4.

2. "On Misunderstanding *Oedipus Rex*," *Greece and Rome* 13.1 (April 1966) 37–49.

3. This is the most usual way that these positions are distinguished in modern times, anyhow, as by J. S. Mill, for instance. Some of the Stoics had rather different ways of distinguishing the two ideas, however. See Cicero's *De fato* 42(18), for example.

4. For the various forms the story took and what can be said for the antiquity and popularity of each, see C. Robert, *Oidipus* (Berlin 1915), also H. W. Parke and D.E.W. Warmell, *The Delphic Oracle* (Oxford 1956) 1.298–300, and R. Lattimore, *Story Patterns in Greek Tragedy* (London 1964) 3–6.

5. In *Tragic Themes in Western Literature*, ed. Cleanth Brooks (New Haven 1955); cf. *Oedipus at Thebes* (New Haven 1957) 38.

6. *Sophocles* (Cambridge [Mass.] 1951) 141.

7. *A Study in Sophoclean Drama* (Ithaca 1958) 73.

8. *Eum.* 286. The manuscripts read καθαιρεῖ, time "destroys" or "cancels," but many editors change the accent to καθαίρει, time "cleanses." Most editors since Musgrave consider the line spurious because 1) it is thought to contradict Orestes' claim to have been absolved at Delphi and 2) by itself (with the MSS accent) it sounds like a proverbial line

meaning "Time destroys (or whisks away) all things eventually." The first of these arguments is based on a misreading of βρίζει, μαραίνεται and πέλει in 281–82, however, and the second is a mere guess.

9. "On the Irony of Sophocles," *Philological Museum* 2 (1833) 483ff. Before Thirlwall, "irony" was used in English only in the ordinary Greek sense of *eirôneia* or as a description of one of Socrates' mannerisms, i.e., pretended ignorance of one sort or another. Thirlwall's choice of this word for unintentional double meanings is comprehensible only if we suppose fate or the gods to be practicing *eirôneia* on Oedipus, i.e., fate seems to allow Oedipus to make sense but it knows better and has a mischievous purpose. Cf. the French *ironie du sort*. In recent decades, however, Thirlwall's new use of the word—*without* any thought of fate—has become almost primary.

10. "History" would be the Communist equivalent, perhaps.

11. Except for some, mostly Protestants, who say that it would be foolish or even impious for us to expect our reason to be able to uncover God's reasoning.

12. This fragment was for a long time known only from Plato's quotation. But see D. Page, *Literary Papyri, Poetry*, Loeb ed. 8. Page makes an interesting case for believing that the sentiment is also at the heart of most Aeschylean tragedy: see his ed. of the *Agamemnon* (Oxford 1957) xxviii f.

13. A. W. H. Adkins, "Aristotle and the Best Kind of Tragedy," *CQ* 16 (May 1966) 96, argues that the loose use of *miaros* in the orators and in comedy (he might also have added *Phaedrus* 236e, *Charmides* 161b and 174b) justifies the assumption that *miaros* is "a piece of 'ordinary language' used generally at the time to condemn works of art that were felt to be shocking." It is a long leap, however, from an angry or jocular use of an epithet meaning literally "you who have committed a pollution-causing violation," but which is used in a non-literal, exaggerated spirit, to "polluted" as a description of the experience of an audience at a play. If *miaron* had come to mean little more than the English "filthy" or "revolting," the characters in Aristophanes would surely have lost interest in it and looked for a stronger word.

14. Perhaps because the notion of kinsman was sometimes felt to include all of one's fellow countrymen, treason too might be thought of as a *miaria*. Socrates' indictment (*Apology* 23d) said he was "*miarôtatos* and a corrupter of the young." At *Republic* 5.470a2 the offer of spoils taken from kinsmen (i.e., any other Greeks) is called a *miasma*. At *Euthyphro* 4c Euthyphro suggests, that a *miasma* is the same whether in the family or not, but Socrates denies it. This is his more usual stand, cf. *Republic* 8.565e, *Laws* 9.872e. We shall look at another, uniquely Platonic, use of the word below.

15. See Page's interesting, if somewhat oversimplified, defense of the innocence of Agamemnon, in his edition of the *Agamemnon* xx–xxix. There is no question of Agamemnon's ignorance; like Orestes, he is compelled by necessity to do the impious deed with his eyes open.

BERNARD KNOX

Introduction to Oedipus the King

This play is universally recognized as the dramatic masterpiece of the Greek theater. Aristotle cites it as the most brilliant example of theatrical plot, the model for all to follow, and all the generations since who have seen it staged—no matter how inadequate the production or how poor the translation—have agreed with his assessment as they found themselves moved to pity and fear by the swift development of its ferociously logical plot. The story of Oedipus, the myth, was of course very old in Sophocles' time and very well known to his audience. It was his use of the well-known material that made the play new. He chose to concentrate attention not on the actions of Oedipus which had made his name a byword—his violation of the two most formidable taboos observed by almost every human society—but on the moment of his discovery of the truth. And Sophocles engineered this discovery not by divine agency (as Homer did) and not by chance, but through the persistent, courageous action of Oedipus himself. The hero of the play is thus his own destroyer; he is the detective who tracks down and identifies the criminal—who turns out to be himself.

The play has also been almost universally regarded as the classic example of the "tragedy of fate." To the rationalist critics of the eighteenth century and still more to the firm believers in human progress of the nineteenth, this aspect of the play was a historical curiosity, to be discounted;

From *The Three Plays*, trans. Robert Fagels, pp. 115–135. © 1982 by Viking Press.

but our own more anxious age has seen in the situation of Oedipus an image of its own fears. In the very first year of our century Sigmund Freud in his *Interpretation of Dreams* offered a famous and influential interpretation of the destiny of Oedipus the King:

> *Oedipus Rex* is what is known as a tragedy of destiny. Its tragic effect is said to lie in the contrast between the supreme will of the gods and the vain attempts of mankind to escape the evil that threatens them. The lesson which, it is said, the deeply moved spectator should learn from the tragedy is submission to the divine will and realization of his own impotence. Modern dramatists have accordingly tried to achieve a similar tragic effect by weaving the same contrast into a plot invented by themselves. But the spectators have looked on unmoved while a curse or an oracle was fulfilled in spite of all the efforts of some innocent man: later tragedies of destiny have failed in their effect.
>
> If *Oedipus Rex* moves the modern audience no less than it did the contemporary Greek one, the explanation can only be that its effect does not lie in the contrast between destiny and human will, but is to be looked for in the particular nature of the material on which that contrast is exemplified. There must be something which makes a voice within us ready to recognize the compelling force of destiny in the *Oedipus*, while we can dismiss as merely arbitrary such dispositions as are laid down in [Grillparzer's] *Die Ahnfrau* or other modern tragedies of destiny. And a factor of this kind is in fact involved in the story of King Oedipus. His destiny moves us only because it might have been ours—because the oracle laid the same curse upon us before our birth as upon him. It is the fate of all of us, perhaps, to direct our first sexual impulse towards our mother and our first hatred and our first murderous wish against our father. Our dreams convince us that this is so. (Trans. James Strachey)

This passage is of course a landmark in the history of modern thought, and it is fascinating to observe that this idea, which, valid or not, has had enormous influence, stems from an attempt to answer a literary problem— why does the play have this overpowering effect on modern audiences?—and that this problem is raised by an ancient Greek tragedy. As a piece of literary criticism, however, it leaves much to be desired. If the effect of the play did indeed depend on the "particular nature of the material," then one would expect modern audiences to be just as deeply moved by a performance of

Voltaire's *Edipe*, whereas, in fact, the play is rarely produced and then only as a museum piece. At any rate, though the primordial urges and fears that are Freud's concern are perhaps inherent in the myths, they are not exploited in the Sophoclean play. And indeed Freud himself, in a later passage in the same work, admits as much: "the further modification of the legend," he says, "originates ... in a misconceived secondary revision of the material, which has sought to exploit it for theological purposes." This "further modification" is the Sophoclean play.

Sophocles' play has served modern man and his haunted sense of being caught in a trap not only as a base for a psychoanalytic theory which dooms the male infant to guilt and anxiety from his mother's breast, but also as the model for a modern drama that presents to us, using the ancient figures, our own terror of the unknown future which we fear we cannot control—our deep fear that every step we take forward on what we think is the road of progress may really be a step toward a foreordained rendezvous with disaster. The greatest of these modern versions is undoubtedly Jean Cocteau's *Machine Infernale*; the title alone is, as the French say, a whole program. Cocteau also worked with Stravinsky on an operatic version of the Sophoclean play (the text in liturgical Latin), and for a recording of this work he wrote a prologue that sums up his compelling vision of man's place in a strange and haunted universe. "*Spectateurs*," says the author in his forceful, rather nasal voice, "*sans le savoir* ... without knowing it, Oedipus is at grips with the powers that watch us from the other side of death. They have spread for him, since the day of his birth, a trap and you are going to watch it snap shut." This is of course much more explicit (and much more despairing) than the Sophoclean play; it stems, like the beautiful and terrifying second act of the *Machine Infernale*, in which the Sphinx and Anubis play their fiendish game with Oedipus, from a modern vision of a death-haunted universe, from the obsessed imagination that gives us also, in the film *Orphée*, the unforgettable images of Death at work: her black-uniformed motorcyclists, enigmatic radio messages and rubber gloves.

Parallel with this modern adaptation of the Oedipus story, serving new psychologies and mythologies of the irrational, goes a reinterpretation of the Sophoclean play itself by scholars and critics along similar lines. Yeats, who translated the play for production at the Abbey Theatre in Dublin, described his reaction to a rehearsal in the words: "I had but one overwhelming emotion, a sense as of the actual presence in a terrible sacrament of the god." Taking his cue from the work of Frazer and Harrison, who emphasize the religious, tribal, primitive aspects of the Greek tradition, Francis Fergusson, in his brilliant book *The Idea of a Theater*, gives us a vision of the Sophoclean masterpiece as an Athenian mystery play, a solemn rite of sacrifice that purges the community of its collective guilt by punishing a scapegoat, one man who perishes for the good of the people—an emphasis taken up and broadened by René Girard in his *Violence and the Sacred*. Some such interpretation must have been the base for the Tyrone Guthrie film of the play's production at Stratford, Ontario: the actors wear hideous masks, for all the world like Halloween goblins, and the effect of the performance is to suggest some Stone Age ceremony of human sacrifice.

All this is a reaction, predictable and perhaps even necessary, against the nineteenth-century worship of the Greek rational "enlightenment"—a vision of ancient Greece dear to the hearts of optimistic Victorians who found in Greece, as each successive generation in the West has done since the Renaissance, their own image. But the reaction toward the mysterious, the irrational, has gone too far. For Sophocles' play, read without preconceptions of any kind, gives an entirely different impression. There is not one supernatural event in it, no gods (as there are in so many other Greek plays), no monsters (like jackal-headed Anubis in Cocteau's play), nothing that is not, given the mythical situation, inexorably logical and human. So far as the action is concerned, it is the most relentlessly secular of the Sophoclean tragedies. Destiny, fate and the will of the gods do indeed loom ominously behind the human action, but that action, far from suggesting primeval rituals and satanic divinities, reflects, at every point, contemporary realities familiar to the audience that first saw the play.

The voice of destiny in the play is the oracle of Apollo. Through his priests at Delphi, Apollo told Laius that he would be killed by his own son, and later told Oedipus that he will kill his father and marry his mother. At the beginning of the play Apollo tells Creon that Thebes will be saved from the plague only when the murderer of Laius is found and expelled. This Delphic oracle, which for modern poets—Yeats, for example—can conjure up mystic romantic visions, was, for Sophocles and his audience, a fact of life, an institution as present and solid, as uncompromising (and sometimes infuriating) as the Vatican is for us. States and individuals alike consulted it as a matter of course about important decisions; Sparta asked Apollo if it should declare war on Athens in 431 B.C. (it was told to go ahead and was promised victory), and at the end of the war young Xenophon asked it whether he should join the expedition of Cyrus and go up-country into Asia Minor as a mercenary soldier fighting against the Great King. The oracle maintained contacts with peoples and rulers all over the Greek and barbarian worlds; it promoted revolutions, upheld dynasties, guided the foundation of colonies—its wealth and political influence were immense.

Its power was based on a widespread, indeed in early times universal, belief in the efficacy of divine prophecy. The gods knew everything, including what was going to happen, and so their advice was precious; the most influential dispenser of such advice was Apollo, so of Zeus. His knowledge is celebrated in a famous passage of the Ninth Pythian Ode of Pindar, who wrote in the same century as Sophocles:

> *You know the appointed end*
> *of all things, and all the ways.*
> *You know how many leaves the earth unfolds in spring,*
> *how many grains of sand are driven by storm wind and wave*
> *in the rivers and the sea.*
> *You see clear the shape of the future*
> *and what will bring it to pass. (44–49 in the Greek)*

In such a faith, private individuals and official representatives of state had for centuries made the journey by land and sea to Apollo's temple in its magnificent setting on a high plateau below Mount Parnassus; in gratitude for the god's advice kings and cities had lavished gifts on the sanctuary and even, built treasuries on the site to house their precious offerings.

When Sophocles was a boy, the Spartan infantry at Plataea, the final battle of the Persian War, had stood motionless under a murderous fire of Persian arrows while their prophets tried (like Tiresias in *Antigone*) to obtain a prediction from their observation of the sacrificial ritual; only when the signs were declared favorable did the soldiers advance against the enemy. The historian Herodotus, who describes this incident in his history of the war, states emphatically in another passage his own belief in the truth of divine prophecy and rejects firmly the arguments of those who deny it. But his protest is the voice of the older generation. In the last half of the fifth century B.C., particularly in Athens, this belief in prophecy and with it belief in the religious tradition as a whole was under attack. Philosophers and sophists (the new professional teachers of rhetoric, political theory and a host of allied subjects) were examining all accepted ideas with a critical eye: the fifth century in Athens was an age of intellectual revolution. Among the younger intellectuals prophecies, especially those peddled by self-appointed professional seers (a class of operator common in ancient Greece but not unknown in modern America), were viewed with skepticism if not scorn; inevitably some of the skepticism spread to embrace the more respectable oracular establishments that claimed to transmit divine instructions. Thucydides, the historian of the Peloponnesian War, dismissed prophecy contemptuously in a couple of cynical sentences, and Euripides attacked it, sometimes lightheartedly, sometimes bitterly, in one play after another. The philosophical attack on it was more radical; the dictum of the sophist Protagoras—"the individual man is the measure of all things, of the existence of what exists and the nonexistence of what does not"—subjected prophecy, and for that matter the gods themselves, to a harsh criterion that found them wanting.

When he chose as the subject of his tragedy a story about a man who tried to avoid the fulfillment of a prophecy of Apollo, believed he had succeeded, and cast scorn on all the oracles, only to find out that he had fulfilled that prophecy long ago, Sophocles was dealing with matters that had urgent contemporary significance; prophecy was one of the great controversial questions of the day. It was in fact the key question, for the rationalist critique of the whole archaic religious tradition had concentrated its fire on this particular sector. Far more than prophecy was involved. For if the case for divine foreknowledge could be successfully demolished, the whole traditional religious edifice went down with it. If the gods did not know the future, they did not know any more than man. These are exactly the issues of the Sophoclean play. When the chorus hears Jocasta dismiss divine prophecy and Oedipus agree with her (948–49), they actually pray to Zeus to fulfill the dreadful prophecies they have just heard Jocasta and Oedipus report. They identify prophecy with the very existence of the gods. Never again, they say, will they go reverent to Delphi or to any oracular shrine of the gods

> *unless these prophecies all come true*
> *for all mankind to point toward in wonder....*
> *They are dying, the old oracles sent to Laius,*
> *now our masters strike them off the rolls.*
> *Nowhere Apollo's golden glory now—*
> *the gods, the gods go down.* (989–97)

By this emphasis Sophocles gave the age-old story contemporary and controversial significance, and he had other ways besides to make his audience see themselves in the ancient figures he brought to such disturbing life on stage. The play opens, for example, with a group of priests begging a ruler for relief from plague, and the first choral ode, a prayer to the gods, rehearses the harrowing details of the city's suffering—

> *children dead in the womb*
> *and life on life goes down*
> *you can watch them go*
> *like seabirds winging west....*
> *generations strewn on the ground*
> *unburied ... the dead spreading death ...* (198–208)

The Athenians were all too familiar with plague; in the second summer of the war, in a city overcrowded with refugees from the Spartan invasion of Attica, plague had raged in the city, and it had recurred over the next three or four years.

But more important for the play's impact on the audience than this grim setting is the characterization of the play's central figure, Oedipus the King. The poet's language presents him to the audience not as a figure of the mythical past but as one fully contemporary; in fact he is easily recognizable as an epitome of the Athenian character as they themselves conceived it and as their enemies saw it too. One trait after another in the character of Sophocles' Oedipus corresponds to Athenian qualities praised by Pericles in his Funeral Speech or denounced by the Corinthians in their attack on Athenian imperialism at the congress in Sparta before the war.

Oedipus is clearly a man of action, swift and vigorous action, and this is a markedly Athenian characteristic. "Athens," said Pericles, "will be the envy of the man who has a will to action"; the Corinthians, from the opposite point of view, say the same thing—"Their nature not only forbids them to remain inactive but denies the possibility of inaction to the rest of mankind." In the play Oedipus' will to action never falters, and it forces Tiresias, Jocasta and the shepherd, in spite of their reluctance, to play their part in the swift progress toward the discovery of the truth and his own fall. The priest in the opening scene appeals to Oedipus as "the man of experience"; experience is the result of constant action and this too—especially their experience in naval warfare—is a quality celebrated by Athens' orators and feared by her enemies. Oedipus is courageous, and it was characteristic of Athenian courage that it rose to its greatest heights when the situation seemed most desperate. This is exactly what we see in the play—Oedipus' most defiant and optimistic statement comes when Jocasta, knowing the truth, has gone off to hang herself, and the audience waits for the appearance of the shepherd who, under duress, will reluctantly supply the last piece of evidence that identifies Oedipus as the son of Laius and Jocasta.

Oedipus is quick to decide and to act; he anticipates advice and suggestion. When the priest hints that he should send to Delphi for help he has already done so; when the chorus suggests sending for Tiresias, the prophet has already been summoned and is on the way. This swiftness in action is a well-known Athenian quality, one their enemies are well aware of. "They are the only people," say the Corinthians, "who simultaneously hope for and have what they plan, because of their quick fulfillment of decisions." But this action is not rash, it is based on reflection; Oedipus reached the decision to apply to Delphi "groping, laboring over many paths of thought"

(79). This too is typically Athenian. "We are unique," says Pericles, "in our combination of the most courageous action and rational discussion of our plans." The Athenians also spoke with pride of the intelligence which informed such discussion: Pericles attributes the Athenian victories over the Persians "not to luck, but to intelligence." And this is the claim of Oedipus, too: "the flight of my own intelligence hit the mark" (453), he says, as he recalls his solution of the riddle of the Sphinx. The riddle has sinister verbal connections with his fate (his name in Greek is *Oidipous* and *dipous* is the Greek word for "two-footed" in the riddle, not to mention the later prophecy of Tiresias that he would leave Thebes as a blind man, "a stick tapping before him step by step," 519), but the answer he proposed to the riddle—"Man"—is appropriate for the optimistic picture of man's achievement and potential that the figure of Oedipus represents.

His solution to the riddle, as he reminds Tiresias, the professional diviner, was a triumph of the amateur; "it cried out for a prophet," he says,

> *Where were you?* ...
> No, but I came by, Oedipus the ignorant,
> I stopped the Sphinx!" (448–52)

So Pericles boasts in the Funeral Speech that the Athenians, though they refuse to regiment their lives for war like the Spartan professionals, can face them confidently in the field. And Oedipus' adaptability to circumstances—he came to Thebes a homeless wanderer and became the admired ruler of a great city—this too is typically Athenian: Pericles claims "that the individual Athenian addresses himself to the most varied types of action with the utmost versatility and grace."

Above all, as we see from the priest's speech in the prologue and the prompt, energetic action Oedipus takes to rescue his subjects from the plague, he is a man dedicated to the interests and the needs of the city. It is this public spirit that drives him on to the discovery of the truth—to reject Creon's hint that the matter should be kept under wraps, to send for Tiresias, to pronounce the curse and sentence of banishment on the murderer of Laius. This spirit was the great civic virtue that Pericles preached—"I would have you fix your eyes every day on the greatness of Athens until you fall in love with her"—and which the enemies of Athens knew they had to reckon with—"In the city's service," say the Corinthians, "they use their bodies as if they did not belong to them."

All this does not necessarily mean that Sophocles' audience drew a conscious parallel between Oedipus and Athens (or even that Sophocles himself did); what is important is that they could have seen in Oedipus a man endowed with the temperament and talents they prized most highly in their own democratic leaders and in their ideal vision of themselves. Oedipus the King is a dramatic embodiment of the creative vigor and intellectual daring of the fifth-century Athenian spirit.

But there is an even greater dimension to this extraordinary dramatic figure. The fifth century in Athens saw the birth of the historical spirit; the human race awakened for the first time to a consciousness of its past and a tentative confidence in its future. The past came to be seen no longer as a golden age from which there had been a decline if not a fall, but as a steady progress from primitive barbarism to the high civilization of the city-state. One of the new teachers, the sophist Protagoras, was particularly associated with this idea; he wrote a book called *The State of Things in the Beginning*, and his outline of human social history is clearly the basis of Plato's re-creation of him in the dialogue entitled *Protagoras*. But much more important, because contemporary, is the clear reflection of his ideas in that chorus of *Antigone* that sings the praise of man the resourceful. "Man the master, ingenious past all measure ... / he forges on ..." (406–8). Three of the most important achievements of man celebrated in that ode are his conquest of the earth, the sea and the animals. And Oedipus, in the images of the play, is presented to us as hunter, sailor and plowman. He is the hunter who follows "the trail of the ancient guilt" (124); the sailor who, in the chorus' words, "set our beloved land—storm-tossed, shattered— / straight on course" (765–66), and he is also the plowman—"How," sings the chorus when the truth is out at last,

> how could the furrows your father plowed
> bear you, your agony, harrowing on
> in silence O so long? (1338–40)

These images, recurrent throughout the play, recall the first decisive steps that brought man from nomadic savagery to settled, stable culture, made him master of the land and sea and the creatures inhabiting them. But Oedipus speaks too in terms that connect him with more advanced stages of human progress. Among these—the culmination of the *Antigone* ode—was the creation of the city-state, "the mood and mind for law that rules the city" (396). Oedipus is a ruling states-man; he is a self-made man who has won and kept control of the state, a master of the political art, and he is conscious of his achievement and its value:

> O Power—
>
> wealth and empire, skill outstripping
> skill in the heady rivalries of life

—he bursts out when Tiresias accuses him, "what envy lurks inside you!" (432–35). The words conjure up the feverish activity, the political ferment of Athenian imperial democracy. And, as head of the state, Oedipus is the enforcer of the law. He is, in the play, the investigator, prosecutor and judge of a murderer. In all these aspects he represents the social and intellectual progress that had resulted in the establishment of Athenian democracy and its courts of law, a triumph of human progress celebrated in the last play of Aeschylus' *Oresteia*.

The figure of Oedipus represents not only the techniques of the transition from savagery to civilization and the political achievements of the newly settled society but also the temper and methods of the fifth-century intellectual revolution. His speeches are full of words, phrases and attitudes that link him with the "enlightenment" of Sophocles' own Athens. "I'll bring it all to light," he says (150); he is like some Protagoras or Democritus dispelling the darkness of ignorance and superstition. He is a questioner, a researcher, a discoverer—the Greek words are those of the sophistic vocabulary. Above all Oedipus is presented to the audience as a symbol of two of the greatest scientific achievements of the age—mathematics and medicine. Mathematical language recurs incessantly in the imagery of the play—such terms as "measure" (*metrein*), "equate" (*isoun*), "define" (*diorizein*)—and at one climactic moment Oedipus, seizing on a numerical discrepancy in the evidence against him, dismisses it with a mathematical axiom: "One can't equal many" (934). This obsessive image, Oedipus the calculator, is one more means of investing the mythical figure with the salient characteristics of the fifth-century achievement, but it is also magnificently functional. For, in his search for truth, he is engaged in a great calculation, to determine the measure of man, whom Protagoras called the measure of all things."

Functional too is the richly developed image of Oedipus as a physician. Hippocrates of Cos and his school of physicians had in this same century founded Western medicine; their treatises and casebooks are still extant, and in them we can see the new methods at work: detailed observations of hundreds of cases, classification of symptoms, plotting of the regular course of individual diseases and then diagnosis, prognosis (these are Greek words, their words). In the play the city suffers from a disease, and Oedipus is the physician to whom all turn for a cure. "After a painful search," he says, "I found one cure: / I acted at once" (80–81). And the metaphor extends throughout the play: the sickness, the cure, and the physician who will find it.

And all these images, like the plot, like the hero, have what Aristotle called their *peripeteia*, their reversal. The hunter catches a dreadful prey, the seaman steers his ship into an unspeakable harbor—"one and the same wide harbor served you / son and father both" (1335–36)—the plowman sows and reaps a fearful harvest, the investigator finds the criminal and the judge convicts him—they are all the same man—the revealer turns into the thing revealed, the finder into the thing found, the calculator finds he is himself the solution of the equation and the physician discovers that he is the disease. The catastrophe of the tragic hero thus becomes the catastrophe of fifth-century man; all his furious energy and intellectual daring drive him on to this terrible discovery of his fundamental ignorance—he is not the measure of all things but the thing measured and found wanting.

The reversal of the tragic hero is singled out for praise by Aristotle because it comes about through recognition, in this case Oedipus' recognition of his own identity. But he recognizes also that the prophecies given to his father and to him by Apollo were true prophecies, that they had been fulfilled long ago, that every step taken to evade them, from the exposure of the child to the decision never to go back to Corinth, was part of the pattern of their fulfillment. "And as I fled I reached that very spot / where the great king ... met his death" (881–82). And this does pose, for the modern reader as for the ancient spectator, the question of fate and, though those spectators could not have expressed the idea in abstract terms, of free will and human freedom.

This basic theme has often been discounted on the grounds that the opposition of fate and free will, providence and chance, determined and open universe, is not explicitly formulated until much later than Sophocles' time, in the philosophical discussions of the late fourth and third centuries. This is true (though it must not be forgotten that we have lost the writings of the fifth-century sophists and, more important still, of the "atomic" philosophers Democritus and Leucippus), but it does not necessarily follow that because a problem had not yet been given philosophical expression, it could not be conceived. The myth of Oedipus itself—like the stories of attempts to escape a predicted fate so frequent in the *Histories* of Sophocles' friend Herodotus—poses the problem in poetic form, and one of the functions of myth in preliterate societies, as Lévi-Strauss has so brilliantly demonstrated, is to raise deeply disturbing problems that will later demand more precise formulation.

Even though what remains of early Greek literature shows no verbal consciousness of the ideas we associate with freedom of the will, there is abundant evidence, from the earliest times, for a related concept that is in fact almost inseparable from it: individual responsibility. No one can be held fully responsible for actions committed under some kind of external constraint, and in early Greek belief such constraint might be exerted by a host of nonhuman powers. When Agamemnon, in Homer's *Iliad*, makes his

apologies to Achilles for the harsh treatment which led to the death of so
many heroes, he tries to evade responsibility; he is claiming, in other words,
that he did not act freely.

> *I am not responsible*
> *but Zeus is, and Destiny, and Erinys the mist-walking*
> *who in assembly caught my heart in the savage delusion*
> *on that day I myself stripped from him the prize of Achilleus.*
> *Yet what could I do? It is the god who accomplishes all things.*
> (19.86–90, trans. Richmond Lattimore)

The context suggests that this is merely an excuse (Achilles, in his reply, does
not even refer to Agamemnon's lengthy development of this theme—over
fifty lines long). But the negative implication of this and many similar
passages is clear: that a man is responsible for those actions which are not
performed under constraint, which are the expression of his free will. The
question of Oedipus' responsibility for what happens (and what has
happened) is, as we shall see, posed in the play; it is also discussed much later,
in *Oedipus at Colonus*, which deals with Oedipus' old age and death.

It is interesting to note that in those later centuries, when the Stoic
philosophers do pose the problem in abstract form, they start from this same
mythical base, the oracle given to Laius. Chrysippus uses this oracle to
illustrate his almost completely determinist position (the only freedom he
allows man is that of a dog tied to a moving cart); Carneades reinterprets the
oracle to allow man a little more freedom; Alexander of Aphrodisias takes up
the challenge on the same ground, and Cicero debates the meaning of this
same oracular prophecy. As long as Greek philosophy lasts, the discussion of
Oedipus' freedom or his subjection to fate goes on—even in the
commentaries on Plato by Albinus in the second and Calcidius in the sixth
century A.D. It is from these endless (and inconclusive) discussions that
Milton draws his famous description of the intellectual delights of the fallen
angels:

> [*they*] *reason'd high*
> *Of Providence, Foreknowledge, Will, and Fate,*
> *Fixt Fate, free will, foreknowledge absolute,*
> *And found no end, in wand'ring mazes lost.*
> (*Paradise Lost* 2.658–61)

The end of Greek philosophy and the triumph of Christianity brought no
end to the argument, only new terms in which to phrase it. St. Augustine

writes his book *On Freedom of the Will* (*De Libero Arbitrio*) just as Cicero had written his *On Fate* (*De Fato*); Augustine is no longer concerned with the oracle given to Laius but he is just as tormented (as he claims all humanity is) by the contradiction between our free will and God's foreknowledge that we will sin. It was of course an argument that was to go further; Bergson, Croce, and Friedrich Engels, to name only a few, continue it into modern times. It has become much more complicated and sophisticated with the years; the terms of the opposition can be, and have been, continually redefined in philosophically elegant formulas that are designed, and may even seem, to abolish it; and of course modern analytical philosophers can dismiss the problem as a mere verbal misunderstanding. But to the ordinary man, now as in Sophocles' day, there is a problem in the coexistence of predictable pattern and free will, whether that pattern be thought of as divine providence, the will of history, or the influence of the stars.

There are two obvious ways of avoiding the contradiction, both of them extreme positions and at opposite poles to each other; one might call them, to use a political metaphor, the right and the left. The right is all for order and pattern; it escapes the dilemma by dispensing with freedom altogether. It sees history, individual and general, as a rigidly determined succession of events in time. If you take such a view, whether Christian with St. Augustine—that all history is God's providential preparation of two cities, one of God, one of Satan, and that certain souls are predestined for salvation (or with Calvin, that other souls are destined for damnation)—or materialist and atheist with Marx and Engels, denying the freedom of history to all classes but the proletariat—"Freedom," wrote Engels, "is the recognition of necessity" (which is a German version of Chrysippus' dog tied to a cart)—if you take either of these determinist views, you have no antinomy, no contradiction. But you have no freedom, and, unless you happen to be one of the Christian or the Marxist elect, you have no future either.

What we have called the left, on the other hand, is all for freedom; to the devil with pattern and order, this party is for anarchy, the human will is absolutely free and nothing is predictable; there is no pattern of order in the universe, which is merely the operation of blind chance. If you deny the possibility of prediction and the existence of order, whether as an "atomic" theorist like Democritus, or out of sheer desperation, as Jocasta does in the play—"What should a man fear? It's all chance, / chance rules our lives" (1069–70)—you have abolished the logical contradiction. But you accept a blind, pointless, meaningless universe—the universe of the absurd.

Both of these extremes are of course repugnant to the human spirit and especially to that of the West, which is that of the Greeks. We want both the freedom of our will and the assurance of order and meaning; we want to eat our cake and have it too, and in this non-Christian and Christian are alike. But no matter what subtle distinctions we invent and refine, the basic contradiction remains. Insofar as any meaningful pattern or divine providence exists it must encroach to some extent on human freedom; if human freedom is unlimited, the possibility of pattern or order is denied. Whenever we are tempted to forget this uncomfortable fact we should look at what happens to the Christian version of the contradiction—God's foreknowledge that man would sin and man's freedom not to—under the scalpel of a satiric critic.

In that now much-neglected classic *Penguin Island*, Anatole France tells the story of an old half-blind Celtic saint, St. Mael, who goes off one day in his miraculous stone boat, is swept north by the current and lands on an ice floe. He is immediately surrounded by a flock of small, inquisitive, chattering creatures and being too short-sighted to see that they are penguins, he baptizes them. This raises grave theological difficulties for the celestial authorities, and in the council in heaven that meets to discuss the problem, doctors of the church and saints debate the fate of the baptized penguins. It is finally decided to turn them into human beings, and they are thus subject to the fate of man—the fall from grace, the expulsion from the garden, sin, work, disease and death, judgment and redemption. (As the Almighty remarks, they would have been much better off if they had gone on being penguins.) He closes the debate with a reminder to himself that though they will certainly fall from grace, they are nonetheless free not to do so. "However, my foreknowledge must not he allowed to interfere with their free will. So as not to limit human freedom, I hereby assume ignorance of what I know, I wind tightly over my eyes the veils which I have seen through, and in my blind clairvoyance, I allow myself to be surprised by what I have foreseen."

France is of course quite right; as a logical proposition, the two concepts are irreconcilable. The only way to believe in the pattern and the freedom at once is not as a logical proposition but as a mystery; the medium of exploration is not philosophy but religion—or art. We can say, as Tertullian is supposed to have said (but almost certainly didn't), "I believe it precisely because it is absurd," or we can express the contradiction in poetic terms that transcend logic. It is significant that Plato's main discussion of the problem is not phrased in the cut and thrust of dialectic, but in the great myths, as in the myth of Er, where Socrates is no longer subject to questioning. Only a mood of religious humility or a work of art can hold in precarious coexistence the irreconcilable concepts. But for one form of art, the drama, this is a particularly dangerous subject. For the power of drama depends on our feeling that the actors are free, that their choice of action is significant. The dramatist who, like Sophocles, dares to base his drama on a story that seems to question if not rule out human freedom of action is walking a perilous tightrope.

The soul of drama, as Aristotle says, is plot—the action that demands and succeeds in engaging our attention so that we are no longer detached spectators but are involved—in the progress of the stage events. Its outcome is important for us; in the greatest plots (and the plot of this play by Sophocles is perhaps the greatest) it is for the moment the most important thing in the world. But this engagement of the audience proceeds from an identification with the figures on stage, and this is not possible if we are made to feel that the action of the characters is not free, not effective. We expect to be made to feel that there is a meaningful relation between the hero's action and his suffering, and this is possible only if that action is free, so that he is responsible for the consequences.

There are of course external factors in our own lives that no force of our will can influence, and no one can object to their presence in the play. But the hero's will must be independent of those factors, not identified with them. As Macbeth, for example, is independent of the prophetic witches. Macbeth *chooses* to believe the witches and the vision of the dagger—and on this subject be says something very revealing:

> *or art thou but*
> *A dagger of the mind, a false creation,*
> *Proceeding from the heat-oppressed brain?*
> *I see thee yet, in form as palpable*
> *As this which now I draw.*
> *Thou marshall'st me the way that I was going ...* (2.1.37–42)

He *was going* anyway. If the witches had bewitched Macbeth, so that the murder of Duncan were not an act of his will, *Macbeth* would not be a tragedy—it would be a sort of science—fiction story in which a man is injected with a drug that makes him carry out the will of some external force. We might sympathize with him but could hardly be expected to engage ourselves emotionally with his actions, presented as a play. If Macbeth were injected with witches' brew or Oedipus with fate-serum, we could not regard them as tragic, or even dramatic.

In a play, then, the hero's will must be free, but something else is needed: it must have some causal connection with his suffering. If through no fault of his own the hero is crushed by a bulldozer in Act II, we are not impressed. Even though life is often like this—the absconding cashier on his way to Nicaragua is killed in a collision at the airport, the prominent statesman dies of a stroke in the midst of the negotiations he has spent years to bring about, the young lovers are drowned in a boating accident the day before their marriage—such events, the warp and woof of everyday life, seem irrelevant, meaningless. They are crude, undigested, unpurged bits of reality—to draw a metaphor from the late J. Edgar Hoover, they are "raw files." But it is the function of great art to purge and give meaning to human suffering, and so we expect that if the hero is indeed crushed by a bulldozer in Act II there will be some reason for it, and not just some reason but a good one, one which makes sense in terms of the hero's personality and action. In fact, we expect to be shown that he is in some way *responsible* for what happens to him.

If so, the hero obviously cannot be "fated," predestined or determined to act as he does. And, to get back finally to the *Oedipus* of Sophocles, Oedipus in the play is a free agent, and he is responsible for the catastrophe. For the plot of the play consists not of the actions which Oedipus was "fated" to perform, or rather, which were predicted; the plot of the play consists of his discovery that he has already fulfilled the prediction. And this discovery is entirely due to his action.

He dismisses Creon's politic advice to discuss the Delphic response in private; he undertakes a public and vigorous inquiry into the murder of Laius. He is the driving force which, against the reluctance of Tiresias, the dissuasion of Jocasta and the final supplication of the shepherd, pushes on triumphantly and disastrously to the discovery of the truth. If it had not been for Oedipus, the play persuades us, the truth would never have been discovered, or at least it would not have been discovered *now*. This presentation of the hero's freedom and responsibility in the context of the dreadful prophecy already unwittingly and unwillingly fulfilled, is an artistic juxtaposition, a momentary illusion of full reconciliation between the two mighty opposites, freedom and destiny. It is an illusion because of course the question of responsibility for what happened *before* the play, of Oedipus' freedom in the context of divine prophecies fulfilled, is evaded. But it makes the play a triumphant tour de force, the like of which no other dramatist has ever attempted. Oedipus is the free agent who, by his own self-willed action, discovers that his own predicted destiny has already been fulfilled. This is why the play moves us as a spectacle of heroic action and why the figure of Oedipus, dominating the stage, arouses our admiration as well as our sympathy. It is noticeable that in Cocteau's masterpiece, where Oedipus is deliberately portrayed as a marionette in the hands of daemonic powers, the greatest dramatic excitement is generated by the action and speech not of Oedipus but of those divine powers, Anubis and the Sphinx.

Oedipus' heroic achievement is the discovery of the truth, and that discovery is the most thoroughgoing and dreadful catastrophe the stage has ever presented. The hero who in his vigor, courage and intelligence stands as a representative of all that is creative in man discovers a truth so dreadful that the chorus which sums up the results of the great calculation sees in his fall the reduction of man to nothing.

> *O the generations of men*
> *the dying generations—adding the total*
> *of all your lives I find they come to nothing ...* (1311–13)

The existence of human freedom, dramatically represented in the *action* of Oedipus in the play, seems to be a mockery. The discovery to which it led is a catastrophe out of all proportion to the situation. Critics have tried, with contradictory results, to find some flaw in Oedipus' character that will justify his reversal. But there is nothing in his actions that can make it acceptable to us. The chorus' despairing summation, "come to nothing," echoes our own feelings as we watch Oedipus rush into the palace.

But this estimate of the situation is not the last word; in fact, it is contradicted by the final scene of the play. Oedipus' first thought, we are told by the messenger, was to kill himself—he asked for a sword—but he blinds himself instead. This action is one that the audience must have expected; it was mentioned in the earlier *Antigone*, for example (61–64), and Oedipus as the blind, exiled wanderer seems to have been one of the invariable elements in fifth-century versions of the myth. But, though the blindness was foreseen by Tiresias, Oedipus' action did not figure in the prophecies made to and about him by Apollo. When the messenger comes from inside the palace to describe the catastrophe he uses words which emphasize the independence of this action: "terrible things, and none done blindly now, / all done with a will" (1359–60). And as Oedipus, wearing a mask with blood running from the eye sockets, stumbles on stage, he makes the same distinction when the chorus asks him what power impelled him to attack his eyes:

> *Apollo, friends, Apollo—*
> *he ordained my agonies—these, my pains on pains!*
> *But the hand that struck my eyes was mine,*
> *mine alone—no one else—*
> *   I did it all myself!* (1467–71)

These two passages suggest that in his decision to blind himself Oedipus is acting freely, that the intricate pattern of his destiny was complete when he knew the truth. To that terrible revelation some violent reaction was inevitable; the choice was left to him. He resisted the first suicidal impulse perhaps (though Sophocles is silent on the point) because of a latent conviction, fully and openly expounded in the last play (*Oedipus at Colonus*, 284–95, 612–16, 1101–31), that he was not to blame. He chose to blind himself, he tells the chorus, because he could not bear to see the faces of his children and his fellow-citizens. But his action has, in the context of this play, an impressive rightness; the man who, proud of his far-seeing intelligence, taunted Tiresias with his blindness now realizes that all his life long he has himself been blind to the dreadful realities of his identity and action.

The messenger's description of the horrors that took place inside the palace has prepared the audience for the spectacle of a broken man. So Oedipus seems to be at first, but very soon this bloodstained, sightless figure begins to reassert that magnificent imperious personality which was his from the beginning. He reproaches the chorus for wishing him dead rather than blind, defends his decision to blind himself, issues instructions to Creon and finally has to be reminded that he is no longer master in Thebes. The despairing summation based on the fate of Oedipus—the great example (as the chorus calls him) that man is equal to nothing—is corrected by the reemergence of Oedipus as his old forceful self. Formidable as of old he may be, but with a difference. The confident tone in which the blind man speaks so regally is based on knowledge, knowledge of his own identity and of the truth of divine prophecy. This new knowledge, won at such a terrible price, makes clear what it was in the hero that brought about the disaster. It was ignorance.

In spite of his name, *Oidipous*, with its resemblance to the Greek word *oida* ("I know")—a theme that Sophocles hammers home with continual word-play—Oedipus, who thought he knew so much, did not even know who his mother and father were. But ignorance can be remedied, the ignorant can learn, and the force with which Oedipus now reasserts his presence springs from the truth he now understands: that the universe is not a field for the play of blind chance, and that man is not its measure. This knowledge gives him a new strength which sustains him in his misery and gives him the courage needed to go on living, though he is now an outcast, a man from whom his fellow-men recoil in horror.

The play then is a tremendous reassertion of the traditional religious view that man is ignorant, that knowledge belongs only to the gods—Freud's "theological purpose." And it seems to present at first sight a view of the universe as rigid on the side of order as Jocasta's was anarchic on the side of freedom. Jocasta thought that there was no order or design in the world, that dreams and prophecies had no validity; that man had complete freedom because it made no difference what he did—nothing made any sense. She was wrong; the design was there, and when she saw what it was she hanged herself. But the play now seems to give us a view of mans position that is just as comfortless as her acceptance of a meaningless universe. What place is there in it for human freedom and meaningful action?

Oedipus did have one freedom: he was free to find out or not find out the truth. This was the element of Sophoclean sleight-of-hand that enabled him to make a drama out of the situation which the philosophers used as the classic demonstration of man's subjection to fate. But it is more than a solution to an apparently insoluble dramatic problem; it is the key to the play's tragic theme and the protagonist's heroic stature. One freedom is allowed him: the freedom to search for the truth, the truth about the prophecies, about the gods, about himself. And of this freedom he makes full use. Against the advice and appeals of others, he pushes on, searching for the truth, the whole truth and nothing but the truth. And in this search he shows all those great qualities that we admire in him—courage, intelligence, perseverance, the qualities that make human beings great. This freedom to search, and the heroic way in which Oedipus uses it, make the play not a picture of man's utter feebleness caught in the toils of fate, but on the contrary, a heroic example of man's dedication to the search for truth, the truth about himself. This is perhaps the only human freedom, the play seems to say, but there could be none more noble.

REBECCA W. BUSHNELL

Speech and Silence: Oedipus the King

The response to prophecy informs all of *Oedipus the King*, beginning with Oedipus's consulting the Oracle to save the city and ending with Creon's sending once again to Delphi for Apollo's sanction. In *Antigone*, Creon's response to prophecy only enhances his portrayal as a tyrant. But Oedipus's entire life is an answer to oracular prediction. As in *Antigone*, the context is political; Oedipus, however, combines the defiance of Antigone and the tyranny of Creon, for even as Oedipus resists the tyrannical silence of the gods, he threatens to destroy the city in his effort to speak his own story.

Like the Sphinx's riddle, which brings together the ages of man, *Oedipus the King* merges Oedipus's many encounters with Apollo and his prophet, which are all encounters with silence. In each incident—his first consultation of the Oracle about his parents' identity, his sending to Delphi about the city's plague, and his conflict with Apollo's servant, Tiresias— Oedipus cannot make god and prophet answer fully. When he asks the Oracle and later Tiresias who his parents are, they tell him only of his future—that he will kill his father and marry his mother, or discover those crimes. When he asks Apollo, through Creon, how he can save the city from the plague, Apollo gives only half an answer: expel the murderer, says Apollo, but he leaves it for Oedipus to name the criminal.

From *Prophesying Tragedy: Sign and Voice in Sophocles' Theban Plays* by Rebecca W. Bushnell, pp. 67–85. © 1990 by Cornell University Press.

Plutarch wrote in his *Moralia* that we learn silence from the gods, speech from man.[1] So in *Oedipus the King* silence is associated with the gods and their mysteries and speech with Oedipus. In Chapter 1, I described the language of the gods as ironic and ambiguous, and thus full of silences. In *Oedipus the King*, when the Oracle speaks, it is only to mask its silence about the truth, which Oedipus must learn. In *Antigone* it is a sign of Creon's desire for godlike tyranny that he would silence others; but *Oedipus the King* marks Oedipus's confrontation with gods by their silences. His original encounter as a young man with the horror of Delphic silence is reflected in his later resistance to any form of silence, but especially the silence of Tiresias, the prophet who imitates Apollo.

Like Antigone, Oedipus is characterized throughout the play as a person who believes in speaking freely. When this play's politically taciturn Creon hesitates to report the Oracle's mandate in front of the citizens, Oedipus insists that he speak publicly (*es pantas auda*, 93). Even in his shame at the end, Oedipus wants to tell the Chorus of his pain, while Creon wishes to shut him away in the house. But he is not content merely to speak himself; he also forces others to speak.[2] His speech is at once, in Benjamin's words, the "free spontaneous utterance of the creature" and a defense against entrapment in the gods' silence; it is through his speech that he tries to control his life and the events in the world around him.

Oedipus's first encounter with "audible" silence in Sophocles' play comes when he asks the Chorus to tell him what they know of Laius's murderer. The text implies two silences: the first after he asks that they reveal the murderer, even if he is one of them (226), and the second after he asks them to tell whether the criminal is an alien (232). These two moments of silence replicate Apollo's partial silence, implicit in the oracle's omission of the murderer's name, and they provoke Oedipus to call a curse of silence down on the unknown silent criminal. If the citizens are silent, he says (*ei d'au siōpēsethe*, 233), protecting either themselves or others, he will order all of them to shun the criminal, "neither receive him nor speak to him" (238). Not only does Oedipus's speech thus evoke (as do all his other speeches) the monstrous silence of the unspoken truth, but Oedipus also calls the curse of silence down upon himself.

Oedipus's struggle with the silence of his people, the prophet, and the gods, which becomes his defiance of prophecy, takes its shape both from the epic tradition and from the Delphic Oracle's political and religious role in Athenian society. On one level, his actions replay the defiance of Hector. On another level, Oedipus's political actions with regard to the Oracle have a double reference. First, his behavior echoes that of Athenian politicians, who knew how to manipulate oracular signs to promote their own policies for

Athens' defense. Second, his abuse of the prophet Tiresias, resembling the behavior of Creon in *Antigone*, identifies him as a *tyrannos*.

Herodotus and Plutarch, believers in prophecy of quite different eras, both relate a well-known incident in Athenian history in which the politician Themistocles is said to have made divine signs fit his own purposes. Herodotus writes that when the Persians threatened Athens, the Athenians consulted the Delphic Oracle and were directed to flee the city since all was lost.[3] Rather than accept this advice, they again went to the Oracle, asking the god "to give some better oracle concerning our country." The Oracle answered once again with the famous oracle of the wooden walls: "Zeus grants this to Athena, that the wooden wall alone shall be unravaged, for the profit of you and your children" (7.1411.6–7). It counseled that they should not wait for the coming of the army, but turn their backs, until the day of battle comes: "Holy Salamis, you shall destroy the children of women, when men sow, or when they harvest" (11–12). The new answer elicited many different interpretations, as Herodotus tells us. Did the Oracle mean the wooden wall of the citadel, or, metaphorically, the "wall" of the fleet? If so, the people wondered what the reference to Salamis signified. Did it not suggest a defeat at the island of Salamis? As Herodotus reports, it was Themistocles, long an advocate of the Athenian fleet, who delivered the city from its quandary: "This man said that the interpreters [*tous chrēsmologous*] had not quite accurately hit on the meaning" (7.143.5–6). Themistocles insisted that if the Oracle meant to predict a defeat at Salamis, it would have used the phrase "wretched Salamis" (*ō schetliē Salamis*) instead of "holy Salamis" (*ō theiē Salamis*), and so he advised them to prepare to fight on their ships, as these were the "wooden walls" in which they had been told to trust. The Athenians found Themistocles' reading preferable to the reading of the interpreters (143.3–5). Themistocles was, of course, proved "right," insofar as the Athenians succeeded brilliantly by relying on the fleet, but it was he who *made* it true through his advocacy of the Athenian navy.

Plutarch, much later, makes explicit what Herodotus only implies, that Themistocles in fact seized control of the Oracle's authority to suit his plan to evacuate the city and rely on the fleet for defense.[4] Plutarch prefaces his account of the same scene with a description of Themistocles' response to the Persian advance. He tells how "then indeed, Themistocles, failing to influence the majority with human reasoning, provided divine signs and oracles for them, just as if he were erecting a machine in a tragedy [*hōsper en tragōidia(i) mēchanēn aras*]; he took as a sign the serpent which seemed to have disappeared then from the sacred precinct; and when the priests found that the daily sacrifices to the serpent were untouched, they announced to the multitude—Themistocles putting the words in their mouth [*tou*

Themistokleous logon didontos]—that the goddess had left the city behind and was leading them to the sea."[5] After that, Plutarch says, he also tried to convince the people with his reading of the oracle of the wooden wall, until finally he got his way. Plutarch thus associates Themistocles' interpretation of the oracle with his invention of the serpent prodigy, in which he "gave the word" to the priests, clothing his own ideas and thoughts in sacred authority when other means failed. Further, both sign and oracle are compared to a tragic *mēchanē*, which can mean contrivance or, more specifically, the machine in which the gods were brought down to the stage. In either case it suggests the application of a "supernatural"—and artificial—solution to a human problem.

It is difficult, of course, to draw any close parallels between Oedipus and Themistocles, or to claim that Sophocles counted on his audience to remember the politician, who died thirty years before *Oedipus the King* was performed.[6] Yet the incident suggests how prophecy might have been understood and used for the city's sake in fifth-century Athens. Themistocles, as a politician, made the gods and prophets speak the words he thought necessary to save his city. In *Oedipus the King*, Oedipus begins by taking up Apollo's oracle as a means to save the city, and then reinforces it with his own curse. Oedipus goes a step further than Themistocles, however; when Tiresias's refusal to name the murderer seems to threaten the civic order, as Oedipus sees it, and prophecy seems inadequate, Oedipus pronounces his *phatis*, his story that Creon and Tiresias conspired to kill Laius, an accusation that reduces Tiresias's words to the manifestation of a political conspiracy. Unlike Themistocles, Oedipus does not simply present his ideas as a divine mandate, contradicting the *chrēsmologoi*. Oedipus competes with the Oracle and Tiresias, setting himself up as the city's only "prophet" by attempting to find explanations for events in human stories and testimony. What happens, of course, is that his efforts lead him eventually to confirm Apollo's and Tiresias's words. It appears that in this play Sophocles is not willing to allow the human word full power to govern the world.

The play's title, *Oedipus Tyrannos*, draws attention to Oedipus's political role in the city, which is inextricably linked to his effort to present himself as a new "prophet" for the city. Most scholars who have contrasted Oedipus and *Antigone*'s Creon find, as Webster puts it, that "Oedipus is the good ruler in spite of his defects, and Creon the bad ruler in spite of his virtues."[7] A comparison of their opening speeches suggests some of the initial differences. In his speech, Creon emphasizes that the citizens must put the state's interests before their own; Oedipus, however, proclaims his own obligation to the citizens, his private pain for the public cause, declaring that while each of them feels only his own pain, "my spirit mourns for the city, for you, and for myself" (63–64). Both Creon and Oedipus each identify their private will with the public opinion. Creon, however, seems to force his will on the city, whereas Oedipus makes the public will his private desire.[8]

The frequent repetition of the word *tyrannos* in the play raises the question whether Oedipus is indeed a "tyrant." In some cases in Greek tragedy the word *tyrannos* is interchangeable with the word *basileus*, "king"; at other places, *tyrannos* means more what we understand by "tyrant," a ruler who has wrongfully seized power and who rules unjustly.[9] While for many scholars Oedipus does not really resemble the Greek tyrant described by Plato in the *Republic*,[10] some see him on the "verge of tyranny"[11] in his irrational anger, his apparently illegitimate Assumption of power (which turns out to be legitimate), and his commission of the "paradigmatic" tyrannical crimes of incest and parricide.[12] Plato and others attribute to the tyrant the transgression of the boundaries that separate human from beast.[13] To them, the tyrant is a monster, a wolf, an animal masked as a human being.[14]

More significant for this study, however, Oedipus has also been suspected of wanting to be a god in Thebes. In the *parodos*, the Chorus come to Oedipus as suppliants, as if to a god,[15] although the priest denies that they equate him with the gods (31). Later, when the Chorus has prayed to the Olympians, Oedipus responds, "You pray [*aiteis*]. If you want what you pray for—if, hearing my words, you accept them and turn back the plague, you will gain strength and relief from evil" (216–17), words which echo the style of the Delphic Oracle.[16] But if he thus seems to embrace a god's role, it is not as Creon did, by imitating the impersonal and severe qualities of the divine voice, but rather by mimicking the god and Oracle in his role as granter of prayers, *sōtēr* or "savior." Oedipus is a "humanized" god, responsive and benevolent, the city's guardian, more father than fate. Further, in contrast to *Antigone*'s Creon, Oedipus, until he argues with Tiresias, seems remarkably pious.[17] When Apollo delivers his mandate to expel the curse on the land, Oedipus takes this as his responsibility, for the sake of Apollo, his city, and himself, proclaiming that "rightly you see me as an ally [*symmachon*], honoring both the land and the god" (135–36). He transforms Apollo's oracle into his own curse on the murderer and those who protect him, identifying his own will and words with the god's.

Oedipus's character as *tyrannos* thus seems different from Creon's. Oedipus is both better and worse than Creon, worse in his crimes that are eventually revealed, but from his first appearance better as a benevolent and god-fearing, if authoritative, leader. He is not seen to pose a threat to the city until the entrance of the prophet Tiresias. Oedipus intends, by sending for Tiresias, to receive further divine assistance in his task. When Tiresias refuses to cooperate, however, Oedipus treats Tiresias's silence as a betrayal of Thebes (330–31). In *Antigone*, Creon's rejection of Tiresias climaxes his rivalry with the gods. In *Oedipus the King*, Tiresias's arrival initiates the conflict between Apollo's signs and Oedipus's voice—a conflict that strikes at the roots of the city's order, which is based on the cooperation between sacred and secular interests.

The Tiresias whom Oedipus encounters is a far more complex figure than *Antigone*'s Tiresias. Sophocles did not strongly characterize the earlier Tiresias, but presented him solely as the gods' representative in Creon's secular world. In *Oedipus the King*, however, Tiresias's character makes him, in Reinhardt's words, a "walking enigma," half "superhuman, half only too human."[18] In a sense Tiresias is Oedipus's double, as Oedipus, too, represents an enigma in the duality of his being.[19] Yet Oedipus and Tiresias are also opposites, the mortal facing the riddling god. Tiresias directly mimics the Oracle, which, in Heraclitus's well-known formula, "does not speak or hide but signifies [*sēmainei*]."[20] On stage, Tiresias is the Oracle, the divine mind in human flesh, a figure of divinity expressed in human speech. Like the Oracle, too, he seems to respond to supplication and yet finally refuses to respond, angering the king.

Tiresias's most vital secret is the secret of Oedipus's past, his parentage, and his crimes. Although later he will tell Oedipus of his future—his discovery, blindness, and exile—the scene focuses on Tiresias's ability to tell the "true" story of Laius's murder. But Tiresias does not tell his story until Oedipus, angered by Tiresias's silence, produces his own solution to the mystery: "Know that I think that you conspired to do the deed—and did it, except for killing him with your hands; if you could see, I would say that you did the deed alone" (348–49). Tiresias's response is swift and brutal: "Is that true [*alēthes*?]? Then I bid you to abide by the decree [*kērygmati*] that you yourself pronounced, from this day on to speak neither to me nor to these people, for you are the unholy polluter of the land" (350–53). Tiresias insists that the truth is strong in *him* (356). Oedipus, however, has already set up the terms of the *agon* as a contest of contradictory stories about the murder.

While Oedipus, like *Antigone*'s Creon, accuses Tiresias of being just another greedy fortune-teller (388–89), his attack against the prophet's authority goes far beyond this accusation, as he attempts to strip him and his words of divinity. Oedipus creates a situation in which Tiresias's words seem to have no value, when, as René Girard says, he makes Tiresias's accusation seem "simply an act of reprisal arising from the hostile exchange of a tragic debate."[21] Tiresias seems to admit this, in effect, when Oedipus asks who taught him this "word" or story (*rhēma*), for he cannot believe it was derived through his *technē*, "mantic craft" (357). Tiresias answers that he "learned" it from Oedipus: "From you—you forced me to speak unwillingly" (358); Oedipus, not divine inspiration, motivated Tiresias's speech.

Oedipus taunts Tiresias further, saying that he has neither the right nor the power to speak the truth. For him, Tiresias's physical infirmity indicates mental incapacity. When Oedipus asks whether Tiresias thinks he can keep on talking this way (368), and Tiresias answers yes, for there is strength in the truth (369), Oedipus retaliates, "Indeed there is, but not in you; in you there is no truth, for you are blind in your ears and your mind as well as your eyes" (370–71).

Oedipus reminds Tiresias that it was he, Oedipus, not the prophet, who was able to solve the riddle of the Sphinx (cf. 390–98). Just as Oedipus claims that his tale of Creon's and Tiresias's conspiracy supplants any Tiresias can tell, so he demonstrates that he, with his own mind, can supplant the prophet in Thebes: "I came, Oedipus who knows nothing, I stopped [the Sphinx], I succeeded, by my intelligence, without learning anything from birds [*out'ap'oiōnōn ... mathōn*]" (397–98). Like Themistocles, Oedipus has taken over when the prophet and gods seem to have failed the city, acting himself both as an interpreter and a provider of answers. Tiresias becomes, from Oedipus's perspective, merely a political antagonist, a schemer in a conspiracy to overthrow the rightful ruler of Thebes.

Thus Oedipus attacks the prophet with a twofold strategy: he attempts to go him one better as a revealer of past secrets and a solver of riddles, and he places the prophet in an essentially political and secular setting, stripping him of sacred privilege. Like Hector, Oedipus is at least temporarily successful in outwitting and debasing the prophet. C. M. Bowra may call Oedipus's tale of conspiracy a "hallucination,"[22] but it has enough reality *in the play* to render Tiresias's words ineffective, insofar as neither Oedipus nor the Chorus believes them. As Oedipus says, Tiresias speaks in vain (*hōs matēn eirēsetai*, 365), when Oedipus does not even seem to hear him, and the Chorus will not convict their king merely on the basis of Tiresias's words. The Chorus, while they respect the wisdom of Zeus and Apollo, question whether "the *mantis*, among men, should be right more than myself, for there is no certain means of judging the truth; but one man may excel another in skill [*sophian*]" (499–503). It is not simply that Tiresias has no proof;[23] Oedipus has made it seem that he and Tiresias are merely rivals, competing in their skill, speaking the same language. In these terms, this is not an oracular consultation, in Oedipus's view, but a citizens' court of law, where men are equal, and the victory will go to the man who speaks better in his own defense.[24]

If Oedipus means to supplant the sacred with the secular,[25] he succeeds, for the moment, with respect to the past. What Oedipus cannot grasp, as Hector cannot, is the riddle of the future. Toward the end of the episode, Tiresias tells Oedipus of his future (412–28), but Oedipus says he hears only absurdities (*mōra*, 433). Tiresias taunts Oedipus, too, with the one secret of the past Oedipus feels he does not know for sure: "I brought forth these things, which you think are absurd," he says, "but your parents, who brought you forth, found them wise" (435–36). Startled, Oedipus asks him who his parents are, but Tiresias only says, "This day shall give you life and destroy you" (438). As the Oracle did, Tiresias answers Oedipus's question about the past with an enigmatic prediction of the future. Tiresias's prophecy thus suggests a radical difference between Oedipus's and Tiresias's language and knowledge, however alike the two men may seem in this scene. While both Oedipus and Tiresias are riddlers, because their language is fraught with double meaning, Tiresias's ambiguity is informed, whereas Oedipus only thinks he speaks without silences, hidden meanings, or ambiguity. The audience, of course, has a double view of the play. They see Oedipus's viewpoint, entirely in the present tense and in a purely secular world, as well as Tiresias's, a view from the future into the present and past.

The stalemate created in this scene, and in the scene with Creon which follows, ends with the entrance of Jocasta, who talks Oedipus into permitting Creon to go unpunished. When Oedipus then complains that Tiresias blames him for Laius's murder, Jocasta argues that no human has true prophetic skill (*broteion ouden mantikēs echon technēs*, 709). She offers to show him *sēmeia* or signs (710) as proof of this contention. Jocasta's *sēmeia*, like Oedipus's accusations, amount to a kind of anti-oracle. She opposes what she believes to be the real story (*phatis*, 716) of Laius's death against the Oracle's *chrēsmos*. So she tells how "an oracle [*chrēsmos*] came to Laius once, I would not say from Apollo himself, but from those under him" (711–12), which said that he should be killed by his own son. "But, as the report [*phatis*] goes" (715), Laius was killed by strangers at the place where three roads meet. In this story, Jocasta in effect repeats Oedipus's strategy against Tiresias. First, she represents the oracle to Laius as human discourse, not the direct words of Apollo but the stories of priests. She thus renders the oracle fallible, just as Oedipus emphasizes Tiresias's human failings to leave him open to doubt. Second, Jocasta, like Oedipus, sets the human word against the mantic sign, her *phatis* against the *chrēsmos*. It is a further irony that the word *phatis* can mean "oracle" or "prophecy," as well as "report" or "rumor."[26] Jocasta has found her own "oracle" in human testimony.

Jocasta's attack against prophecy has a different result than Oedipus's attack: her *phatis* contains a phrase, "the place where three roads meet" (716), which catches Oedipus's attention. Oedipus sees suddenly that he indeed might be Laius's murderer, having killed a man at such a place. Afraid that "the prophet can see after all" (747), he calls for the herdsman, the only surviving witness, to retell his story, and he narrates for Jocasta his flight from Corinth, the murder at the crossroads, and his triumphant arrival in Thebes. Rather than turning to the god, Oedipus again relies on human testimony to establish his guilt or innocence. When Jocasta wants to know why Oedipus is so eager to see the herdsman, Oedipus responds, "If his words match yours, I shall escape suffering" (839–40). Jocasta had said that the herdsman spoke of robbers who killed Laius, not just one man (842), and if the herdsman holds to the same number (844–45), Oedipus is innocent. Oedipus thus focuses not on the correspondence of his experience with the prophet's words but rather on matching his experience to the herdsman's story. In his search for the murderer, the question of prophecy's truth seems secondary.

Jocasta and Oedipus give the herdsman's story an authority that supplants that of prophecy. To reassure Oedipus, Jocasta insists that the herdsman "cannot retract [his story] now" (*kouk estin autō[i] touto g'ekbalein palin*, 849), having once told his story as she retold it. She attributes to his words the immutability of the prophetic word, echoing what Tiresias says in *Antigone* when he boasts that his words, once spoken, can be neither called back nor avoided. The herdsman himself is the only person other than Tiresias who knows the secret of Oedipus's birth and crimes. When confronted by Oedipus, he acts as Tiresias did—he, too, would rather not say what he knows and pretends to have forgotten (1141). But the herdsman is also different from Tiresias in that words are not enough to make him speak. By twisting back his arms, Oedipus makes him suffer pain, which he does not inflict on Tiresias and cannot inflict on Apollo. It is this last step, the infliction of pain to break silence, which forces Oedipus's own initiation into inexpressible pain.

Indeed, it is the herdsman's *phatis* that brings Oedipus to realize that Apollo's oracle has been fulfilled. Oedipus and Jocasta contend that simple facts and human testimony contradict and thus invalidate the oracles from Delphi. When Oedipus confesses his earlier visit to the Oracle, Jocasta relies on an apparent fact—the destruction of the infant Oedipus—to invalidate the Oracle's predictions. The Messenger's report that Polybus is dead, too, seems certain proof that all oracles and signs mean nothing, as Oedipus exults: "Why then," he asks, "look to the hearth of the Pythia, or the birds that cry above, who prophesied that I would kill my father?" (964–68). In his rejection of the oracle, Oedipus depends on the Messenger's accuracy, an expectation the Messenger lives up to only too well, for he knows Polybus is not truly Oedipus's father. When Jocasta finally realizes that Oedipus is her son, she attempts to discredit the Messenger, just as she had earlier devalued prophecy, calling the Messenger's words just vain speech, empty talk (*ta de rhēthenta boulou mēde memnēsthai matēn*, 1057). But Oedipus pushes through to the end, as the herdsman's report intersects with the oracle, and the story that Oedipus believed would contradict Apollo's oracle becomes identical to it.

As the play approaches this *peripeteia*, Oedipus's attempt to create a secular order through human stories seems less and less an affirmation of the city's concerns and more a tyrannical attack on order. At the play's beginning, when he is faced with a world that seems confused and inexplicable, Oedipus tries to control the city's crisis by finding the words for it, first in his invention of Creon's and Tiresias's conspiracy, and when that strategy fails, through his attempts to reconstruct the past. But as that effort becomes more and more personal, a question of *Oedipus*'s past, Oedipus seems to threaten directly the stability that the fulfillment of oracles represents, without establishing any new structure. After Jocasta first declares that prophecy has no meaning, the Chorus sings of its fear that Apollo's oracles will not be fulfilled, even though their fulfillment means disaster for Oedipus: "Never again will I go, reverent, to the sacred navel of the land, nor to the temple at Abae, or Olympus, if these oracles are not fulfilled for all mortals to point at" (898–903). "Why should I dance?" the Chorus asks (896): If oracles are not fulfilled, there is no divine prescience, or even presence on earth, and Oedipus's own words and presence do not seem a sufficient substitute.

Oedipus himself, nearing the moment of recognition, thinks less of the city's misery than of the mystery of his own identity, as he is willing to sacrifice civic order, or at least those fictions that maintain civic order, to gain complete autonomy and self-knowledge. Trying to encourage Oedipus, Jocasta asks, "Why do men fear, when chance rules, and there is no clear foresight [*pronoia*] of anything?" (977–78). So Oedipus, on the verge of knowing his birth, proclaims that "I count myself the son of Chance" (1080), who is the goddess who personifies lack of cosmic order.[27] It is at this moment that Oedipus comes closest to tyranny, insofar as his will diverges furthest from the city's interests. The moment demands Oedipus's rapid recognition of the oracle's fulfillment for the city's sake, as the vindication of the gods' words and their order at whatever cost. Here the playwright seems ultimately on the side of the gods, who, as Benardete says, "want the authority of all the oracles, i.e., their own authority, maintained even at the expense of human morality."[28] Oedipus loses in his attempt to govern his city and himself through his own speech, when fighting against the power of religious and civic fictions of order.

Taking Oedipus's recognition of the oracle's truth as the "lesson" of the play, some scholars describe the last episode as a portrayal of a humbler yet wiser Oedipus, broken by the gods.[29] Others see Oedipus reasserting his authority and intelligence even in his suffering.[30]

Oedipus's own words about his relationship with Apollo are quite complex. When the Chorus asks him which of the *daimones* drove him to blind himself (1328), Oedipus answers that it was both Apollo and himself: "He brought to pass these evils and my sufferings, but I, in my misery, struck my eyes with my own hands" (1330–32). This intersection between the god's words and Oedipus's actions and words also appears in Oedipus' demand that Creon fulfill the Oracle's mandate to expel the murderer, thereby also fulfilling his own curse. When Creon hesitates to decide Oedipus's fate, Oedipus reminds him that the Oracle has already spoken, asking for the murderer's death or banishment: "The voice [*phatis*] of the god was clear to all—to destroy the parricide, myself, unholy" (1440–41). But as Oedipus calls on Apollo's authority, he acknowledges that he, too, has commanded, as he says to the Chorus: "I deprived myself, myself commanding that all should shun the blasphemer" (1381–82). Oedipus thus apparently sees in his disaster not simply the tyranny of the god's word over his own life but a consonance between his commands and the god's pronouncements, even as human stories came to correspond with the Oracle's version of Oedipus' past. At the same time, he certainly tries to gain control of his own future, giving orders to Creon for the burial of his wife and for his children's future.[31] But Oedipus clearly pushes Creon, the city's new leader, too far. When Oedipus begs that his daughters not be taken away, Creon reminds Oedipus that he must no longer wish to rule in all things (*panta mē boulou kratein*, 1522). Like Creon at the end of *Antigone*, Oedipus no longer has *kratos* ("authority"), and his voice has lost the power to command in the city and direct its future.

Yet while Oedipus has lost his power to command, he has not lost his voice. Oedipus does not slip into the life of silence he has cursed upon himself and which indeed he seems at first to seek, when he asks that Creon drive him out of the country "to where no one will ever speak to me" (1437). As at the play's beginning, in the end Oedipus finds silence unbearable; he must speak his pain, even though his crimes are unspeakable and his pain impossible to articulate. When Oedipus first appears before the Chorus after the catastrophe, he does indeed seem broken, unconscious of his own voice in his pain. He cries out to the Chorus, "Where is my voice [*phthogga*] flying, so violently?" (1310). His very voice seems "disembodied,"[32] not his own, in the initial moments of his pain. Yet, even as he asks these questions, he responds to the Chorus as the sound of another human voice: "I recognize your voice, clearly, even in this darkness" (1326–27). The final episode suggests that for Oedipus, the human voice, with human touch, is more than ever the identifying mark of human nature, the mark of the presence of others and of himself.

For Oedipus, stripped of his position in the city, blind and helpless, his last resource of power is his voice.[33] Although he loses the power of the political command, he never loses the authority of self-naming, as Creon does in *Antigone*. Creon calls himself "nothing more than nothing"; Oedipus, however, proclaims his name to the Chorus in all his shame: "This," he says, "is the lot of Oedipus [*tout'elach' Oidipous*]", (1366). In contrast to Creon, whose authority is defined solely by his political and familial position in *Antigone*, Sophocles' Oedipus is meant to have authority by "nature," which is revealed even in the experience of his suffering, when he alone has the right to speak of what it is to be Oedipus.

Can it be said, then, that in this play Oedipus ends, as Hector does, by discovering his own prophetic voice? He has come, certainly, to know the past as Tiresias does and to understand his present identity and condition, but does Sophocles bestow on him a vision or right to speak of the future? Charles Segal concludes that Oedipus is at the end "a second Tiresias," with an "inner sight of blindness," a vision like Hector's, coming "not as a gift of the gods but as the hard acquisition of his human experience and suffering."[34] Oedipus does seem to anticipate his own future as he says to Creon: "This I know, that neither disease nor any other ill shall destroy me; I would not now have been saved from death if it were not for some terrible evil" (1455–57). But while he anticipates the future, he does not have a clear knowledge of future events, such as Hector obtains in his death. At the play's end, he has a sense of himself as a man with a future, but he does not yet have the right to know or determine it.

In this play, as in *Antigone*, Sophocles dramatizes a crisis in which humans try, and fail, to write their own stories. Oedipus's attempt to have his "plots" win out over those of the prophet and the Oracle—and the playwright—fails, because the play makes the fulfillment of prophecy a necessity for the city's survival. Sophocles suggests, in the moment when the Chorus hesitates between Tiresias's and Oedipus's versions of the past, that it might have been otherwise. Indeed, some critics see that Oedipus makes himself a scapegoat, accepting the others' story of the murder without sufficient proof and giving in to "oracular idolatry."[35] Even as Sophocles allows for the myth and the oracle to be criticized, he grants the oracle the power of truth through the agency of Oedipus himself. The playwright respects the social order such fulfillment represents, at whatever cost for the individual. Yet *Oedipus the King* also celebrates the power of human speech to represent a self, even in such a defeat. The tension between the two impulses is evident, and the only solution is to move Oedipus out of the city.

For Oedipus, as for Antigone, even in disaster the human voice achieves a dramatic or apostrophic significance without power to command. As *tyrannos*, through his abandonment of the city's cause in the search for his own identity and autonomy, Oedipus risks and loses his authority as king, and his voice is stripped of the power to rule. When Oedipus speaks at the end of the play, however, his words have little to do with politics. Sophocles moves him out of the sphere of city and gods, into the state of exile, where we find him at the beginning of *Oedipus at Colonus*, about to violate the silent grove of the Furies.

Notes

1. *Moralia* 505f.

2. See Charles Segal, *Tragedy and Civilization: An Interpretation of Sophocles* (Cambridge: Harvard University Press, 1981), p. 244.

3. Herodotus 7.141–43. There is some question of the authenticity of this story; what is important for our purposes is that Herodotus seems to have regarded such behavior as patriotic rather than reprehensible. See Joseph Fontenrose, *The Delphic Oracle: Its Responses and Operations with a Catalogue of Responses* (Berkeley: University of California Press, 1978), pp. 124–28, and Roland Crahay, *La Littérature oraculaire chez Hérodote* (Paris: Belles Lettres, 1956), pp. 294–304, on the authenticity of this oracle. Fontenrose states, "So we must conclude that these two responses are dubious at best; if authentic they are extraordinary and unusual pronouncements of the Delphic Oracle" (p. 128).

4. See Martin P. Nilsson, *Cults, Myths, Oracles, and Politics in Ancient Greece* (Lund: Gleerup, 1951), p. 124.

5. Plutarch, *Life of Themistocles*, 10.1. Text from *Plutarch's Lives*, vol. 2 (Cambridge: Harvard University Press, 1948).

6. Bernard Knox suggests in *Oedipus at Thebes* that Oedipus himself resembles Themistocles, as the intelligent amateur, "the Thucydidean archetype of the Athenian democratic character at its best" (New Haven: Yale University Press, 1957; rpt. New York: Norton, 1971), p. 73.

7. T. B. L. Webster, *An Introduction to Sophocles* (Oxford: Clarendon, 1936), p. 63. See also Victor Ehrenberg, *Sophocles and Pericles* (Oxford: Blackwell, 1954), and Thomas Gould, "The Innocence of Oedipus: The Philosophers on *Oedipus the King*," *Arion* 4 (1965): 582–611, esp p. 599; and Knox. pp. 53–61.

8. See Seth Benardete, "Sophocles' *Oedipus Tyrannos*," in *Sophocles: A Collection of Critical Essays*, ed. Thomas Woodard (Englewood Cliffs, NJ.: Prentice-Hall, 1966), pp. 105–21, on the private and public in relation to Oedipus.

9. On the meaning of *tyrannos* as simply "king" or "tyrant," see Ehrenberg, pp. 66–67; Gould, p. 599; Knox, pp. 53–61.

10. Knox, p. 59. See also Diego Lanza, *Il tirano e il suo pubblico* (Torino: Einaudi, 1977), pp. 140–48.

11. Ehrenberg, p. 67.

12. Benardete, p. 108. See also Vincent Farenga, "The Paradigmatic Tyrant: Greek Tyranny and the Ideology of the Proper," *Helios* 8 (1981): 1–31.

13. See Farenga, p. 2.

14. See Plato, *Republic* 8.566.

15. Ehrenberg, p. 67: "The suppliant people approach him almost as a god (2.31f.), and he is honoured as a saviour, as *Soter* (46f.)"; see also Knox, pp. 59–60, and Cedric H. Whitman, *Sophocles: A Study of Heroic Humanism* (Cambridge: Harvard University Press, 1951), p. 12–5.

16. Knox comments that Oedipus's words "accept and promise fulfillment of the choral prayer ... and are phrased in what is a typical formula of the Delphic oracle" (p. 160).

17. See Ehrenberg, p. 67: "He is also a pious man who believes in oracles, respects the bonds of family, fears and hates impurity."

18. Karl Reinhardt, *Sophocles*, trans. H. Harvey and D. Harvey (1947; rpt. New York: Barnes & Noble, 1979), p. 104.

19. Jean-Pierre Vernant and Pierre Vidal-Naquet, *Tragedy and Myth in Ancient Greece*, trans. Janet Lloyd (Atlantic Highlands, N.J.: Humanities Press, 1981), p. 90.

20. Frag. 93, in H. Diels, *Die Fragmente der Vorsokratiker*, 7th ed. (Berlin: Weidmann, 1954). See Reinhardt, p. 104; Benardete, p. 113.

21. René Girard, *Violence and the Sacred*, trans. Patrick Gregory (Baltimore: Johns Hopkins University Press, 1977), pp. 70–71.

22. C. M. Bowra, *Sophoclean Tragedy* (Oxford: Clarendon, 1944), p. 195.

23. As Whitman says, "Tiresias offered no proof for what he said, but based it simply on his prophetic art, which is not sufficient in this case to convince even the naive Chorus" (p. 131).

24. Knox, in his analysis of this scene, notes that it resembles a legal trial (p. 86).

25. Benardete, p. 114.

26. Segal, p. 237.

27. Knox, p. 166.

28. Benardete, p. 113.

29. See Bowra, p. 210, and Gould, e.g.

30. See Whitman, p. 142; Knox, chap. 5.

31. See Knox, p. 189.

32. Segal, p. 242.

33. Reinhardt, p. 130.

34. Segal, p. 246.

35. Sandor Goodhart, "*Leistas ephaske*: Oedipus and Laius' Many Murderers," *Diacritics* 8 (1978): 67, who follows Girard. See also Cynthia Chase, "Oedipal Textuality: Reading Freud's Reading of *Oedipus*," *Diacritics* 9 (1979): 54–68.

FREDERICK AHL

Oedipus and Teiresias

Not only has Creon served as Oedipus' ambassador to and interpreter of Apollo's oracle, he has also advised Oedipus to consult Teiresias (287–89, 555–56). Oedipus, in relying so heavily on Creon's advice and on his interpretations of the oracle, places himself squarely in Creon's hands. Yet not until Teiresias appears do we begin to realize that Oedipus' reliance on Creon is counterbalanced by fear and distrust of him. What he most trusts is that which he also most suspects, distrusts, and fears.

THE PREAMBLE

After Creon leaves the stage, the play's chorus enters. The chorus, we have been specifically told, represents the Theban people and gathers in response to Oedipus' injunction at line 144 that the *Kadmou laon*, the "laity" of Cadmus, convene. The first two-thirds of their song (151–89) is a complex of prayers addressed not only to Apollo but also to Athena, and reinforces the priest's comments about the plague at the play's opening. But there is an added sense that the singers are reaching out to the ancient audience's own circumstances in their special appeal to Athena, Athens' very particular goddess. The final third of their song (190–215) moves even further into the writer's contemporary world, appealing to Zeus,

From *Sophocles' Oedipus: Evidence and Self-Conviction* by Frederick Ahl, pp. 67–102. © 1991 by Cornell University Press.

Apollo, Artemis, and Bacchus in the hope they will strike down with their various weapons and emblems of power—thunderbolts, arrows, and Bacchic *thyrsus* ("staff")—the god who is dishonored among gods"—Ares, the god of war.

In the chorus' thoughts, then, the plague is accompanied by a war, and it is above all the war that they want ended. The verb they use to ask Zeus to destroy Ares, *phthison* (201), is the same verb the priest uses twice to describe the destructive effects of the plague upon Thebes in lines 25–26 (*phthinousa*).[1] What war could the chorus have in mind? There is nothing in the mythic context of Sophocles' play to suggest that Thebes is currently at war with anyone. The great wars of Theban tradition follow the reign of Oedipus. On the other hand, the great war between the Athenians and the Peloponnesians (who were allied with Thebes) was well under way as Sophocles wrote. The chorus, then, in its first utterances, has assumed a very fifth-century Athenian identity.

OEDIPUS AND THE CHORUS

Oedipus' opening words after the choral song indicate that he has heard at least the last part of the chorus's prayer. He must either have remained onstage throughout, as I suspect, or have reentered in time to catch the final words of the choral song. Oedipus begins his speech (216–20)

> You are praying. Now regarding your prayers,
> if you're willing to listen to my words,
> to use them on the plague, you could achieve
> strength—and reduction of your suffering.
> I will speak them as an outsider
> both to what was reported and to what
> was done.

Oedipus adopts an authoritative, oracular tone, as if he really has an answer to offer the chorus. He also specifically dissociates himself from Laios' death and the reports of it that he has just heard. He then goes on to explain his inability to act on his own in an investigation (220–26):

> I could not track things by myself,
> and get far. I lack evidence. But now,
> a latecomer and fellow resident,
> I proclaim to all you Cadmeans:

If any of you knows the man who killed
Laios, the son of Labdacus, I command
that he communicate it all to me.

He demands information from the chorus to get his investigation under way. But notice that he has not revealed any particular plan of action to cope with the problem; that he again refers to the killer in the singular; and that his description of Laios as son of Labdacus (the first mention of Labdacus in the play) shows that he knows more about Laios than was evident from his earlier conversation with Creon. There he said only that he had heard of Laios.

Oedipus mentions various categories of people who might give information. He starts by allowing for a confession by the (singular) killer himself, with a promise of clemency (227–29):

If he fears for himself, he shall evade
full penalty if he just brings the charge
against himself. He will suffer nothing
unpleasant. He will leave the land unharmed.

He continues by allowing for the possibility that the murderer was not a Theban (230–32):

Or, if someone knows the man who struck the blow
came from elsewhere, let him not be silent.
I will reward him; he'll be duly thanked.

But no one has yet interrupted. So Oedipus proceeds to threaten (233–45):

But if you're silent, if someone holds back,
fearing for a friend, or for himself,
then he should hear from me what I shall do.

I proclaim that no one must receive
this man, whoever he may be, within
this land whose throne I now control,
no one must speak to him, no one take part
with him in prayers or sacrifices, none
share with him the cleansing holy font.

No, everyone must shun him from their homes.
He's the defilement on us, as the god
of Delphi has just now revealed to me
in prophecy. I thus ally myself
with the god's will, also with the deceased.

Oedipus offers, as yet, only words—a proclamation that the murderer (still singular) must be shunned. More curious, he speaks as if he personally had received the word from Apollo at Delphi. He does not allude to Creon's intermediacy, much less to the fact that it was Creon's *interpretation* of the oracle that established the connection of the plague with the death of Laios.

Finally Oedipus proceeds to his action: a ritual curse on the murderer (or murderers, this time) and those who harbor him (246–48):

I lay a curse on him who did this deed,
whether just one man has eluded us
or whether there were more to help him out:
May this wicked man in wickedness
wear down a wretched, homeless path through life.

There is no strong threat of punishment, only whatever power may reside within the imprecation itself.

Now Oedipus assures the people that, if the killer lives in his palace, he himself does not know it. He is not necessarily alluding only to himself. Creon, for instance, might have a motive for killing Laios. Jocasta might also have a motive, as we will see. He continues (249–54):

I lay a curse, if he is in this house
and shares the hearth, my very own,
with my full knowledge: may what I just prayed
for others fall upon me with its spell.
I set responsibility on you
to do just as I ask on my behalf,
on god's, and for this land so ruined now,
deprived of fruitfulness and god's presence.

It is worth at least passing notice that Oedipus places himself first in the order of those on whose behalf he asks the chorus to act. Had he stopped here, we might have summed up what he says as a vain and ineffectual gesture that tries its best to be evenhanded. But this apparent peroration is in fact the prelude to the most astonishing part of his declaration (255–64):

Even were this a matter where the gods
made no demands, it would be like leaving
a moral stain uncleansed, to overlook,
not hunt, its cause. A noble man, a king (*basileôs*),
has perished. Now, since I am in control,
possessing the power he once possessed,
possessing his marriage, the woman who
drew semen from us both, some common bonds
would surely have been born between us from
children, had there not been such bad luck
in terms of his own offspring. Since, then,
Luck came crashing down upon his head, I'll take
their place, as if he were my own father.

Oedipus avows a moral responsibility quite independent of specific oracular demands. A king's death demand a inquiry, especially since Oedipus is himself that king's successor. It is worth noting that on this occasion, as opposed to his earlier comment to Creon in line 128 he refers to Laios as a king, *basileus*, rather than as a tyrant, perhaps because numerous people in Sophocles' Athens would find the killing of a *basileus* more morally reprehensible than the killing of a tyrant. The *basileus* at Athens was an important figure in the religious functions of the state and was not the subject of antityrannical legislation.[2]

Oedipus goes to such pains to establish virtually a blood relationship between himself and the dead monarch that he represents himself as charged with the duty to avenge kindred blood. This claim, like his representation of Laios as a *basileus*, not only intensifies the demand that an important, unresolved crime be cleared up, but attempts to bolster his own rights to act as litigant. As R. G. Lewis points out in connection with the procedures in the prosecution of a case of homicide at Athens, "a litigant had to be a citizen and (normally anyhow) kin of the victim."[3] Further, an Athenian homicide trial (*dikē phonou*) required a proclamation not only by the litigant but by the *archôn basileus*, the "king" archon, who "retained the responsibility for many of the older religious ceremonies of the city throughout his year of office."[4]

When Oedipus declares that he will act as if Laios were his father and describes Laios as a *basileus*, he is drawing himself, rhetorically, within the citizen and family community of the state so as to justify his proclamation. And his stress on the fact that he is now the husband of the former *basileus'* wife, whom Athenians called the *basilinna*, "queen," seems designed to authorize his own acting as both litigant and "king" archon in making his proclamation. For the *basileus* shared important ritual duties with his wife.[5]

Thus Oedipus, who is neither a citizen nor a *basileus*, seeks to justify his religious authority by virtue of his relationship to the *basilinna*, Jocasta, and the *basileus*, Laios, whose place he has taken.

In justifying himself as the man entitled to bring a curse upon Laios' killer, of course, Oedipus is describing himself both as Laios' son and as Jocasta's son and husband. He has created enough of a figured description of his relationship with Laios by this act of speech that the mere discovery that he had killed the old king would, in terms of most Herodotean oracles, show him as having killed his father and married his mother.

Oedipus reveals something else of importance here: that he knows more about Laios' personal life than he has indicated earlier: either Laios and Jocasta had no children, or something unfortunate happened to them. But what is surely most troublesome is his metaphor of Laios' death as "Luck crashing down upon his head." For, we later learn, Oedipus remembers striking down an old man at a crossroad with a lethal blow from his staff (810–12). He also claims himself to be "a child of Luck" (1080–81). Our sense that Oedipus knows more than we at first assumed about his predecessor's family is firmly reinforced by the complete genealogy of Laios he gives in the following lines (265–68):

> I'll fight for him, I will go everywhere,
> laboriously seeking how to catch (*labein*)
> the man who killed the son of Labdacus,
> son of Polydorus, Cadmus' son,
> the child of Agenor from long ago.

Of course Oedipus will not really go everywhere in the search. He stays in Thebes and will conduct his investigation from just outside the palace. Others will come to him.

Finally, we have the real peroration, both curse and benediction (269–75):

> To those who do not act: I pray the gods
> no produce may sprout from the land for them,
> that their wives bear no children, but that they
> will wither with the doom that strikes them now—
> and even worse than this.
> > But then for you,
> you other Cadmeans who do approve,
> may justice be your ally, may the gods,
> all gods, be with you and be kind always.

The chorus, representing the citizen body of Thebes, promptly disavows either killing or knowing who killed Laios, and takes exception to Apollo's vagueness—a point on which Oedipus agrees with them (276–81):

Chorus:	As you have made me subject to a curse,
	my lord, I'll state outright: I did not kill,
	I can't point out the killer. But Phoebus,
	since he sent us on the search, should then
	explain just who it was who did the deed.
Oedipus:	You're right, that would be just. But no one man
	can force the gods to do what they don't wish.

It is worth noting that the chorus say it can't point out, rather than that it does not know, the (singular) killer. So Oedipus is left with the possibility that someone unknown—or at least offstage—is (or is harboring) the killer, or that he himself may be (or be harboring) the killer.

The chorus realizes it has just deflated Oedipus' grandiloquent announcement of his nonexistent plan to deal with the plague and offers its own suggestion for a course of action, which Oedipus avidly accepts (282–83):

Chorus:	Then could I say what I judge second best?
Oedipus:	If there's a third best, don't miss telling me!

Oedipus, who began by pompously advising the chorus to listen attentively to him, awaits the chorus's response with almost childlike eagerness. And the response is crushing (284–86):

As lord (*anakt'*) equal to lord (*anakti*), identical
in sight to Phoebus is Teiresias:
this I know, absolutely. Anyone
who looked to him, my lord (*ônax*), in this matter
would learn deeply. He'd make things very clear.

Apollo will not give the answer, but Teiresias, who is Apollo's equal in foresight, can and will. The use of *anax* ("king, lord") to describe both Teiresias and Apollo sets them above Oedipus. Calling him *anax* too seems merely formal courtesy, if not irony. There is nothing the citizens of Thebes can now learn from the man who destroyed the Sphinx.

Oedipus responds with something like pique (287–89):

> I did not consign even this to lists
> of what could be put off. When Creon raised
> the subject, I twice sent him embassies.
> He's long past due and so amazes me.

There is a strange confusion in Oedipus' phrasing which critics have imputed to Sophocles' (rather than to Oedipus') haste or loss of balance. The verb I have rendered "consign," *epraxamên*, does not yield the meaning editors want the sentence to carry, namely: "I did not leave this among things neglected" or "Well, I have not neglected this point either."[6] The verb suggests to me, rather, that Oedipus is taken aback a little by the chorus's response, that he shows a hint of reluctance to deal with Teiresias. Note how carefully Oedipus points out that Creon suggested consulting Teiresias. In contrast, he takes all the credit for the mission to Delphi himself and does not even mention Creon's role to the chorus. Oedipus also notes that his approaches to Teiresias have been made through unspecified emissaries rather than directly—and that they have been sent twice without success.

The chorus hurriedly changes the subject (290–93):

Chorus: Then there's the silly talk of times long past.
Oedipus: What was it? I'm surveying every word.
Chorus: Word was he got killed by some travelers.
Oedipus: I heard so too—and someone saw it all.
              But no eyes see the man who saw it all.

Oedipus instantly takes the bait when the chorus mentions ancient rumor. Then he gives a biting retort when he assumes that he is hearing a reiteration of what Creon had just told him. But the last word before Oedipus takes over again is not "brigands" but "travelers." Perhaps, as Dawe suggests obliquely on line 292, "travelers" (*hodoiporôn*) might have some sense akin to "highwaymen" in English.[7] Oedipus does not follow up this difference, which is at least as marked as that between the singular and plural of the word "brigand" which so bothers him, because he is too quick to assume he knows what they are going to say and too eager to point out, in a snide manner, that what he had expected to hear after his proclamation has not emerged: the identity of the supposed witness who could presumably say who killed Laios.

Oedipus has in fact noticed something important. Why does no one point out the man who saw the killing, despite the fact that Creon and, later, Jocasta imply that what the witness said was publicly stated and thus general knowledge? At the same time, however, Oedipus himself has not yet made a single move to ascertain the identity of the alleged witness, much less summon him, other than by this proclamation.

The chorus adopts the attitude that the man (witness or, more likely, the killer) will probably go away (294–96):

> *Chorus*: Well if he's subject to portentous fears,
> he won't stay when he hears curses like yours.
> *Oedipus*: If deeds don't scare him, words won't frighten him.

These three lines undermine many assumptions on the basis of which Oedipus invokes his curse on the killer and those shielding him. The curse will have effect only if *the killer fears such pronouncements*, and Oedipus admits that someone who does not stop at killing will not be deterred by a mere verbal formula.

In short, Oedipus' grandiloquence has led him only toward a close association of himself with Laios, to whom he now plays the role of avenging son. The Thebans have given him no information. Although they treat him with formal respect, they make it clear that they admire and value Teiresias much more. The blind seer, like Creon, will be the center of attention as he comes onstage.

TEIRESIAS *ANAX*

As Teiresias arrives, he is hailed by the chorus as the person who will be able to cross-question and refute (*houxelenxôn*) the killer (297–99):

> The man who will cross-question and refute
> the killer has arrived: the godlike seer
> these men are leading in before us now,
> the only human in whom truth is born.

Skill in cross-questioning and refutation seems more rhetorical and Socratic than prophetic. The guard who arrests Antigone, for instance, tells Creon (*Antigone* 399) to "judge and cross-examine (*exelenche*)" her to assure himself of her guilt. In what sense would we imagine that Teiresias is such a master of *elenchos*, of dialectic? *Elenchos*, to use Aristotle's definition in *De Sophisticis Elenchis* 170B1, is "the proof of the contradiction of a given thesis." Similarly, in the Aristotelian *Rhetoric to Alexander* 1431A7–8, *elenchos* is "that which cannot be otherwise." Dawe, commenting on *Oedipus* 297, finds it odd that the chorus should talk of refuting the killer since the killer's identity is unknown. "Until it is known," Dawe observes, "examining, cross-questioning, refuting, have no place."[8] Unless, of course, the chorus suspects or knows that there is going to be an argument. For Teiresias is Oedipus' cross-questioner and refuter in the dialogue that follows: the only person in the play to accuse Oedipus outright of killing Laios, and to suggest that he was the child of Laios and Jocasta. He turns Oedipus from principal investigator into the accused. And such is his success that by the end of the play everyone, including Oedipus, accepts the full sweep of Teiresias' charges.

True, Oedipus *attempts* both to cross-question and to refute Teiresias. But in the hostile interchanges that follow, Oedipus is verbally routed. Teiresias earns the chorus's title of the great refuter. We should ask ourselves, however, why the chorus feels so sure at the outset that Teiresias, rather than Oedipus, merits this honorific. Although it was Oedipus who solved the verbal riddle of the Sphinx, who refuted her, the chorus is absolutely confident that Teiresias is "the only man in whom truth is born (*pephyken*)" (298–99).[9]

To engage in public debate with such a man before a choral audience already disposed to believe that one's interlocutor has some inborn access to the truth could be most dangerous. To augment Teiresias' stature, Oedipus himself delivers a flattering introduction to the seer, extending from line 300 to line 315, which reinforces the chorus' high opinion, endowing him with a Delphic prophetic authority, and casts aside, albeit temporarily, the uneasiness he seemed to feel about the seer when talking to the chorus a few lines earlier. No less important, Oedipus' words immediately inform everyone (including Teiresias) that Oedipus makes no distinction between Phoebus' prophecy and Creon's interpretation of it. Again Oedipus shows he has accepted that it was Phoebus, rather than Creon, who connected Laios and his death with the plague:

> Teiresias, observing everything
> that can be taught and all things that defy
> expression, what is in the skies above
> or walks upon the earth! You cannot see,
> and yet your reason shows you our city,
> and the plague afflicting it. My lord (*ônax = ô anax*),
> we are discovering that only you
> can be her savior, champion (*prostatês*), and spokesman.
> Phoebus—in case you have not heard the news
> from messengers—sent us his answer.
> For we had sent to him for his advice.
> The only release from this disease

could come if we clearly identified
those who killed Laios and then killed them
or drove them out in exile from this land.
Don't grudge us what the auspices have said,
or any other pathway that you have
which yields prophetic insight, and protect
yourself, the city—and protect me too
from all the blight this dead man brings on us.
For we are in your power. To help a man
with all your might is real nobility.

The extravagant admiration expressed for Teiresias' rhetorical prowess, insight, and truthfulness deserves close attention, because such praise commits those who give it to a rhetorically inferior position either real or, as with Socrates, feigned. The chorus and Oedipus give all outward signs that they expect Teiresias to be able to provide truthful answers. Oedipus not only calls Teiresias *anax,* "king, lord" as the chorus just did, but even acknowledges: "we are in your power." Events prove the assessment correct. Oedipus and the chorus are transferring to Teiresias the power to decide what actions are appropriate.

RHETORIC AND DECISIONS

"The purpose of rhetoric," Aristotle observes, "is to control decision making" (*heneka kriseôs estin hê rhetorikê* [*Rhetoric* 2.1377B]). Our ability to control decision making is affected by how we are perceived by others. Aristotle continues (ibid.): "One must look not only toward one's speech so it will demonstrate one's point and be believable, but set both oneself and the decision maker in the right perspective."

Aristotle here assumes that the speaker, that is, the rhetorician, and the decision maker are not one and the same. The speaker's task is to control, by rhetorical skill, the reactions of the decision maker. So, as Aristotle makes absolutely clear in the second book of his *Rhetoric,* rhetoricians must understand what the emotions are and how they work. They must know how to play upon the emotions of their audience; and they cannot play upon emotions until they learn what these emotions are and how they can *predict* the circumstances under which a given emotional response will be triggered. Thus rhetoric is as much a matter of what we would nowadays call psychology as it is of the artifices of speech. The most persuasive rhetorician must have a good sense of what the object of manipulation will do when subjected to given stimuli.

There is no question, then, that Oedipus has put the chorus and the audience in a very receptive mood toward Teiresias by giving him what we would call a good "buildup." He has also put himself at a rhetorical disadvantage by making himself—the tyrant, the decision maker—dependent on the rhetorician. Thus the chorus' description of Teiresias as the "cross-questioner" or "refuter" is fundamentally valid. Teiresias can say anything he wishes. He, not Oedipus, controls the dispersal and interpretation of information. And he does so with Oedipus' consent.

TEIRESIAS THE RHETORICIAN

Teiresias' first statement is oracular in its ambiguity and apparently addressed to himself (316–18):

> Alas: reason's power! How formidable (*deinon*)
> when reason does not pay. I know this well.
> But I forgot it, or I'd not have come.

He berates himself for having come at all. Or perhaps it is wiser to say that he conveys the appearance of berating himself. For precisely what he means is not at all clear. His first word in the Greek text—after his exclamation of grief—is *phronein* (to have "reasoning power"). *Phronein* is also his last word as he departs in line 462. Could the formidable quality of the rational mind to which he refers be somehow akin to the great speaker's traditionally formidable tongue? Is Teiresias *deinos phronein* ("formidable in reasoning"), as Plato's Socrates was apparently *deinos legein* ("formidable in speaking") according to his accusers (*Apology* 17A)?

Formidable power in speaking, as in thinking, is potentially devastating to rhetorical adversaries; but it can also mean trouble for its master. Socrates, after all, was brought to court and ultimately put to death on charges of being, among other things, *deinos legein*. There is, then, a sense in which one can suggest that what is fearsome (*deinon*) is the ability to speak (*legein*) or think (*phronein*). And this is how Teiresias begins: with a comment on the drawbacks of intelligence under certain circumstances. Critics usually assume that he is reacting to his own dilemma, and that he wishes he did not have the intellectual power that is his. But it is surely no less possible that Teiresias is reacting to the irony of Oedipus' laudatory introduction—that he is commenting on the drawbacks of Oedipus' rationality rather than on the drawbacks of his own intelligence. Such an interpretation might make better sense of the extraordinary observation Teiresias adds: that he knew how formidable a thing powerful reason was but had forgotten until this moment.

Oedipus either fails to hear or fails to understand Teiresias' words. He notes only that the seer seems depressed (319): "What *is* this? You come in so listlessly." Teiresias responds (320–21):

> "Send me home. Do as I say, then you'll
> cope best with your affairs and I with mine."

Teiresias' response is curiously phrased: he does not say "I'm going home" or "Let me go home," but "Send me home." Oedipus has assumed responsibility for summoning Teiresias. Teiresias is now leaving him the responsibility for his dismissal—something Oedipus seems hardly likely to do. Further, Teiresias adds that such a dismissal would be in their mutual interests—though he makes no mention of the interests of Thebes.

Oedipus understandably responds by rebuking Teiresias for his lack of concern for the city; but Oedipus in turn is knocked back into place by the blind seer's needling and personal retort, ironically introduced by the verb "I see" (322–25):

> *Oedipus*: What you suggest runs contrary to law,
> and is not kind to this city. It nourished
> you, yet you deprive it of wise words.
> *Teiresias*: I see you voicing words not right for you
> or the occasion. Let me not do so too.

Oedipus lets the insulting innuendos slip by and resorts instead to the humblest statement he voices in the play (326–27):

> Since reason rules your mind, don't turn from us.
> We are your suppliants; by the gods we all
> beg you, shower kisses at your feet.

The dramatic image of a tyrant so humbling himself before a seer might well elicit a gasp from most ages and societies other than our own. Certainly nowhere else in surviving Greek tragedy does an unconquered ruler prostrate himself before another person. But Teiresias, instead of acknowledging Oedipus' gesture of self-humiliation with at least a courteous refusal, turns on the prostrate monarch with withering condescension (328–29):

> Precisely. *All* of you lack reason. I myself
> will never give my best advice. I'll thus
> avoid revealing your bad news to you.

Again, Teiresias says nothing about the city's suffering. Nor does he comment this time on any troubles to which he himself might be susceptible. He alludes only to his own knowledge of *Oedipus'* misfortunes and thereby sets up a dialectical opposition between himself and the tyrant from which the city is pointedly excluded.

Oedipus manages to contain himself somewhat and still insists on linking his inquiries to the city's interests more than to his own (330–31):

> What's this you say? You know, and will not speak?
> You plan to sell out, ruin the city?

Oedipus' multiple questions, however, show more than a trace of anger and indignation. Teiresias' next haughty response could hardly fail to make things worse, when he intones (332–33):

> I cause myself no pain and none to you.
> Why cross-question (*elencheis*) me further on this?
> You could not find the answer out from me.

Teiresias' selection of the word *elencheis* is especially effective, given our recollection of the chorus' observation that the seer is himself "the great refuter." I won't let you play the role of the cross-questioning attorney, Teiresias is saying. But is this his statement or his challenge? The seer certainly does not maintain his uncommunicative pose very long. Seventeen lines later he starts to level charges against Oedipus—to say all the things that he now avers could not be drawn from him.

THE ANGERED OEDIPUS

The immediate result of Teiresias' condescension is an explosion of anger on Oedipus' part. Oedipus expects answers from Teiresias. Yet he has created a situation in which his requests and unparalleled self-abasement have been met with rudeness. Here is their exchange (332–49)

> *Oedipus*:   You evil man, you'd temper a heart of stone!
>   You just won't speak? You will appear, yet be
>   inflexible and leave things unresolved?
> *Teiresias*:   You mind my temperament yet have no eyes
>   to see your own. And you despise me for it.
> *Oedipus*:   Who could control his temper when he hears
>   your words which now dishonor this city?

Teiresias:	Fate comes, though I wordless and quietly go.
Oedipus:	Since it comes, don't you *have* to let me know?
Teiresias:	No sense in saying more. So counter that
	with all the wildest temper of your heart.

Oedipus' expectations have been frustrated. Predictably, he becomes angry. Aristotle observes that we are liable to be specially angered when "things turn out the opposite from what one expects" (*tanantia tychêi prosdechomenos* [*Rhetoric* 2.1379A24)). Indeed, the first emotion he treats in the second book of his *Rhetoric* is anger. After discussing the mental disposition of those who are angry, the objects of their anger, and the reasons for their anger—the *pôs* ("why") the *tisi* ("at whom"), and the *dia poia* ("on account of what kinds of thing")—Aristotle points out that people, when angry, are always in some kind of pain. "And the person who is in pain is in search of something" (*ephietai gar tinos ho lypoumenos* [*Rhetoric* 2.1379A]); "whether a person is deliberately getting in your way, preventing, say, a thirsty man from drinking, or whether he is not doing so deliberately but *appears* to be; he could be working against you—or not working with you."

One of the orator's tasks may be precisely "to arrange what he is saying so as to make his hearers inclined to anger" (*kataskeuazein tôi logôi toioutous hoioi ontes orgilôs echousi* [*Rhetoric* 2.1380A]). But if so, the orator in this scene between Oedipus and Teiresias is Teiresias. We surely cannot miss the very overt challenge in Teiresias' last words in the passage cited above: "So counter that with all the wildest temper of your heart." Unfortunately, it takes Oedipus a disastrously long time to realize that he has played into the refuter's hands. By appearing to force Teiresias to speak in public against the latter's own declared better judgment, Oedipus endows in advance whatever the seer says with public authority. And the seer's professed reluctance to speak undermines Oedipus' later contention that Teiresias has conspired with Creon against him.

We cannot rule out, then, the possibility that Teiresias' opening words are part of a deliberate strategy rather than a bumbling confession of absentmindedness, particularly if he is, as the chorus suggests, the master cross-questioner and refuter. Teiresias leaves the impression that he has the answers everyone in seeking but does not want to reveal them. And by pointedly focusing on Oedipus' problems, he implies that his reticence arises from unwillingness to get his ruler in trouble.

Teiresias' words and conduct arouse Oedipus' curiosity as well as his anger. They may well be designed to do precisely that. If so, Teiresias has adopted a powerful rhetorical strategy, given both the chorus's and Oedipus' avowed respect for the accuracy of his prophetic skills. Further, Teiresias' words make it quite clear that the news he has for Oedipus is bad. So if Jocasta is right about Oedipus' vulnerability to someone who speaks to his fears, Oedipus is in Teiresias' power from this point on.

Teiresias creates an opposition between himself and Oedipus in almost every utterance early in the scene. He refers to his *own* misfortune in contrast to Oedipus' (e.g., 321, 329, 331). In his first seven interchanges with Oedipus, none more than three lines long, Teiresias uses the emphatic personal pronoun "I," *egô*, six times, and both "me" and "my" in the one response where he does not use *egô*. Oedipus, in contrast, uses a first-person singular pronoun only once in these interchanges: as the very last word of line 342 when he has lost his temper with the reticent seer: "You must tell me (*emoî*)."

Oedipus concludes, ironically, that Teiresias is setting himself above ruler and country. I say ironically, because Oedipus does not comment on the fact that both he and the chorus—the country, if you will—have placed Teiresias on that very platform above them on which he now stands, abusing his monarch. Oedipus comments only on the arrogance of Teiresias' insistent and apparently haughty *egô* and on his refusal to take any account of the city itself.

Oedipus now finds himself facing an especially difficult task. He must reestablish his authority and his status as tyrant not by rising from his throne in anger but by rising from the floor where he has been groveling at the feet of the man he now realizes is his adversary. So he resorts to the tyrannical and authoritarian first person. Once Oedipus' angry, tyrannical, and egotistical response occurs, Teiresias does not use *egô* again for, roughly, the next fifty lines. He has, I suspect, elicited the angry response he sought. He, like the chorus, has the opening advantage of knowing there would be an argument with Oedipus.

OEDIPUS' ACCUSATIONS

In response to Teiresias' challenge to get angry, Oedipus exclaims (345–49):

> Yes! Such is my temper that I'll hold
> nothing that I know back. For you should know
> that I suspect you helped father this act,
> indeed, you did it—all but with your hands.
> If you had eyes, I'd claim you worked alone.

Teiresias' refusal to speak drives Oedipus to declare with passionate religious logic that Teiresias must have planned Laios' murder. For if

Teiresias has known the criminal and has not spoken out as bidden, he is not only under the curse that Oedipus has placed on the murderer or murderers of *Laios* and on those who may be sheltering him or them, but also responsible for the destruction of the Theban people, the *laos*, who will continue to perish until the murderer is found. Teiresias must therefore be responsible for the murder of Laios—though his blindness at least means that he did not actually commit the crime himself. Oedipus' conclusion is perfectly logical for someone who believes first that an unsolved murder really has caused the plague and second that Teiresias really knows who the killer is. Oedipus probably assumes that Teiresias, as a holy man, accepts the same religious logic too. But there is no reason to assume that Teiresias the rhetorician does.

It is no less ominous that Oedipus talks of Teiresias "fathering" or "begetting" the crime (*xymphyteusai*). It may be more than coincidence that Oedipus' mind seems yet again, as when he invoked the curse on the killer and those who might be harboring him, to be linking Laios' death and fatherhood, an association that becomes quite critical later in this scene.

Oedipus, then, lets anger get the better of him and unleashes upon Teiresias charges that have neither basis nor substantiating evidence. Is Oedipus simply being irrational and foolish, or is there rhetorical method in this apparent madness? If Oedipus has suddenly realized that Teiresias is about to point the finger at him, it could be quite advantageous to forestall Teiresias' accusation with one of his own. For any accusation from the seer would then appear to be only a retaliation in kind.

Indeed, Teiresias, who seconds earlier was saying that Oedipus did not have the power to drag his secret from him, does in fact retaliate with accusations of his own: he declares that Oedipus is the pollution upon the city (350). And we should note that this is also the first time Teiresias makes any reference to the city and its suffering (350–56):

Teiresias:	Is that true? I bid you now honor
	your proclamation: from this very day
	speak neither to these people nor to me!
	You are this land's unholy, sickly curse!
Oedipus:	You see no shame in starting such rumors?
	Where do you think you'll get away to hide?
Teiresias:	I've got away. I nurse the truth—it's strong.

Oedipus is understandably enraged at the accusation and the public humiliation, for the people, we recall, are present during the interchange. Yet Teiresias never offers a shred of evidence—now nor later—to substantiate his claim that Oedipus is guilty. Instead, he reiterates the words *alêthes*, "true," and *alêtheia*, "truth" (350, 356, 369). And the chorus, we will recall, has praised Teiresias as "the only human in whom truth is born" (299).

TEIRESIAS AND THE TRUTH

Oedipus now faces the much more difficult task of assailing Teiresias' credibility as a purveyor of truth. To do so, he falls back on the conventional arguments which we find again and again in fifth-century Greek writers on the fraudulence of prophecy. The case would have more rhetorical merit had Oedipus not prefaced his interrogation of Teiresias with a speech that seemed to show traditional honor and respect for the seer's profession. Here is Oedipus' attack and Teiresias' response (358–59):

> *Oedipus*:   Who taught you it? It's not part of your trade.
> *Teiresias*:   You taught me, made me speak against my will.

Oedipus' taunt does not elicit a defense of prophets and prophecy from Teiresias as Pentheus' taunt draws out Teiresias in Euripides' *Bacchae* 248–327. The Sophoclean Teiresias simply hurls the insult back in his accuser's teeth, just as he does when Creon insults the prophetic trade in *Antigone* 1033–90. The Sophoclean Teiresias will not let his interlocutor escape from the personal nature of the conflict.

But angered as Oedipus is, he is still listening. Nothing Teiresias says is lost on him (359–60):

> *Oedipus*:   Speak what? Say it again, so I'll learn more.
> *Teiresias*:   You did not catch it—or you're testing me?

Why does Oedipus ask Teiresias to repeat his accusation? Dawe suggests (on line 359) that it is an authorial device "so that the audience may fully grasp some important point ... or because the demands of stichomythia [the rapid interchange of single lines of verse] require a line to be delivered but the sense really requires nothing."[10] This explanation leaves me uneasy, since both alternatives assume there need be no dramatic justification from the speaker's point of view. I find it hard to see how the audience would not have caught the point the first time around and think it does Sophocles little credit to suggest he resorted to "filler." So we must explore alternatives.

Teiresias has just suggested, sarcastically, that he has learned the truth from Oedipus who forced him to speak. Now Oedipus is feigning not to understand the drift of Teiresias' words; he places himself in the position of a slow learner at Teiresias' feet, thus subtly undermining Teiresias' contention that he learned from Oedipus. Oedipus' words are not hostile but matter-of-fact: he is not, as tyrant to subject, forcing Teiresias to speak; he is, as student to teacher, requesting him to repeat what he said before. Oedipus' response throws Teiresias off balance for the first time in this scene. Confused and suspicious, he must be reassured by Oedipus before continuing (361–63):

> *Oedipus*:   Not to my best knowledge. Say it again.
> *Teiresias*: These murderers you hunt: I say they're you.
> *Oedipus*:   You'll not say this a second time scot-free.

Teiresias rephrases his original accusation with greater precision. We note that it assumes the connection between the plague and Laios' murder which was not made by Apollo's oracle but suggested by Creon, then given definitive form by Oedipus himself in his opening address to Teiresias. It is, of course, possible that Teiresias had heard news of Creon's consultation before Oedipus summarizes its outcome for him, as Oedipus concedes at the beginning of the scene (305). But we don t have to make this assumption.

A conflict of testimony now exists between Creon and Teiresias, as the chorus and Oedipus should realize. Creon insisted that Laios was assailed by many attackers: Teiresias implies that Oedipus was the only killer. And general opinion on this matter, if Creon is right, favors Creon's notion of the multiplicity of killers. Jocasta indeed explains later that the alleged witness to Laios' death publicly declared that the former king was attacked by several men.

Teiresias' declaration, then, conflicts with what most people at Thebes believe. But it does not necessarily conflict with what Oedipus believes. For Oedipus, we have noted, oscillates between accepting that plurality of killers and the possibility that it was just one—although he has not yet explained why he oscillates. We have not yet been told that Oedipus remembers having killed an old man at a crossroads. We have yet to grasp that he is worried by a fear still not clearly enunciated: that he himself may be the killer(s) he seeks.

For the present, let us simply note that Oedipus does not protest his innocence. He reacts with sufficient nonchalance that Teiresias seems almost dissatisfied with the results of his statements (364–65):

> *Teiresias*: Should I speak on to fan your temper more?
> *Oedipus*:   As much as you feel need. You're wasting words.

Teiresias now openly admits that he intends to anger Oedipus, confirming our previous suspicion that such may have been his intention all along. But the positions have changed. Now Oedipus tells Teiresias he is wasting time trying to provoke him further. Earlier, Teiresias claimed Oedipus could not compel him to speak.

Teiresias cunningly recaptures the initiative in three steps. First he returns to his protests of truthfulness—where he must reestablish his credentials. Then he intimates that Oedipus is guilty of some family sexual crime, possibly incest, which, as we will discover, Oedipus greatly fears he may commit (or has committed). Finally the blind prophet opens up for Oedipus an obvious path along which to counterattack. He accuses his ruler of blindness to the real truth of the situation (366–69):

> Teiresias: The truth eludes (leLÊTHEnaî) you; you associate
>   in vile sin with those dearest to you
>   yet don't see where you are in evil's grasp.
> Oedipus: Do you have the illusion you can talk
>   this way for ever with impunity?
> Teiresias: If truth's (aLÊTHEias) strength is not illusory.

Teiresias uses an etymologizing wordplay to reinforce his point, much as Plato later suggests the "truth" of Er's vision at the end of the *Republic* (10.621A–D). There Socrates reports that Er wandered in the divine world of disembodied souls who are about to be reincarnated. He journeys with them to the plain of the *LÊTHÊ*, "forgetfulness" and camps beside the river of indifference. A person who drinks (*PiONTA*) from this river forgets everything (PANTÔn LAnTHAnesthai). But Er is prevented from drinking and therefore remembers everything. Since knowledge, to the Platonic Socrates, is recollection, it would also be in a sense nonforgetfulness, that is to say, *A-LÊTHE-ia*: the truth.[11] Plato gives us, in short, an etymologizing assurance of the truth. And Socrates suggests it will be useful to remember Er's message when we come to cross the *LÊTHÊ* too. Similarly Teiresias, by suggesting that knowledge has eluded (*le-LÊTHEnai*) Oedipus, is undermining in his listeners the possibility that Oedipus could know the truth.

The etymologizing force of Socrates'—and Teiresias'—suggestion finds interesting confirmation in Plato's *Cratylus* 421B, where Socrates defines truth, *ALÊTHEIA*, as *THEIA ... ALÊ*: "heavenly wandering," which is no more than an anagram of *ALÊ THEIA* and an interesting reinforcement of the ideas that Er's journey is a heavenly wandering toward the truth. We must give this ancient etymologizing careful attention in Sophocles' *Oedipus*, no matter how bizarre or even silly it may sound to modern ears. For Oedipus himself will go on to accept an etymologized identity for himself, derived from the assertion that his name, Oedipus, means "swollen foot."

THE PROPHECY OF BLINDNESS

The bait to which Oedipus rises, however, is not the issue of the truth itself. It is Teiresias' boast that, though blind, he has special sight. Blindness, one might—and Oedipus does—suggest, could be an obstacle to discerning the truth (370–77):

Oedipus:	It's strong, but not in you. In you it's dead.
	Your ears and mind are sightless as your eyes.
Teiresias:	You are pathetic, taunting me the way
	that soon the whole world will be taunting you.
Oedipus:	Child of unbroken darkness, never could you
	harm me or anyone who sees life's light.
Teiresias:	Fate does not set your downfall by my hands.
	Apollo wants to finish this himself.

We see again the success of Teiresias' tactics: he provokes Oedipus' insults and accusations, then turns them against him. In this instance we find Teiresias' only prophetic statement in the play. It immediately prompts the question that should always arise when prophecies are addressed to believers in prophecy: is prophecy in such cases proof of the seer's foreknowledge of subsequent actions, or is it the *cause* of what follows? Let us remind ourselves that there is *nothing* in Apollo's oracle, even as reported by Creon, that said anything about the killer blinding himself. And there is nothing in what Oedipus subsequently reveals about his own visit to Delphi to suggest that he will blind himself. The statement that he will do so comes from a blind prophet whose blindness and prophetic powers Oedipus has insulted.

Here we gain a glimpse of what ought to be a central issue in the discussion of Sophocles' *Oedipus*. Yet it has not been, for the simple reason that readers and critics themselves make a curious act of faith: that Teiresias is actually speaking the truth. The reasoning that precedes the act of faith is quite straightforward. Because Oedipus ultimately blinds himself, Teiresias must be a purely objective clairvoyant. How else would he know that Oedipus will take such drastic action against himself?

The counterexplanation is not particularly hard to grasp: that Oedipus' behavior, based on prior observation, is predictable. He will respond to a given stimulus in a given and predictable way. It is not only the biologist but the witch doctor and the psychologist who understand this principle. We see from the beginning of the play that there is an element in Oedipus that makes him take prophecy seriously. Thus he risks allowing prophetic utterances to control his life, whether he acquiesces in his "doom" or tries to avoid fulfilling it.

The danger is that if he is convinced one prophecy is correct, he will accept other prophecies as similarly binding. If he concludes that he has killed his father and married his mother, as he fears he will, because Apollo prophesied that he would, Oedipus may go on to blind himself, in the belief that he is not only fulfilling his doom but justly punishing himself. We are dealing with the huge power of suggestion that is often wielded over the superstitious, in this case by a blind prophet whose trade and whose blindness Oedipus has just insulted. Here is the difference between Teiresias and an attorney in court: Teiresias is trying to persuade *the accused* of his guilt, not the jury.

The same vagueness in Oedipus' thinking that makes him assimilate Creon's explanation to the oracle reported makes him assimilate what Teiresias says to the prophecy of matricide and incest. It thus makes little sense to argue that Oedipus can accept the efficacy of Apollo's prophetic powers without believing in those of Teiresias. We have seen how readily Oedipus accepts not just Apollo's word but whatever is reported as Apollo's word. Hence the force of Teiresias' attribution of the fulfillment of Oedipus' destruction to the prophetic god whose oracles Oedipus fears and respects: Apollo.

The Theory of Conspiracy

Oedipus is not, however, so hopelessly naive as immediately to accept at face value Teiresias' insinuation of Apollo into the argument. The moment Apollo is mentioned, in fact, he sees a link between Creon and Teiresias. There is a plot: Creon is in league with Teiresias. Oedipus asks (378): "Creon or who came up with these findings?"

Oedipus realizes he may have been trapped by his dependence on religious sources, by his use of Creon to consult Apollo, and by calling Teiresias. To make things worse, he has conducted his investigation in public. The people of Thebes have heard Creon speak; they have witnessed the accusations of Teiresias. Oedipus is in deep rhetorical and political trouble. Teiresias tries to turn Oedipus back on himself again with the immediate retort (379): "Creon is not your problem, you are your own." This time, Teiresias fails. Oedipus explodes into a denunciation of Creon and Teiresias (380–89):

Riches, tyranny, and skillfulness
surpassing others' skill makes for a life
much coveted. The envy that stands guard
upon you is so great! I did not ask
the city to put in my hands the power
to be first lord. The city gave it me,
this power for which Creon, a trusted man,
a friend from my first days of lordly rule,
now yearns to throw me out. He secretly
creeps on me from behind, quietly works in
a plot-weaving, king-making charlatan,
a treacherous liar who sees personal gain
but was born sightless in the trade he plies.

There is no overwhelming reason to suspect, on the basis of what has been said thus far in the play, that Creon has been plotting with Teiresias against Oedipus to take over Oedipus' *tyrannis*, his position as tyrant (380). We, of course, do not have access to any prior "knowledge" such as Oedipus might have to support such charges in his own mind. True, we have noticed that Creon is curiously reticent in reporting the oracle, blurring the lines between what the oracle may have said and his own interpretation of it. The motive Oedipus attributes to Creon, envy, is not impossible, given Creon's reasonable expectation that he might have become ruler after Laios' death—as he does in some versions of the myth.

Indeed, envy could also explain Teiresias' hostility toward Oedipus. For Oedipus' strongest single claim to superiority over Teiresias is that he, not Teiresias, solved the riddle of the Sphinx. He now knows he must publicly match his credentials in riddle solving against Teiresias'. He abruptly adopts the skeptic's position on oracles and divination, then turns on Teiresias with the haughtiness of God to job: where were you when I solved the riddle of the Sphinx? Here is his attack (390–403):

Come on now, prove your clear prophetic powers.
When the riddle-singing bitch was here,
how was it you said nothing to release
these fellow citizens of yours? Here was
a riddle needing power of prophecy,
not an accidental passerby to solve.
But you did not come forward with your birds
or words of god to make it known. Then I,
Oedipus, no wit at all (*mêden eidôs Oidipous*), passed by.

And I defeated her, not by learning
from birds, but by using my intellect.

This is the man you now try to turn out,
thinking you'll stand up close to Creon's throne.
But I think you will weep, both you and he
who organized all this. Did I not think
that you were old, you would have learned by now
what your reasoning power had brought you to.

Oedipus here offers his strongest possible evidence that he is intellectually superior to Teiresias and casts in his teeth Teiresias' claims to "reasoning power." He might well have gone on to reestablish his own credentials as savior of the state, had he pursued further the matter of the Sphinx and its riddle. The question is indeed interesting. If Teiresias is the "only human in whom truth is born," and if he has great reasoning power, why was he unable (or unwilling) to solve the riddle? Oedipus, however, mixes up the issue of Teiresias' professional competence with accusations of political plotting. And his explosion of anger provokes the chorus to intervene, censuring both men and asking them both to return to the central issue (404–7):

The words he spoke seem shaped in temper and
yours too, Oedipus. That's what we think.
The situation does not call for this.
Rather one must look for the best way
to break down, answer the god's prophecies.

Teiresias, however, has been let off the hook and has no intention of returning to it. He takes advantage of Oedipus' political accusations to reply in astonishing political kind. He does not engage Oedipus on the latter's strong ground—his solution of the Sphinx's riddle. Nor does he deny involvement in a conspiracy. Instead he focuses on Oedipus himself, on the nature of his power, and on the personal insults Oedipus has directed toward him, especially the insult to his blindness. And he picks up on two political words Oedipus has used.

The first word is *tyrannis*, which Oedipus used in reference to Laios' power in lines 128–29 and again, in Teiresias' presence, in line 380. Oedipus, himself a tyrant, understandably has no sense that *tyrannis* is a politically "negative" word. But Teiresias is not so naive. He uses Oedipus' general description of absolute power as a means of accusing Oedipus of behaving tyrannically. Teiresias is in fact, the first person in the play to describe Oedipus' rule as tyrannical (*tyrannein*) in an overtly negative sense (408). Tyrants, proverbially, are the enemies of free speech. So with rhetorical aplomb, Teiresias demands the right to reply, which no one has denied him. Indeed, the problem earlier was precisely Teiresias' *refusal* to speak (408–9):

> Though you're the tyrant, still, equality
> must be allowed at least in equal time
> to make reply. In this I too have power.

The second word is *prostatês*, "sponsor, champion," a word Oedipus had used flatteringly of Teiresias himself in line 303 as the seer was entering: "only you can be her [Thebes'] savior, sponsor (*prostatês*), and spokesman." This is how Teiresias picks up and uses the term (409–11):

> I live as Apollo's slave, not yours,
> so don't enroll me as an alien
> with Creon as my sponsor (*prostatou*) and spokesman.

The last line cited carries some extraordinary undertones which smack of fifth-century Athens rather than mythic Thebes, and which I am quite sure would have jolted Sophocles' audience. So we must digress briefly to discuss some of them here.

CREON AS CHAMPION

The word *prostatês* ("sponsor, champion") and its associated adjective *prostatêrios* ("protecting, championing") are often used by Sophocles of divine rather than human patrons.[12] In fact, when Oedipus calls upon Teiresias as sole *prostatês* and savior in the plague (303), he is using language that, as Dawe observes on that line, "can be used unaltered of a god."[13] More often, however, *prostatês* carries political resonances. The word came, Victor Ehrenberg observes, to denote "the political leader of the people," though the first clear use of the term in that sense does not occur until Aristophanes' *Peace* 684, some time after the production of *Oedipus*.[14] We saw in Chapter 1 how such a champion of the people can be a threat to democracy and lead to the imposition of tyranny. A comment by Orestes, in Euripides' *Orestes* 772, shows that the *prostatês* can be a demagogue in tragedy as well as in Plato: "The populace is a formidable entity when it has mischievous champions (*prostatas*)."

The earliest and most common political use of the word, however, is that exemplified in Aeschylus' *Suppliants* 963, where king Pelasgus is described as "sponsor of the future metics [resident aliens]." And this is the particular sense of the word that Teiresias seems to have in mind here.

Jebb paraphrases Teiresias' sentiments (cited above) as follows:

> You charge me with being the tool of Creon's treason. I have a right to plead my own case when I am accused. I am not like a resident alien, who can plead before a civic tribunal only by the mouth of that patron under whom he has been registered.

"Every *metoikos* [resident alien] at Athens," Jebb continues, "was required *epigraphesthai prostatên*, i.e. to have the name of a citizen, as patron, inscribed over his own." The allusion to the need for resident aliens in the Athens of Sophocles' own day to speak "through" a citizen patron is fascinating in many ways.[15]

Sophocles' audience was composed not of literary scholars but of ordinary citizens who understood political issues most readily in terms of their own experience of government. The same Athenian citizens, gathered in the Assembly, were the city's legislative body, and gathered in the various courts, the judiciary. As Ehrenberg observed, the Greek tragedian was not "a private person writing beautiful poetry in an ivory tower," and tragedy itself was "an event of public life in which the trends of people's minds were reflected, discussed, and displayed."[16] Sophocles himself had taken a prominent part in Athenian public life, and almost certainly served as general with Pericles in 441/40.[17] He was not simply a professional writer who observed politics from a distance, but a man at the very hub of political activity, and in political contact with those most active in government.

We must then look once more at the role of Creon as *prostatês* and F. J. Parsons's note on Aristotle's *Rhetoric* 3.8 (1408B) makes a good starting point:

> Emancipated slaves, like the *metoikoi* [resident aliens], seldom arrived at the dignity of Citizens, or were allowed to manage business in their own names; but were obliged to select some one of the Citizens as their "Patron," (*prostatên, epitropon,*) under whose name to be enrolled, and to whose care and protection to be committed. Compare Sophocles' *Oedipus Tyrannus*, 411 [Teiresias' remark about Creon, cited above].... The popularity of the demagogue Cleon, of course, caused many to solicit his "Patronage," indeed so many, that the boys in the street anticipated the close of the Crier's proclamation on these

occasions [i.e., when the Crier asked who would speak on someone's behalf] by calling out "Kleona."[18]

Creon's role as *prostatês*, as intermediary and spokesman for the ordinary person, combined with his overt "popularizing" could hardly fail to evoke thoughts of the Athenian demagogue Cleon, who was one of the major political forces in Athens in the years following Pericles' death—the very years during which Sophocles must have written *Oedipus*: 429–25 B.C. Cleon was bitterly hated by the historian Thucydides and mocked again and again by Aristophanes in his comedies where Cleon's control over the Athenian people is savagely satirized.[19]

Thucydides saw him as the main driving force of the prolonged and ultimately disastrous war Athens waged against Sparta, as the agent of the most callous Athenian imperialism, who again and again prevented the conclusion of a just and advantageous peace by stirring up war fever in the gullible populace. It was he who used his power as a champion of the people to build the basis of a personal authority in the state which no one was able to challenge successfully until his death. Cleon paved the way for a succession of popular leaders who were able to wrest control of the state from more genteel and aristocratic leaders. In Aeschylus' day a *prostatês* may have been a kindly champion of the dispossessed. But this was no longer true in the later years of the fifth century, as we have seen from Orestes' comment in Euripides' *Orestes* 772: "the populace is a formidable entity when they have mischievous champions (*prostatês*)."

The passage in Aristotle (*Rhetoric* 3.8[1408B]) that drew Parsons's attention to Teiresias' remark about Creon deserves, then, our special attention:

> The form of one's prose style should not be either metrical or unrhythmical. If it is metrical it is unpersuasive because it appears contrived. It is at the same time distracting because it prompts the audience to look out for when similar occurrences will again arise—the way the children do when they anticipate the answer when the heralds ask: "Who does the freedman choose as his patron?" "Cleon!" they say.

Cleon had been dead for more than fifty years when Aristotle wrote. Yet Cleon's popularity as champion of resident aliens was still proverbial, as it was for Aristophanes in the *Frogs*, written twenty years after Cleon's death. A hostess who considers herself to have been wronged by Heracles calls upon Cleon as *prostatês* (*Frogs* 569): "Go and call Cleon to act as *prostatês* for me."

How much more striking, then, must Teiresias' *metrical* reference to the need for a *prostatês* have been in Sophocles' *Oedipus*, written when Cleon was at the pinnacle of his career, and when there were fears that he, like the *prostatês* of Plato's *Republic*, might make himself a tyrant.

CREON AND CLEON

The names Cleon and Creon are not far apart upon the Athenian aristocratic tongue. The letters *r* and *l* were readily confused by the Greeks, and their confusion is even the subject of a famous epigram by Palladas (*Anthology* II.323): "Rho and Lambda are the only things separating ravenous crows (*korakas*) from craven flatterers (*kolakas*). So the raven and the craven would both rob a shrine. Be on your guard, good friend, against this creature, knowing that among the living, cravens are as ravens." In Aristophanes' *Wasps*, a play focused on Cleon and produced in the year of Cleon's death (422 B.C.), this confusion of *l* and *r* emerges prominently in the opening scene. Sosias describes a dream in which he saw the politician Theorus with a crow's head (*kefalên korakas* [*Wasps* 42]). As the dream continues, Alcibiades, a young aristocrat and nephew of Pericles, came up to him and said (*Wasps* 45): "*olas. Theôlos tên kephalên kolakos echei.*"[20] Alcibiades lisped, in Greek fashion, substituting *l* for *r*: instead of *oras*, "you see," he said *olas*, which means (more or less) "you destroy." The name Theorus, which suggests a pilgrim, "one who goes to see god (*theos*)," becomes Theolus, "destroyer of god." His head becomes that of a flattering craven (*kolakos*), not a raven (*korakos*). With the Greek *r*'s the line means: "You see? Pilgrim Theorus has a raven's head." With the Greek *l*'s, the changed meaning is something like: "You destroy? Pogrom Theorus has a craven's head."

It should be noted that the Theorus mentioned by Aristophanes is one of Cleon's friends. At the end of the *Wasps*, in fact, when Philocleon and his son Bdelycleon are imagining themselves at a drinking party among Cleon's entourage, Bdelycleon gives us the image of Theorus lying at Cleon's feet (*pros podôn*), holding his right hand and singing (1236–37).[21]

The same speech impediment that makes Theorus Theolus makes Creon Cleon; it also has a name most appropriate to the tale of Thebes: Labdacism (*labdakismos*). Labdacism, Quintilian says (*Instructing the Orator* 1.5.32), along with iotacism, solecism, and so forth, are mistakes that "happen through sounds, and which cannot be shown in writing because they are errors of speech and of the tongue" (*per sonos accidunt, quae demonstrari scripto non possunt, vitia oris et linguae*). I mention Quintilian's use of the Greek term to demonstrate that "la(m)bdacism" was used in antiquity to describe this particular speech problem. It is not just a modern coinage used by speech therapists.[22]

Laios, the son of Labdacus, then, was killed while leaving his native people to consult the oracle: *theôros* ... *ekdemôn*, as Creon reports. And through Labdacism and Labdacus, a link is forged between the myth of Oedipus and Sophocles' contemporary Athens. For a fleeting instant, Creon and Cleon, mythic Thebes and fifth-century Athens, merge in Teiresias' words.

Curiously, another way Creon resembles Cleon is in his role as intermediary between Oedipus and the sources of oracular wisdom. He is Oedipus' envoy to Delphi; he prompts Oedipus to consult Teiresias; finally he suggests that Oedipus himself go to Delphi to check out the validity of the report he has brought. Similarly, in Aristophanes' *Knights* 61, a complaint is made that the Paphlagonian slave (sometimes identified as Cleon) bewilders Dêmos (i.e., the people) by chanting oracles (*aidei de chrêsmous*). In fact the speaker suggests to his fellow-slave that they steal the Paphlagonian's oracles while he is asleep (1109–10). As Fontenrose observes: "Kleon is in effect a chresmologue who possesses a collection of Bakis' oracles, which help him to keep Demos under his control (*Knights* 109–143, 195–210, 960–1096)."[23]

It is in his role as purveyor of oracles that Creon influences Oedipus' actions in Sophocles' play: an inquiry which will lead Oedipus to the conclusion that he is, as Teiresias suggests, a native-born son of Thebes (*engenês Thebaios*), not a resident alien (*xenos* ... *metoikos*) (452–53). Oedipus, then, owes his citizen status to the oracle Creon brings from Delphi.

I am not trying to suggest that Sophocles' Creon *is* Cleon, but rather that Sophocles uses the suggestive resonances of Cleon in the play to color his presentation of Creon. He might thus, and reasonably, expect his audience to react more skeptically to Creon's rhetoric than many modern critics do, when they choose to see in him an honest and detached observer, fulfilling his citizen duty in a forthright way. In a world where Cratylan etymologies are taken seriously, we must not just privilege the etymology of Oedipus' name in this play. After all, Creon's own name is nothing more than the adjective *kreôn*, "the ruler."

PARENTS AND DEFEAT

Let us return now to the exchanges between Oedipus and Teiresias. After contemptuously dismissing the possibility that he is conspiring with Creon (though with words, as we have seen, that might arouse rather than quell our suspicions), Teiresias resumes the theme of his (and Oedipus') blindness (412–28):

You taunt my blindness. Therefore I shall speak.
You don't see where you are in evil's grasp,
though you have eyes, or where you make your home,
or who you share it with.
                              Who gave you birth?
Do you know this?
                              Does it elude you that
you are an enemy to relatives
both buried and alive upon the earth?
And yet the curse of mother and father,
moving its inexorable feet,
will strike a double blow, some day drive you
out of this land. Now you can see well,
then you'll see darkness. Oh what place, what place
will not give harbor to your scream that day?
Will Cithaeron not quickly sing with you
when finally you understand the tune
of your own wedding hymn with which you sailed,
with what smooth sailing, straight into a home
that had no proper berth for your vessel?
There is a host of other evils too
which you don't grasp but which will make of you
an equal to your very own children.

Counter that by throwing mud at Creon
and at my own face! There is no mortal
who will ever appear more vile than you
when the veneer is some day scraped away.

The allusions are much more explicit in this third announcement of
Oedipus' "crimes." But there is now no reference to their more public
nature. Teiresias focuses on the pollution Oedipus has been within his own
family. Then, after these accusations of incest, he returns to a more political
tone and, with consummate rhetorical bravado, rebukes *Oedipus* for
mudslinging (425–26).

At this point Oedipus' rhetorical defeat begins to become a rout. He
understandably, but feebly, protests (429–31):

Must I hear these insufferable slurs
from this man? Go to hell! Turn round and back
and get out of this his house. And make it quick!

But Teiresias turns the very dismissal against him (432): "I'd not have come. But then you summoned me." Oedipus tries bravely to retort, hoping, perhaps, that he can get Teiresias to respond to one insult with another, and thus shift the focus away from himself. But Teiresias, ignoring the taunt, intensifies the focus on Oedipus (433–36):

> *Oedipus*:   I did not know you'd talk such idiocy,
>   or I'd have waited before asking you.
> *Teiresias*: We are what we were born. Idiots, you think.
>   Those who begat you thought me rational.

Teiresias is not simply making a point of his superior age and experience when he says he was respected as a prophet by Oedipus' parents. He is implying that he knew Oedipus' parents and they him.

Teiresias has baited a rhetorical trap for Oedipus and, as we will see from Oedipus' response, obviously starts to walk off the stage. His answers, like those of Euripides' Dionysus, are designed to make his questioner curious. There has been no indication up to this point that Oedipus is uncertain about his parents' identity. And there is no reason to assume that the chorus was previously concerned with the issue.

The audience, however, familiar with the Oedipus myth in other forms, is certainly ready to pounce on Teiresias' words. So too, it happens, is Oedipus (437):

> "Who were they?
>   Stay!
>   Who is my real father?"

By calling Teiresias back to consult him at this moment, Oedipus loses any rhetorical momentum he has gained and ruins his contention that Teiresias is a fool. He again approaches the seer as an oracular authority with true answers, implying that Teiresias may know the secret answer to a riddle about his own existence. Oedipus has instantly and publicly rebuilt Teiresias' credentials as a prophetic authority. He has also, in effect, conceded Teiresias' truthfulness.

Teiresias' oracular response sets up the rhetorical coup de grace for Oedipus (438–40):

> *Teiresias*: This day will start your life. Destroy it too.
> *Oedipus*:   Your words are all too riddling and obscure.
> *Teiresias*: Weren't you born best at finding riddles out?

Teiresias' enigmatic utterance elicits an objection from Oedipus that he is baffled. Teiresias leaps on the error. Any momentary success that Oedipus' mention of his triumph over the Sphinx may have registered a few lines earlier has been neutralized.

Oedipus, sensing his blunder, does not pursue the question of his birth. He only retorts, pitifully (441): "Keep taunting me with this! You'll find me great." To which Teiresias responds (442): "It was just luck, and now it's ruined you." Teiresias claims total victory and voices the professional's view of amateur success, a view that finds some vindication in the play. If intelligence and skill enabled Oedipus to destroy the Sphinx, why doesn't he even try to repeat that success, relying on his own wits instead of on the established sources of religious and political power which rarely have any love for the interloper? Perhaps it was just "beginner's luck." Indeed, as we have seen in the Introduction, there are traditions that have Oedipus find the solution to the riddle in a prophetic dream rather than by his own intellectual force. Oedipus himself seems to adopt Teiresias' view later when he claims to be the "child of Luck," or "child of Fortune."

However much Oedipus may be an amateur in Teiresias' world, he is not so unaware of his humiliation as is sometimes suggested. Oedipus now accepts the possibility that he is, as Teiresias suggests, destroyed and declares that it was all worthwhile (443): "Well if it's saved this city, I don't care." Satisfied, Teiresias prepares, yet again, to leave. But Oedipus tries one parting shot (444–46):

> *Teiresias*:   I'm going then. Come, boy, you take me out!
> *Oedipus*:   Yes, take him out! When here you're under foot,
>   stir trouble. When gone, you can cause no more pain.

Go, Oedipus is saying, you cannot make things worse for me. Thus challenged, Teiresias does makes things worse. He modifies his assertion that he is leaving by setting forth his charges in all their details in a speech that opens with these words (447–49):

> I'm going once I've said what I came here
> to say. I'm not afraid of your facade.
> You do not have the power to destroy me.
> So I speak.

Teiresias claimed that he intended to say nothing and could not be forced to say anything when he first came on stage. Was that disclaimer no more than a pretext, the bait for the cruel hook, the red rag to Oedipal bullishness? We may recall, as we reflect on this brilliant scene between Oedipus and Teiresias, part of what Quintilian says of persuasive speech in court, cited in the Introduction in our discussion of ancient *emphasis* (*Instructing the Orator* 9.2.71–72):

> Use of the emotions helps a lot. It's good to break the flow of your speech with silence, to hesitate. Then you may be sure the judge will search out that certain something which he probably would not believe if he heard it actually stated. You may be sure he will believe what he thinks he himself has discovered.... In sum: *the judge is most likely to believe what is figured in our speech if he thinks we are unwilling to say it.*

In Quintilian's words we see the power of Teiresias' hesitation, and we remember that the chorus called Teiresias "the cross-questioner," "the refuter." But we also see the vulnerability of the judge to the suggestions implanted by the speaker. Oedipus does not appear to believe what Teiresias says when the charges of his guilt are made overtly. But Teiresias knows the seed of the idea is planted as he moves into his peroration where he spells everything out again, then orders Oedipus inside to think over what has been said (449–62):

> This man you've lately sought,
> threatened and publicly outlawed: this man,
> this Laian killer, is here with us now.
> Word is that he's a foreign resident.
> But he'll become a Theban, native born,
> though this turn of events will not please him.
> Now he sees, but then he will be blind,
> now rich, a beggar then, groping his way
> upon a staff into a foreign land.
> He'll become brother as well as father
> to his children in his house, both son
> and husband to the woman who bore him,
> he'll sow his semen where his father sowed,
> and kill his father.
> Go inside your home.
> Figure it out. And if you catch me lying,
> claim I'm devoid of mantic reasoning.

This time Oedipus musters no response at all. He leaves, dismissed by the prophet he himself summoned, then sought to dismiss.

The professional seer has triumphed over the man who once triumphed over him by solving the riddle of the Sphinx—perhaps by sheer luck rather than reasoning. Indeed, when Teiresias first entered, he seemed depressed that reasoning seemed to count for so little at Thebes (316–18):

> Alas: reason's power! How formidable (*deinon*)
> when reason does not pay. I know this well.
> But I forgot it, or I'd not have come.

Perhaps these were the reflections of a man who had had to take second place to a *parvenu* ever since that *parvenu* solved the riddle of the Sphinx by a stroke of luck, which he certainly was able to make pay. But now, at the end of the scene, his power of reasoning seems vindicated. The word *phronein*, "reasoning," is the last as well as the first word Teiresias speaks. He has used his rhetorical skill to refute Oedipus as utterly as Oedipus had refuted the Sphinx. Indeed, Teiresias has made Oedipus the new Sphinx plaguing Thebes. And he, like the Sphinx of Old, will be destroyed by words. Proceeding inexorably from the top of the social scale to the bottom, his interlocutors will cause his undoing: Creon, his presumed rival and future ruler; Teiresias, the prophet smarting from his defeat in solving the Sphinx's riddle; Jocasta, his queen; an anonymous Corinthian of uncertain status who solves a riddle of feet; finally a slave. But it is Teiresias who most clearly sets Oedipus on the road to self-destruction in this play.

Teiresias' power of refutation is "formidable." Like a curious variant of Socratic *elenchos*, it is designed to win, and wins, an admission of defeat, either overt or tacit, from the baffled interlocutor. Oedipus presents no evidence to support his charge of conspiracy against Teiresias. But neither does Teiresias present evidence of Oedipus' guilt. It is all a matter of rhetoric and psychology. Teiresias' words expose a raw nerve in Oedipus: his doubts about his father's identity—doubts as old as Greek literature. Homer's Telemachus tells Athena that although his mother claims he is Odysseus' son: "I don't know. No one ever really knows in himself who his father is" (*Odyssey* 1.215-b). The reader, "knowing" the Oedipus myth, is confident Teiresias is right about Oedipus' parents. Oedipus fears Teiresias is right. Yet the chorus members, innocent of myth and fear, incline to see a feud at the root of this confrontation. The "great refuter" has *not* convinced *them*. Indeed, they now begin to doubt his mastery of truth.

NOTES

1. Oedipus also uses the verb later (in the form *ephthito*) to summarize what he has concluded from the Corinthian's ambiguous description of Polybus' death (962). Oedipus

supposes Polybus must have died either through treachery or of disease and, after the messenger speaks, concludes that the cause was disease.

2. See H. W. Parke, *Festivals of the Athenians* (Ithaca, 1977), 17: "In Athens, as in Rome, when the kingship was abolished as a political institution, it was still retained for ritual functions."

3. R. G. Lewis, "The Procedural Basis of *Oedipus Tyrannus*," *Greek, Roman, and Byzantine Studies* 30 (1989): 44.

4. Parke, *Festivals of the Athenians*, 110.

5. Ibid., 110–11.

6. See the notes by R. C. Jebb, *Sophocles: The Plays and Fragments*, Part 1: *Oedipus Tyrannus* (Cambridge, 1893), 49, and R. D. Dawe, *Sophocles: Oedipus Rex* (Cambridge, 1982), 121–22. Dawe mentions M. Schmidt's emendation *eiasamên* as one solution to the "dilemma."

7. Dawe, *Oedipus*, 123.

8. Ibid., 124.

9. For a detailed study of the Teiresias myth in antiquity, see Luc Brisson, *Le mythe de Tirésias: Essai d'analyse structurale* (Leiden, 1976).

10. Dawe, *Oedipus*, 124.

11. Marcel Detienne discusses the connection between *LÊTHÊ* and *aLÊTHEia* in "La notion mythique d'ALÊTHEIA," *Revue des Études Grecques* 73 (1960): 27–35, and "*Les maîtres de verité dans la Grèce archaique*" (Paris, 1967), 75–77. W. G. Thalmann, *Conventions of Form and Thought in Early Greek Epic Poetry* (Baltimore, 1984), 147–49, expresses the idea this way: "*Aletheia* personified is thus a mythic double of Mnemosyne, Memory, and the Muses are intimately associated with it" (147). See also my discussion in *Metaformations: Soundplay and Wordplay in Ovid and Other Classical Poets* (Ithaca, 1985), 47 and 321–22, and "*Ars est Celare Artem*: Art in Puns and Anagrams Engraved," in *On Puns: The Foundation of Letters*, ed. Jonathan Culler (Oxford, 1988), 17–43.

12. See, for example, *Electra* 637 and *Trachiniae* 209.

13. Dawe, *Oedipus*, 124.

14. Victor Ehrenberg, *The People of Aristophanes* (Oxford, 1951), 353; cf. 146 and 355–57 and his long discussion in *Sophocles and Pericles* (Oxford, 1954), 75–105. See also Gerhard Thür, "Wo wohnen die Metöken?" *Demokratie und Architektur. Der Hippodamische Stadtebau und die Entstehung der Demokratie,* ed. W. Schutter, W. Hoepner, E. L. Schwander (Munich, 1989), 117–22.

15. Jebb, *Oedipus Tyrannus*, 65.

16. Ehrenberg, *Sophocles and Pericles*, 7.

17. See P. Karavites, "Tradition, Skepticism, and Sophocles' Political Career," *Klio* 58 (1976): 359–65; M. H. Jameson, "Sophocles and the Four Hundred," *Historia* 20 (1971): 541–68; Martin Ostwald, *From Popular Sovereignty to the Sovereignty of Law: Law, Society, and Politics in Fifth-Century Athens* (Berkeley and Los Angeles, 1986), 340–41. For a different view, see Harry Avery, "Sophocles' Political Career," *Historia* 22 (1973): 509–14.

18. F. J. Parsons, *The Rhetoric of Aristotle* (Oxford, 1836), 287–88.

19. Aristophanes, *Knights* 1–5, 137, 191–93, 256, 275–76, 296–98, 392; *Wasps* 592–93; *Acharnians* 215–17, 223–32, 289–91, 299–302; *Peace* 637, for example. Aristotle in *Constitution of Athens* 28.3 speaks of Cleon's manner and approach to politics in highly disparaging terms, and Thucydides, who had personal reasons for his hatred of Cleon, gives him perhaps the roughest treatment of all (3.36.6; 5.10.9). See W. R. Connor, *The*

New Politicians of Fifth-Century Athens (Princeton, 1971), especially 132–34; also Ostwald, *Popular Sovereignty*, 201–34.

20. Major work on this wordplay has now appeared in articles by Michael Vickers (who kindly gave me the opportunity to see some of them prior to publication): "Alcibiades on Stage: *Philoctetes* and *Cyclops*," *Historia* 36 (1987): 171–97; "Lambdacism at Aristophanes' *Clouds* 1381–82," *Liverpool Classical Monthly* 12 (1987): 143; "Alcibiades on Stage: *Thesmophoriazusae* and *Helen*," *Historia* 36 (1989): 267–99; and "Alcibiades on Stage: Aristophanes' *Birds*," forthcoming in *Historia*.

21. Bdelycleon pretends to be Cleon himself and sings the song about Harmodius, the tyrant-killer. "What a man!" sings Bdelycleon. "What a thief!" his father responds (1223–27). Bdelycleon warns his father to be careful what he sings about Cleon, since the latter threatens to "destroy you, wipe you out, and banish you from the land" (1228–29); Plutarch also records the story in *Alcibiades* 1.3–4.

22. One might reach this erroneous conclusion from reading A. D. MacDowell's note on *Aristophanes' Wasps* (Oxford, 1971), 133–34.

23. Joseph Fontenrose, *The Delphic Oracle* (Berkeley and Los Angeles, 1978), 159.

PIETRO PUCCI

Introduction: What Is a Father?

Recent criticism on the *Oedipus Tyrannus* has focused on two main problems: the nature and destiny of the Sophoclean hero, as the tragic operator who symbolizes the limits of human possibilities and drives; and the question of Oedipus's *parrincest*.[1] When we attempt to define the tragic nature of Oedipus in *Oedipus Tyrannus*, we are confronted by several critical riddles. First, how should we construe Oedipus's heroic destiny within the projections of the oracle that announces this destiny and to some extent seems to fulfill it? Recent critics generally agree that the oracle does not constitute a predestination, and that Oedipus has always been free. This conclusion is a neat resolution of a vexing age-old question, but elegant as it is, it risks leaving the oracle and its effect dangling nowhere, as if they did not really count. To neglect the working of the oracle in the play is dangerous enough in itself, but the consequences of this neglect become even more serious when one considers the second question, which in some ways encroaches on the first—that of the parrincest. For the oracle does not predict simply that Oedipus will commit some awful crime; it specifies that Oedipus will murder his father and commit incest with his mother. Both criminal deeds are represented and elaborated in the text with insistent imagery and deep-seated references to the acts of fathering or begetting in nature and in the divine world. Oedipus's destiny is not that of discovering

From *Oedipus and the Fabrication of the Father: Oedipus Tyrannus in Modern Criticism and Philosophy* by Pietro Pucci, pp. 1–15. © 1992 by The Johns Hopkins University Press.

and suffering a generic catastrophe but specifically that of being destroyed by his parrincest.

It is this destruction that reveals to Oedipus his tragic destiny, and forces him to stand erect before his deceptions and to realize the fundamental necessity of the law of the father, as the principle of one's being and status. It is this specific destruction that shows to the audience the unavoidable force of the law of the father that is identified with the voice of the gods. In the edifying view of Sophocles, only this voice is straight and fulfilling: all the other voices and narratives are merging with the mere randomness and drifting of human affairs.

To begin with the question of parrincest: it is a fact that most humanist and academic critics have paid relatively little attention to the specific crimes into which Oedipus unwittingly falls. They concentrate on the process of the discovery, specifically on the self-destructive effect of Oedipus's discovery that casts Oedipus out of his family and out of power, but they scarcely consider the nature of Oedipus's crime, the specific type of transgression.

Indeed, for many critics the rejection of the psychoanalytic reading of the play has meant a relative indifference to the specific nature of Oedipus's transgression of the family's bonds. But psychoanalytic critics, since Freud, have seen in the drama a lucid illustration of the Oedipus complex, and the more intent the psychoanalytic critics become on capturing the subtleties of the Greek text, the more exhaustive their psychoanalytic appropriation of the drama becomes.[2]

Yet the extraordinary richness of these psychoanalytic readings leaves unfocused one question that to me seems essential in *Oedipus Tyrannus*. The central question is, What is a father? Freud has assumed the father to be a hypothetical function of the main experiences of the unconscious. To this extent, Freudian psychoanalysis surrounds the father with a certain "mystery," to speak with P. L. Assoun. A careful analysis of the Freudian writings shows the complexity of the functions Freud attributed to the father: the father as a relation in its different versions, identification with the father, and the ambivalence of the father figure for the child. This analysis, however, does not substantially contradict the popular views on Freud's interpretation of the father figure in his early reading of the *Oedipus Tyrannus* as the object of the son's hostility because of his love for the mother. This definition psychologizes the father and already presents him from the point of view of his law that prohibits incest: it immediately puts the child in the guilty role and the mother in a relationship of complicity. This formulation, in other words, defines the father from the point of view of the law he gives to the son, from the "discourse" with which the father makes a differential entrance into the mirrorlike relationship of mother and son. This role appears in the play, but a more original situation exists, as we shall see.[3]

Facing this response, what should we do with this play in which a father tries to murder the son, who at his turn murders his father without recognizing him? Should we at all costs read in the silent text Oedipus's repressed knowledge that the man he kills is Laius? Or should we recognize the great wisdom of the old poet, as he suggests that the father is in principle a white page, although all is written down by and for the son? Indeed, the text of the play presents at least four functions of the father.

The reason the father has so many faces is that the father is a figure of the logos. The father comes into being not by sowing his seeds, but with the logos: for only humans have a father, though animals are often begotten like humans. A father is a figure that, within the strategies of the logos, acquires a set of meanings and functions—source of the son's legitimacy, provider of livelihood and cares, holder of authority. Thus the father is a fountainhead of goods, an inspiration for the moral life of the son. In a word, he may be equated to a sort of transcendental signified.

But it is easy to see that this description follows a moral and metaphysical pattern in which one can also inscribe the figure of Father God. Simultaneously one perceives analogies between this pattern and that which attributes to the logos an anchorage in the world of being, a relation to things as they are, a power to tell the laws of god.

Faced with this indissoluble knot of analogical relations that holds together the logos, the father, the god, and the laws, we must analyze them and study their function in the shaping of the father figure.[4] The text of *Oedipus Tyrannus* exhibits these analogical relations in a clear light, and shows how they encroach in the shaping of the father. For when the figure of the father is felt to be absent, unable to present itself with his law, with the oracular words of a father god, then the society is endangered; then confusion and chaos ensue.

Why is the absence of the father possible? And prior to this question, what is the discourse or logos that shapes or forms the father? For if we assume that the logos that shapes the father is itself deficient and sick, as Oedipus at another register defines himself (60–61), we may understand why the father may appear without any authority and as an absence.

The father is both he who creates the son and he whom the son creates in order to fill up an absence, to give it the force of an origin and of a destination (*telos*). For otherwise the father would be the author of a life by a mere stroke of chance. No one felt the all-embracing force of this teleological origin and destination as the Greeks. Most of the epithetical nouns that describe and ennoble the epic heroes are formed through such father names as Peleiades ([Achilles], the son of Peleus) and Laertiades ([Odysseus], the son of Laertes). Sophocles in *Oedipus Tyrannus* offers an extraordinary example of this technique that mentions the son by silencing his name under the weight of the father's names. At 2.67–68 Oedipus evokes Laius: "The son of Labdacus [i.e., Laius] descended from Polydorus, and from old Cadmus and from ancient Agenor." This resounding pile of names "means" Laius, but the name Laius does not appear.

The son must attach his life and his meaning to a source and he must supplement this source—that is, add it as a source and an origin in a place that may stand as an absence. For if the father were able to present himself, as father, that is, as source of meaning and law, he would not need to beget a son who merely represents him, and desperately tries to mirror in himself such meaning and law. If the father, as source of meaning and law, were absolutely present, it would not appear so only in the blinded eyes of the son.

In *Oedipus Tyrannus* four figures of the father emerge each with its own ideal and imaginary foundations. We recognize (1) the king as a Father of his citizens, (1) Polybus as the provider of cares and affection for the son, (3) Laius as the biological father, and (4) Apollo—and Teiresias, his priest—as a divine Father insofar as he gives an irrevocable *telos* to the son. All these figures constitute for the son an imaginary (and real) beginning, a source of continuity, of authority and law, and are therefore identifiable with a *telos*, a finality. But, though this is the perception Oedipus seems to have of these figures at different moments and in different context, we will see that these notions of origin, continuity, and finality—in a word, teleology—are contiguous with an encroaching upon the notions of indeterminacy, chance, and arbitrariness—in a word, *tukhê*. Besides, Oedipus has a mother that the text explicitly identifies with the notion of chance (*tukhê*). Consequently, the parental figures that limit the horizon of Oedipus's coming into being and becoming what he is are inscribed in an ideological realm and in ideological narratives in which *telos* and *tukhê* are simultaneously in conflict and in complicity.

Let us sketch some of these parental figures. The first words of the play, "O sons, young nurslings [*trophê*] of the old Cadmus," open the issue of royal paternity, in a line of notorious polysemy, where, to limit the ambivalence to the problems that are relevant for us, the "sons" could be the Thebans descending from Father Cadmus or the "children" sitting as suppliant on the stage. Moreover, Cadmus could be the old founder of Thebes or the city itself. However we may take the line, we have to understand that these "young nurslings" (or "youthful care") are now the responsibility of Oedipus. The name of Father Cadmus—if we so take the line—opens the play as a teleological point of origin, which reaches Oedipus and, through him, continues to provide care for the Theban children. There is a chiasmus between "Cadmus of old" and "the young nurslings" that underlines the parallelism and the opposition as well between the two terms. The use of the word *trophê* (for the "nurslings" or the "care) evokes both the material and spiritual gifts the father provides, but simultaneously it prepares us for the various "nourishments" and "cares" that fathers and mothers will provide in the play. To begin with Oedipus, this caring and noble father of the children who are sitting at his knees and, by extension, of all the Thebans provides them, unwittingly, with an ugly plague, "nurtured" in Thebes (*tethrammenon*, 97).[5] The father is far from being only a savior, and the "teleological" force that his function evokes goes along with the chancy ways of Oedipus's destiny and errancy. This sinister nursing by the father repeats the pattern of Laius's attempted murder of his son Oedipus, and it shows the initial situation of specularity in violence between father and son. I call this paternal violence an absence in the sense of the absence of his teleological presence for the son.

Then we find Apollo (376–77) sustaining with the force of truth his seer Teiresias and this, at his turn, nursing (*trephô*, 366) the force of truth as a father does. However, Apollo's truth has been for a long time absent from Oedipus, so that he has never recognized the divine signs. This absence seems congenital since even Teiresias, when he finally reveals his truth, does so only under compulsion and provocation. Meanwhile, Oedipus could kill his father, marry his mother, beget children, and live happily in this monstrous family for years, before the god—which god?—sends the plague and forces Oedipus to recognize his pollution and crimes. Even so, had not Oedipus shown heroic desire to go through the inquiry and to accept all the risks that at each moment become clearer, the oracular truth might have remained hidden forever.

Already in these first notes of the play, the father figure appears ominous, difficult to define in relation to his sons, for whom he is at once teleological and chancy, a creator and a ruin. This, however, is not all. Oedipus and the Thebans assume that Oedipus comes, as a tyrant, from Corinth, and that therefore he does not belong to the Theban stock. To be a *turannos* (tyrant) means to be a king "by chance" (*tukhê*). Yet the audience knows well that he is the legitimate son of Laius and the legitimate king of Thebes, so that it realizes that the legitimate king may happen to sit on the throne by a mere stroke of chance.

The contrast between father Polybus and father Laius is interesting. The former is a gentle figure for whom Oedipus feels filial affection. In fact, because of this affection he decides to leave Corinth when the oracle tells him that he will kill his father and marry his mother. Though the reason for his desertion is legitimate and noble, it remains no less true that his leaving constitutes a sort of betrayal, a metaphorical murder. The son must blind himself and efface the figure he treasures. It is remarkable that this shade of oedipal conflict takes place within a familial relationship that is created by the mere play of chance, since Polybus has simply adopted Oedipus.

Laius and Oedipus present, as I have suggested, a more specular relationship that radicalizes the nature of the relationship between father and son. By unwittingly murdering the father, Oedipus doubles what I call the absence of the father and creates the "Father." For, when he recognizes that he has killed his father, he retroactively realizes that that transgression had been written all the time and he accuses his destiny. The reason for this potentially inevitable condition is that the father with his good or bad contingent behavior can become a Father—that is, an absolute and teleological figure—only if the son transgresses that contingent and absent father and violently doubles his absence.

A certain absence of the father can be traced also in the previous patterns of paternity. We have seen how Apollo never gives to Oedipus recognizable signs of his control and of his law, and how Polybus for all his care and affection does not affect at all Oedipus's destiny (*telos*).

We recognize a fourth pattern of father–son relationship, that between Apollo and Oedipus. In particular Apollo's oracle, by destining Oedipus to kill his father and marry his mother, verbalizes the father's law. In fact, the oracle, in spelling out Oedipus's destiny, foresees also that Oedipus will break the sanctity of the father's bed and person. By sending the plague, Apollo—if he has some responsibility in its occurrence—acts as the Father who manages to punish the son for the breaking of the law.

The different roles of the father are parted in our play among four different characters—Laius, Polybus, Teiresias, and Apollo. This separation of roles, which in life are customarily acted out by a unique person, complicates the interpretation of the father figure in *Oedipus Tyrannus*. In particular, the role of Apollo has never been, as far as I know, described as that of a metaphysical father of Oedipus.

Furthermore, the double action that takes place simultaneously in the drama—the one limning Oedipus's activity about the plague and his reaction to the accusations that are raised against him, and the other producing the reenactment by memory of his past—confuses the sequence and the effects of events. For instance, the search for Laius's murderer(s) goes on without encroaching, until very late, Oedipus's discovery of his father. The audience may have the feeling that the final target of Apollos oracle risks many times being lost and missed, though on the other hand they perceive that he is unmistakably active from the beginning.

All the patterns of fatherhood I have sketchily described are grounded on different narratives. For instance, the royal paternity that Oedipus represents for the Thebans is grounded on mythical stories that begin with Cadmus and continue without break until Oedipus, designing a teleological line of good and caring masters and kings. Polybus's paternity is supported by narratives that Polybus and Merope themselves defend against other narratives that question their statements. Apollo's paternity of Oedipus's true destination is essentially upheld by the oracle and by Teiresias. Laius's paternity of Oedipus is upheld by the stories of the oracles and by the eyewitnesses of his infancy and of his deeds. Even the play, of course, has a father, Sophocles, and he becomes father by appropriating the mythical narrative about Oedipus and producing it in a theatrical context.

All these narratives raise questions about the father by presenting issues like his legitimacy, his position as origin and source, his care, his law—in a word, his teleological function. Yet these narratives are constantly encroaching upon narratives that present the father figure as being deprived of these edifying functions, upon narratives that, for instance, show his mere biological and chancy function. The question of what constitutes a father is therefore inscribed in a series of narratives that present themselves as teleological and chancy, grounded on an irrevocable truth and in the fleeting appearances of chance phenomena. Accordingly this question—What is a father?—ultimately points to narratives that present different and conflicting modes of truth, meaning, and certainty in the world.

In linking the notions of *telos* and *tukhê* with the narratives that fashion the figure of the father and the destiny of the son in *Oedipus Tyrannus*, we discover that the text suggests a complex and unstable vision of the father figure and of its roles, far from the one-dimensional object of some popular psychoanalytic literature, and from the unfocused one of many literary critics. More specifically, we recognize how the question of what constitutes a father does not implicate the question of truth in an instrumental or metaphorical way as it sometimes is conceived in the readings of the play, when critics assert that Oedipus's search for his real self exemplifies or illustrates his desire to discover the truth about himself. The Father figure is the figure of the anchorage of any discourse to a fixed origin, to a transcendental signified, and therefore, in the play, he is not simply the figure of Oedipus's real biological origin, but the figure around whose constitution and fabrication the possibility of truth pivots for every discourse in our world.

Clearly the notion of *telos*—by which I imply the irrevocable fate of Oedipus in accordance with the word of Apollo (1329–30)—is an important and active notion in the narratives that make up the play. Modern scholars have vigorously attacked the notion that fate is the dominating force in the plot of *Oedipus Tyrannus* and have insisted correctly that Oedipus acts in full freedom. Reinhardt, Knox, and Dodds among others realize that the notion of predetermination that earlier critics use is false and ahistorical.[6] Knox argues that the play enacts not the fulfillment of Apollo's prophecies, but Oedipus's discovery of that fulfillment. This point is correct for it locates the action of the drama in Oedipus's consciousness as he becomes aware that he acted freely and fulfilled the prophecies against his will. Nevertheless, this placement of the action of the drama in Oedipus's process of self-discovery does not efface the *reader's* constant awareness and Oedipus's late recognition that the prophecies, by becoming true, prove to have an unavoidable destination (*telos*). For although Oedipus never experiences any constraint or determination while he is acting, the reader perceives that he is following an already written path unknowingly, and when Oedipus himself discovers his true situation, he recognizes that Apollo was responsible for the entire chain of events. Fate is therefore visible and mysteriously active. We cannot help resorting to some idea of fate, however we label or describe it, in order to understand the inevitable outcome (*telos*) of the Apollonian oracle and its necessary destination in the specific form of parrincest.

Schelling systematized the function and the position of "fate" in *Oedipus Tyrannus*, and in Greek tragedy in general, with his view that in these plays a conflict unravels between the program of fate—representative of the power of the objective world—and human freedom. The superior power of fate dooms the tragic hero to perish, but since he resists and fights back, he must be punished for his defeat itself. This defeat, in Schelling's reading of the play, testifies to the herds freedom and, indeed, turns out to honor his freedom.[7]

When we recognize that throughout the recent critical history of *Oedipus Tyrannus* the conflicting terms of the play have been so often identified with various aspects of "fate" and "freedom," we can see that the view of a tragic conflict between necessity and freedom has become largely conventional. Indeed, it still predominates. On the one hand, the various facets and compulsion of objective reality that critics have evoked as the forces that Oedipus discovers to have led him to parrincest are often figures of what Schelling called "fate"; on the other hand, the notion of "freedom" has generally been understood as Oedipus's drive to knowledge, specifically to self-knowledge. To cite but one example of the permanence of these conflicting terms, though under different labels, the Freudian interpretation of the play singles out the son's desire for the mother and hostility toward the father as the specific "fate" of man, and might interpret the relentless process of Oedipus's discovery as a manifestation of the hero's freedom, or at any rate of his quest.[8] Freud's strategy is noteworthy because he resisted and dismissed the interpretation, conventional at his time, of *Oedipus Tyrannus* as a tragedy of destiny;[9] but ultimately he retained the notion of "fate" simply by identifying the fate that operates in the tragedy with that of the Oedipus complex.[10]

Analogously, in modern critical readings the oracle may stand for some inevitable condition inherent in the human situation. For Reinhardt, this condition is our existence in a deceptive world of appearances that confuses and snares us. For Vernant, Oedipus is the model (*paradeigma*, 1192) of the tragic fate of human nature: blind and seer, king and scapegoat (*pharmakos*) he appears to be at once sublime and monstrous. The fact that Oedipus's destiny is programmed by the oracle is instrumental in producing this double and enigmatic nature of man.[11] For Segal, the oracle's dramatic function in building up—beyond Oedipus's awareness—a dense network of enigmatic situations seems so clear that he accounts for the working of the prophecies only inasmuch as they are part of the same tragic world of ambivalence and of disintegration of differences.[12]

I begin my analysis with a careful commentary on the workings of "fate" and of the other force or notion—chance—that propel the action in the play. Oedipus is indeed destined to commit parrincest, and he does so unwillingly and unwittingly, following his destiny. The action of the play, however, begins when he has already committed parrincest and therefore consists essentially in following the process through which Oedipus becomes aware of his crime. Since Oedipus is unaware that his actions follow a specific program, he attributes some of his most fatal actions to chance (*tukhê*). Oedipus is not alone in evoking the power of chance: even Teiresias, who should know that Oedipus follows a divine track and moves directly to the goal (*telos*) foreseen by the oracle, defines Oedipus's solution of the riddle as a stroke of chance, a casual event or his destiny (*tukhê*, 442). We must therefore assume that in the world of the play *tukhê* and fate collaborate, notwithstanding their opposite nature, the one drifting at random, the other moving straight toward a goal (*telos*).

This collaboration and complicity are problematic not only conceptually but also linguistically, for it is often difficult to distinguish the nature of the one force from that of the other. And this difficulty stems from two conditions. The Greek word *tukhê* is strongly ambivalent, because it has a wide range of connotations, implying both the providential (and unexpected) intervention of a god and the secular notion of randomness, and chance. Thus, according to the first connotation, *tukhê* does not oppose the notion of divine fate but corroborates it, through emphasizing the aoristic aspect of the event rather than the perfective one of the set program. The second connotation, however, conceptually suspends the notion of gods' providence or intervention.

The consequence of this ambivalence may be serious when we assess the nature of the forces that propel the action. For Oedipus's final discovery of the parrincest, by validating the *telos* of the oracle, re-marks a posteriori the entire chain of events that up to that point have appeared as more or less effects of *tukhê*, that is, accidentality and free will. It even gives to Oedipus's transgression the force and the status of a law, the law of the father.

Of which *tukhê*? Because of this re-marking, we cannot know whether these events are effects of *tukhê* as divine providence or as random accident. There are several passages in which the connotations of *tukhê* are clear: in a few cases the notion of randomness is so explicit that it becomes almost impious. But when Teiresias, who knows the workings of fate, defines Oedipus's solution of the riddle as an event of *tukhê*, we have grounds to question whether he refers to some divine *tukhê* or to the mere accidentality of that event.

Despite these difficulties, the issues at stake are too important to neglect the analysis of these two notions and of the two narrative modes that they set in motion. For the *telos* of fate and the drifting of *tukhê* evoke two different modes of narrative, each proceeding with its own set of images, figures, and metaphysical underpinnings as it relates how events are determined. For instance, even Oedipus's two main qualities, his nobility and his intelligence, can be seen as aspects of *telos* and *tukhê*, because his nobility is a permanent asset, whereas the successful achievements of his intelligence depend on the fluctuations and the whims of the occasion. His very name, "Oidipous," was given to him by chance and itself suggests two readings: Swollenfoot, allied to the element of finality, and Knowfoot, partaking of the element of chance.

It seems certain that Sophocles' text purposefully combines the two narrative and ideological modes. In the extended passages of tragic irony, the text obviously follows two tracks, so to speak, one tracing Oedipus's ignorance and the other—heard only by the audience[13]—expressing the oracular finality that has already been accomplished. "The language of Oedipus," Vernant writes, "appears as the place where two different discourses weave themselves and confront each other in the same language: a human discourse, a divine discourse. In the beginning the two discourses are quite distinct, as if cut off one from the other; at the end of the play, when all is made clear, the two discourses are rejoined; the riddle is solved."[14] This scriptural project of weaving together the human (chance) and the divine (teleological) discourses is carried out with extraordinary subtlety and forcefulness. The sudden events, the unexpected diversions that seem to confirm the characters' presumptions and false perceptions of the situation but in fact only prove their self-deceptions, are too well known to require mention. Everyone admires the timeliness of the announcement of Polybus's death, which momentarily soothes Oedipus's gnawing anxiety, only to make the subsequent destruction of his newly gained assurance all the more pathetic.

These details among others demonstrate the text's purpose in interlacing the modalities and narratives of divine *telos* with those of accidental *tukhê* and of forcing one into the subjection of the other in order to prove that the *telos* of the oracle is always fulfilled, even if through unorthodox and unexpected ways. This textual purpose, then, does not simply satisfy the rules of suspense, which of course it does, but could be an edifying and religious purpose, as critics have repeatedly affirmed,[15] with the aim of upholding the law of Father Apollo, the truth of the divine word, and the sanctity of the great gods.

If the text aims at such a luminous end, it nevertheless reaches it in such a belated, enigmatic, and confused way as to throw doubts on the simplicity of this edifying purpose. Besides, the two narrative strategies mark each other, and accordingly the narrative of divine *telos* also turns out to be affected by the randomness and wriggling movement of *tukhê*. This interference is made visible in a conspicuous way. On the one hand, the combination of purposeful facts and of random events that satisfy the rules of suspense in the narrative barely hides the lack of cogency and consistency in the action itself. An enormous number of undetermined narrative details, confusing bits of information, unfinished searches, ambivalent and even contradictory pieces of evidence mar the straightness and clarity of the *telos* narrative to such a degree that some critics maintain that the text does not offer sufficient evidence for us to prove that Oedipus is indeed guilty of murdering Laius.[16] The work of *tukhê* endangers the "truth" of the narrative that presents Oedipus murdering, unwittingly, his own unknown father. If Laius is not Oedipus's father, the word and the *telos* announced by Apollo mean nothing any longer. They have been false and unfounded.

Yet, if we resist the temptation of recognizing the confusing and arbitrary work of *tukhê* at this macroscopic level and prefer to accept Oedipus' recognition of his crime as correct, we encounter the destabilizing work of *tukhê* in all the religious and edifying tenets of the narrative, and especially in the destabilization of the notions of fatherhood and of truth.

NOTES

1. For economy's sake I condense the naming of Oedipus's crimes into parrincest, uniting the words *patricide* and *incest*.

2. Rudnystky (1987) provides a good example of this reading.

3. Nicole Jaquot (1988), 28: "If it seems that psychoanalysis has to be responsible for the question about the father [la question du père] (to assume it and to uphold it as a question), nothing in the work of Freud, or in that of Lacan allows us to hope that psychoanalysis may give an answer."

See also Assoun (1989), 27 and 311ff. J. Laplanche (1961), 43–44, elaborates how, in the absence of the father's law, in the vacuum of this absence—as a result of which the father's name is never admitted in the subject's signification system—psychoanalysis identifies the cause of the disturbance of psychosis.

4. Here I refer to the exemplary work "Plato's Pharmacy" of Jacques Derrida.

5. *Tethrammenon* and *trophê* are respectively perfect passive participle of and the noun connected to the verb *trephô*, "I nourish, I tend, I care for."

6. Reinhardt ([1933] 1947), English translation (1979, 98: "Fate as predetermination does not exist before the Stoa and the victory of astrology." Knox (1957), 4ff., Dodds ([1960] 1968), 22, calls the definition of the play as a tragedy of fate, a "heresy." See also Leach ([1917] 1952).

7. See text and arguments in Lacoue Labarthe (1978), 196ff. Schlegel (1809), 174, 204, etc., sees this conflict between fate and man's moral freedom in *Oedipus Tyrannus*.

8. Freud ([1900] 1965), 296: "His [Oedipus's] destiny moves us only because it might have been ours—because the oracle laid the same curse upon us before our birth as upon him. It is the fate of all of us, perhaps, to direct our first sexual impulse towards our mother and our first hatred and our first murderous wish against our father." See also p. 294: "The action of the play consists in nothing other than in the process of revealing, with cunning delays and with mounting excitement—a process that can be likened to the work of psychoanalysis—that Oedipus himself is the murderer of Laius"; and p. 296: "Its [the play's] effect does not lie in the contrast between destiny and human will, but in the particular nature on which that contrast is exemplified."

9. Freud (1985), 272: Freud to Fliess, Oct. 15, 1897; Freud ([1900] 1965), 295.

10. See Dodds ([1960] 1968), 22. Here Dodds recognizes that Freud took the play as a tragedy of "fate," but neglects to say that Freud radically transformed that notion by placing Fate in Oedipus's unconscious, so that only the reader sees the work of Fate, while Oedipus feels free. And despite its dogmatic tone, not even Dodds's interpretation is immune from a certain notion of theological necessity, for Dodds reads the play as a text written in defense of the necessary truth of the oracles and in an "objective world-order" (28). On Freud's position, see also Bollack (1986), 3–4, who illustrates the type of *Schicksalsdrama* against which Freud reacted and Freud's originality in defining a *universal* necessity in *Oedipus Tyrannus*.

11. Vernant ([1970] 1988), 481: "Oedipus thus finds himself, by a divine curse as gratuitous as the election from which the other heroes of legend profit, cut off from the social bond, thrown outside humanity." See also p. 495: "Superhuman and subhuman are joined and mixed together in the same person. And as this person is the model of man, all limits which would permit one to delineate human life, to fix unequivocally its status, are erased. When he wishes, like Oedipus, to pursue the investigation of what he is, man discovers himself enigmatic without stability or a domain proper to him, without fixed

connection, without defined essence, oscillating between the equal of a god and the equal of nothing. His real greatness consists in the very thing which expresses his enigmatic nature: the question."

12. Segal (1981) reveals the enigmatic nature of the prophecies (of both gods and men) and their slippery language; see 241ff.

13. Todorov (1977), 26–27, calls the former "utterance" and the latter "speech act."

14. Vernant ([1970] 1988), 478. Vidal-Naquet's description—he says that the text weaves the time of gods and the time of men ([1986] 1988, 101ff.)—is also apt.

15. This is the thesis, for instance, of Dodds ([1960] 1968).

16. Here I am referring to the thesis of Tycho von Wilamowitz (1917), and others after him. Girard (1972) and Goodhart (1978) have developed their critical interpretations of the play around just this lack of cogent evidence.

References

Assoun, Paul-Laurent. 1989. "Foncionnes freudiennes du père." In *Le père*, edited by Anne Muxel and Jean Marc Rennes, 25–51. Paris: Denoel.

Bollack, Jean. 1986. "Le fils de l'homme." *L'écrit du temps* 12: 3–26.

Derrida, Jacques. [1972] 1981. *La dissemination*. Paris: Seuil. Translated by Barbara Johnson under the title of *Dissemination*, 63–171. Chicago: University of Chicago Press.

Dodds, E. R. [1960] 1968. "On Misunderstanding the *Oedipus Rex*." In *Twentieth Century Interpretations of Oedipus Rex*, edited by M. J. O'Brien, 17–29. Englewood Cliffs, NJ: Prentice-Hall.

Freud, Sigmund. [1900] 1965. *The Interpretation of Dreams*. Translated by James Strachey. New York: Avon Books.

———. 1985. *The Complete Letters of Sigmund Freud to Wilhelm Fliess*. Translated and edited by J. M. Masson. Cambridge: Belknap Press of Harvard University Press.

Girard, René. [1972] 1977. La violence et le sacré. Paris: Grasset. Translated by P. Gregory under the title of *The Violence and the Sacred*. Baltimore: Johns Hopkins University Press.

Goodhart, Sandor. 1978. "*Leistas ephaske*: Oedipus and Laius' Many Murderers." *Diacritics* 8: 54–71.

Jaquot, Nicole. "Oedipe ou l'histoire d'un lien 'consanguinaire.'" In *(Le) père*. Actes du colloque de Nice 1986, edited by C. Nahun, 26–34.

Knox, B. M. W. 1957. *Oedipus at Thebes*. New Haven: Yale University Press.

Laplanche, Jean. 1961. *Hölderlin et la question du père*. Paris: Presses Universitaires.

Leach, Abby. [1917] 1952. "Fate and Free Will in Greek Literature." In *The Greek Genius and Its Influence*, edited by Lane Cooper. Ithaca: Cornell University Press.

Reinhardt, Karl. *Sophokles*. Translated by Hazel Harvey and David Harvey under the title of *Sophocles*. Oxford: Blackwell, 1979.

Rudnytsky, Peter L. *Freud and Oedipus*. New York: Columbia University Press, 1987.

Schlegel, A. W. 1809. *Vorlesungen über dramatische Kunst*. Vol. 1. Heidelberg: Mohr und Winter.

Segal, Charles. 1981. *Tragedy and Civilization: An Interpretation of Sophocles*. Cambridge: Harvard University Press.

Todorov, Tzvetan. 1977. *The Poetics of Prose*. Translated by Richard Howard. Ithaca: Cornell University Press.

Vernant, Jean Pierre. [1970] 1988. "Ambiguité et renversement." In *Échanges et Communications, Mélanges offerts à Claude Lévi-Strauss*. Paris, 1970. Translated by Page duBois in *New Literary History* 9 (1978): 475–501. Republished in Jean Pierre Vernant, Pierre Vidal-Naquet, *Oedipe et ses mythes*. Paris: La Découverte 1986. Reprint: Brussels: Editions Complexe.

Wilamowitz, Tycho von. 1917. *Die dramatische Technik des Sophocles*. Philologische Untersuchungen 22. Berlin: Weidman.

MARTHA C. NUSSBAUM

The Oedipus Rex *and the Ancient Unconscious*

I shall be discussing the practical nature of the ancient unconscious—its preoccupation with questions of good and bad fortune, control and lack of control, security and insecurity. I shall be arguing that these questions are more central to its workings than questions of sexuality narrowly construed, indeed, that sexual anxieties function as just one species of practical anxiety about control and security. It therefore seems appropriate to begin with a dream, to all appearances sexual, which really has, according to the ancient interpretation, a nonsexual practical significance for the fortunes of most of the contributors to this volume—people, that is, who make a living giving lectures and exchanging arguments. In the first book of Artemidoros of Daldis' work on dream interpretation (*Artemidori Daldiani onicocriticon libri V*), in a section—to which I shall return—on dreams whose content is that which violates convention in sexual matters, Artemidoros, a professional dream analyst of the second century C.E.,[1] interprets the dream that one is performing oral sex on a stranger.[2]

In general, Artemidoros says, this dream is a bad one, indicative of some bad fortune to come—this in keeping with the pervasive Greek view that such intercourse is unclean and base (Winkler 1990, 37–38; Henderson 1975, 22, 25, 183–86). But there is an exception. With his characteristic pragmatism and flexibility, Artemidoros notes that the dream is a happy one,

From *Freud and Forbidden Knowledge* edited by Peter L. Rudnytsky and Ellen Handler Spitz, pp. 72–95. ©1994 by New York University Press.

indicative of future good fortune and security, "for those who earn their living by their mouths, I mean flutists, trumpet-players, rhetors, sophists, and whoever else is like them." The sexual act is cheerfully read as a metaphor for the successful practice of one's profession. Beyond the information it imparts, so interesting to the professional academic, this example begins, I hope, to give a sense of some profound differences between ancient Greek and Freudian attitudes toward what the unconscious mind contains and how to decipher its contents. These differences—and also their significance for the reading of Sophocles' *Oedipus Rex*—will be the subject of this essay.[3]

I have often felt discomfort when hearing discussion of the Freudian Oedipus complex in connection with Sophocles' play. For while it seems plain that both Freud's theory and Sophocles' play explore important aspects of human experience and evoke in their readers a valuable sort of reflection about experience, I have (along, I suspect, with many readers of the play) much difficulty finding the closer link that Freudian interpretations of the play wish us to discover. For it seems difficult to avoid the conclusion that the play itself is not very much concerned with sexual desire as such, or with deep-hidden sexual urges toward one's parent, combined with aggressive wishes toward one's parental rival. Its subject matter does very much appear to be that of reversal in fortune. So it has been understood since Aristotle's *Poetics*, where it provides the central illustration of the concept of *peripeteia*—and, it appears, with good reason. Incest seems to figure in the plot as that which, when discovered, causes Oedipus to plummet from the summit of good fortune to the very bottom. It is, of course, crucial to the plot that Oedipus is not experiencing desire toward the person whom he takes to be his mother, toward the woman who raised him as a mother, nor, indeed, toward any woman who nursed, held, or cared for him at any time. So far as the intentional content of his desire is concerned, Jocasta is simply a well-placed eligible stranger. It is also perfectly clear that his aggressive action against Laios is in and of itself culturally acceptable, a counterattack in self-defense.[4] Nor is there any sign that Oedipus has at any level hidden knowledge about the identity of the stranger he kills. How could he, when he would never have looked upon his face, even in infancy? Finally, the whole question of erotic desire does not appear to be salient in the play's treatment of the marriage to Jocasta. The marriage is a political one, and is never described as motivated by *erôs*. *Erôs* is mentioned frequently in Sophocles—but not in this play. In short: the play *seems*, as Aristotle says, to be concerned with the vulnerability of even the best fortune to abrupt disaster. And it is crucial to its construction that the collocation of circumstances that strikes Oedipus down is not regarded, by him or by anyone else in the play, as the product of his sexual intentions, whether conscious or unconscious.

To say all this is to state the obvious. And yet we post-Freudians have learned to doubt the obvious. We have learned to look in the play for signs of the repressed desires, erotic and aggressive, that Freud made the subject matter of his theory of the Oedipus complex and his reading of the play. Peter Rudnytsky's book (1987) persuasively documents the history of Freud's reading, setting it against the background of nineteenth-century German views of tragedy. It would be instructive to couple this history with a history of the avoidance, in that same period of post-Kantian German thought, of the apparently unseemly conclusions of ancient tragedy about the vulnerability of human flourishing and even of virtuous action to changes in fortune.[5] But if we are to move from understanding how Freud's account of the play came about to assessing it as an account of the play that Sophocles wrote, we must ask whether, in fact, an ancient Greek audience would have made the connections a Freudian makes between the surface of the play and deeper questions of sexuality, or whether, on the other hand, my initial hunch about the gulf between the play's preoccupation with security and Freud's preoccupation with sexuality is correct. But in order to know this we need, in turn, to know a great deal more than Freudian interpreters characteristically tell us about *ancient* attitudes to the unconscious mind and its decipherment.

This is a vast task, but I intend at least to begin it here, arguing that in some salient and, I think, representative pieces of the evidence we find that the ancient Greeks, unlike orthodox Freudians, did not think that sexuality lies behind every other wish. Instead, they understood the mind's deepest and most anxious preoccupations to be preoccupations—frequently unconscious on account of their upsetting character—about control and lack of control, security and the absence of security. Thus it will turn out, I think, that the best reading of the tragedy does present material bearing an account of what the unconscious mind contains—but not in the way that the Freudian supposes.

Now of course if one believes that Freud's theory is correct, and universally so, one will not be much deterred from the Freudian interpretation of Sophocles by the discovery that the Freudian interpretation is culturally anachronistic. For it will seem plausible to suppose that Sophocles' brilliance has put him in touch with truths that other members of his culture were slow to discover. And, on the other side, I confess that the explanatory power and the general human plausibility of ancient protopsychoanalytic views is, for me, a part, at least, of the appeal of reading the play in conjunction with these views, rather than with the Freudian views. But if we leave to one side the question of psychoanalytic truth, we can still see that setting the play in its cultural context promotes a much more economical and unstrained reading of the text, one that can recognize as salient what the text itself presents as salient, rather than searching for signs of what it nowhere says or implies.

I shall devote most of the chapter to the examination of two very different ancient Greek accounts of the unconscious mind and its symbolic and motivational activity. First I shall examine a portion of the dream book of Artemidoros, which, though written in the second century C.E., gives us the most extensive evidence we have about popular beliefs concerning these matters and testifies, it is clear, to deep and persistent cultural beliefs about the crucial importance of "external goods" in the structure of the mental life. Artemidoros confines his account to the reading of dreams, which is, of course, his trade; he has no theory comparable to Freud's concerning the motivational role of repressed unconscious desires in one's waking life. I shall therefore turn next to the one ancient theory of the mind known to me that does develop in some detail such a motivational account—namely, to the Epicurean theory of unconscious fears and longings, and their role in explaining behavior. I shall draw some tentative conclusions about the common ground between these two views, and then turn more briefly to the play, to see what light, if any, this background might have shed on how we might approach it. Finally, I shall briefly and tentatively suggest that there is a contemporary psychoanalytic approach that comes closer than Freud's does to tapping the play's central preoccupations—namely, the "object relations" approach.

ARTEMIDOROS: INCEST AND FORTUNE

The dream book of Artemidoros of Daldis has recently been the subject of some valuable analyses: by Michel Foucault in the third volume of his *History of Sexuality* (1986)—more convincing, I think, than the second volume (1985) as a reconstruction of Greek popular thought[6]—and by John J. Winkler in his recent book *The Constraints of Desire: The Anthropology of Sex and Gender in Ancient Greece* (1990, 17–44, 210–16).[7] Winkler's analysis is, I think, more fine-tuned and generally more incisive than Foucault's, especially in its stress on the flexibility and individuality of Artemidoros' dream-readings. I have the highest respect for Winkler's work on the dream-material (see Nussbaum 1990a); what I say here does not go very far beyond what he has already done. But I wish to connect this material with some more general observations about ancient ideas of the mind, and other texts dealing with the mind, in order to prepare the way for a contrast with the Freudian view and for a confrontation with Sophocles. For this reason I shall be looking more closely than Winkler does at certain sections of the text—especially, at its account of bodily parts as dream-signifiers, and its account of dreams of incest with the mother.

First, some general observations. Artemidoros is important to anyone who wants a better understanding of ancient attitudes to dreaming and sex (and many other things besides) because, although he is himself an expert practitioner with a theory, the theory operates through a detailed understanding of popular cultural symbolism and deeply rooted cultural attitudes (Winkler 1990, 28ff). To find out what a dream signifies, Artemidoros needs to know the various symbolic associations of the parts of the dream-content. Usually he does this in general cultural terms, since he is writing a general handbook. But he makes it clear that the good interpreter must really always take into account the peculiarities of the dreamer's own history, his or her own personal variations on the cultural symbolism. In a nonjudgmental way he must seek to uncover the facts about the dreamer's own practices and associations, so that no relevant symbolic connection will have been overlooked. In my opening example, the interpreter needs to know the dreamer's profession—for this will inform him that the dream of giving sexual pleasure with one's mouth, which has dire associations for most people, has associations with profit and success for the dreamer, as member of one of the occupational groups named. Elsewhere he makes it clear that he also needs full information about the dreamer's sexual practices, if dreams with a sexual content are to be correctly understood. In two cases where males dreamed, one of performing cunnilingus on his wife, the other of being fellated by his, Artemidoros at first expected something bad to happen. He was amazed when it did not, and this seemed to him most "unreasonable." But later the puzzle was solved. He discovered (he does not tell us how) that the two men in question actually had all along had a personal taste for oral-genital activity, a taste that they had not reported to Artemidoros, presumably because of the cultural stigma attached to it. "Both were in the habit of doing that, and not keeping their mouths clean. So it was plausible that nothing happened to them, since they simply saw what excited them" (4.59).[8] Thus, though many dreams refer to future events, their significance must be read—as in the case of Freudian interpretation—in terms of the dreamer's own personal history, wishes, and associations (Winkler 1990, 29).[9]

Artemidoros in general divides dreams into two types: *enhupnia* and *oneiroi*. *Enhupnia* are dreams that directly express a current physical or emotional state. For example, "a lover necessarily sees himself with his beloved in his dreams, and a frightened man sees what he is afraid of, the hungry man eats, the thirsty man drinks" (1.1). The significance of such dreams is simple and relatively superficial: they signify the dreamer's current state in a transparent way (Winkler 1990, 32). In general, the presence in a dream of such indications of strong current desires tends to disqualify the dream from having a more complex significance: "Having sex with a known and familiar woman [sc. in a dream] when one is feeling sexy and desires her in the dream predicts nothing, because of the overriding intensity of the desire" (1.78). And, as we have seen, the fact that the two clients turned out to be devotees of oral sex disqualified their dream from predictive significance, even though they were not necessarily in a state of sexual arousal at the time of their dreams.

On the other hand, when dreams do not derive from the dreamer's immediate state, they can have a far more profound meaning. The class of such dreams, *oneiroi*, are the subject matter of Artemidoros' trade—and, he makes clear, of many competing theories and practices of interpretation, prior to and contemporary with his. The interpreter approaches the dream as a complex whole-looking not just at one or two images, but at "the systematized totality of the dream images" (4.28).[10] And this whole is regarded as a kind of symbolic coded language in which the dreamer's soul speaks to itself about matters of the greatest importance. Much of the code, as I said, is common and cultural; that is why it is possible for Artemidoros to write a general manual of dream interpretation. But a most important part of it is personal, as we have seen. To give another example of this, this time from a clear member of the class of *oneiroi*, a dream of beating one's mother, which would usually have been ill-omened, is auspicious for a particular potter, who came into a profit afterwards—the interpretation being that he beat clay (mother earth) for a living, and that the dream used a coded personal language to point to the profitable exercise of his profession (4.2). The art of the interpreter consists in unraveling such complex codes.

If one now asks about the place of the sexual in all this, three dramatic differences between the Freudian theory and the ancient theory will immediately emerge. The first and clearest difference is that for Artemidoros all dreams, sexual dreams included, signify future contingent events, usually events of the near future, whereas for Freudian analysis their significance is usually to be read in terms of the remote past, which is seen as having decisively formed the personality. This is a profound difference; but one should not, I think, overemphasize it, taking it to imply that the Artemidoran theory is magical and of no psychological interest. For Artemidoros as for Freud (as Freud himself saw) dreams are ways the soul has of talking to itself about deep and important things, usually by speaking in a condensed and displaced associative language. If Artemidoros believes the soul can have access to the near future, his dream contents still reveal, no less than Freud's, patterns of significance within the dreamer, and connections so deep that they are not always understood by the dreamer, perhaps because they lie too deep to be confronted in waking life without anxiety. *Oneiroi*, Artemidoros insists, "are the work of the soul and do not come from anything outside" (4.59). In the case of both theorists, then, dream-interpretation is the decoding of people's cryptic and hidden messages to themselves.

Second, again a rather obvious point, one is struck, in studying the sections on dreams of the sexual, by the complete absence of any belief in infantile, or even childhood, sexuality. In Book I, Artemidoros arranges the dream-contents according to the time of life depicted in the content, from birth to death. Dreams of intercourse come right in the middle, after dreams connected with being an ephebe, going to the gymnasium, winning athletic contests, and going to the baths—in other words, as phenomena connected with adult mid-life.[11] Artemidoros is not alone in this, clearly. In all the competing ancient philosophical theories about the natural and first desires of the infant, sexual desire is not advanced as a candidate by anyone.[12] Epicureans ascribe to the infant a basic desire for freedom from pain and disturbance. Stoics defend, instead, the desire for self-preservation. Aristotelians back, in addition or instead, a desire for cognitive mastery. So far as I am aware, no theorist even mentions sex in connection with the infant, and I think ancient readers would have found this idea absurd. (Longus' *Daphnis and Chloe* gives one representative example of the fact that sexual desire was taken to awaken at puberty for both males and females, therefore earlier for females than for males.) The radical and unconventional nature of the Freudian view is easy to overlook, since by now the view so infuses our popular culture. (One dramatic reminder of its radical and sudden nature can be found in Rousseau's *Emile*, the greatest account of the development of desire and emotion in the child in the centuries immediately before Freud. For there it is taken for granted—very much as in the ancient world—that sexual desire will awaken in the male at age sixteen. Much is made of this fact in accounting for the [late] genesis of other-regarding emotions like pity, and the related ethical dispositions.)

The fact that Freud's ideas on this subject are completely absent from the ancient Greek world is not a trivial one for my project. For if we are to manage to ascribe to Oedipus *any* formation of sexual desire in connection with his parents seen as such, we will obviously have to push this desire back into very early infancy, before his exposure. Whether we are even entitled to do this is, of course, unclear, since the play does not tell us whether this baby ever looked on its mother's face, or was held in her arms. Jocasta gave the baby to the herdsman in person, so much is clear; but presumably she did so soon after the birth, without nursing the child, and we have no reason even to suppose that she would have held the baby herself. Certainly the play gives us no reason to suppose the baby ever set eyes on Laios, even in the most early and attenuated sense, a fact which the remoteness of ancient Greek fatherhood (especially upper-class fatherhood) would in any case render most unlikely. Even if it is marginally possible that this infant had some vestigial awareness of its parents, the complete silence of the play about such matters—although nursing and holding might very easily have been mentioned—together with its emphasis on the fact that Oedipus' only real nurse was Cithairon, should make us wary of reading into the text any interest in infantile patterns of desire. The cultural evidence that such desire was not recognized by the Greeks in general should make us far more wary still.

But the most striking aspect of Artemidoros' view about sexual dreaming, for the post-Freudian reader, is the type of significance he attaches to the sexual in the interpretation of the soul's deliverances. The post-Freudian interpreter is inclined to seek for a sexual meaning beneath apparently nonsexual dream-contents. The deepest point at which one can arrive, in unraveling the mind's symbolic language, is a point at which one arrives at some sexual wish. Artemidoros moves, on the whole, in just the opposite direction. For him, even dreams that have an overtly sexual content are, like all other dreams, read off as having a significance for the rise and fall of the dreamer's fortunes, his or her command or lack of command over important items such as money, status, friendships, and the other important things in life.[13] In fact, if one reads the text in connection with the history of philosophical ethics, one notices a striking coincidence between the list of important signifieds to which Artemidoros' account recurs again and again, and the lists of "external goods" or "goods of fortune" that figure in Aristotelian and other accounts of *eudaimonia* (see Nussbaum 1986a, chs. 11–12). The items in question include: wealth, health, reputation and status, family and children, friendships, political roles—in short, all the things generally thought pertinent to *eudaimonia* (whether as instrumental means or as constituent parts)[14] that are not securely and stably possessed or controlled. Their importance in life is therefore a source of much anxiety to most ordinary Greeks, an anxiety that motivates a variety of reconstructive philosophical projects aimed at greater self-sufficiency.[15] Dreams, for Artemidoros, and sexual dreams among them, signify the dreamer's (future) command or lack of command over these significant external goods.

Sex can sometimes figure on the other side of an interpretation, as something signified by a dream content. For sex figures in various ways among the external goods, being an element in marriage, a necessary condition for childbearing, an aspect of one's status and self-assertion as a citizen,[16] and (in the case of unlawful sexual activity) the source of a diminution of status or citizenship. But it is in this connection with external goods that dreams are read, on the relatively rare occasions when they are, as being about sex. Much more frequently, one discovers an apparently sexual dream being read as "really" about external goods such as standing and reputation (see also Winkler 1990, 34–35).

A corollary of this emphasis on external goods and the dreamer's position in the world is that the interpreter must carefully scrutinize the specific details of the apparently sexual dream, taking note of the type of sexual activity performed, and above all of the positions of the actors. For the very same activity that might be auspicious if one is oneself penetrating another will be extremely inauspicious if one is on the receiving end. There is no clearer example of this—and of my general point about the nonsexual significance of the sexual—than in Artemidoros' matter-of-fact discussion of dreams of bestiality. Whatever the animal species in question is, says Artemidoros, if one dreams that one is mounting the animal, then one "will receive a benefit from an animal of that particular species, whatever it is." But if one dreams that one is being mounted by an animal, one "will have some violent and awful experience. Many, after these dreams, have died" (1.80).

The claim that sexual dreams are "really" about command over external goods can be illustrated from any number of passages in Artemidoros' account—and not least from its overall construction. For sexual dreams occupy only a brief three chapters, slipped in between dreams of being given a crown and dreams of being asleep. But for our comparative purposes it will be useful to focus on two portions of Artemidoros' analysis: the account of the manifold significance of the penis, and the account (within the three-chapter section on intercourse) of dreams of incest with the mother. Artemidoros discusses the penis as a signifying dream-content in the course of discussing, each in turn, the parts of the body. It is important to note that it is not more significant than many other parts. It is analyzed after the liver and before the testicles (which are said to signify pretty much the same thing as the penis). Although it takes up a fair amount of space in the discussion (27 lines of text, slightly more than the 18 allotted to the chest, the 20 to the legs, and the 25 to hands, just under the 28 given to feet and the 29 to the tongue, but far less than the 79 allotted to hair and baldness, the 84 to teeth and the loss of teeth)—it is not, as these numbers show, singled out as having any very special significance, or as a central focus of anxiety. The poignant anxieties surrounding baldness and the loss of teeth seem clearly to be far more pressing items in the soul's internal discourse.[17] In fact, the penis takes up as much space as it does only because there are so many slang terms for it, giving rise to a variety of verbal associations. Here is Artemidoros' report on the associations connected with the penis in general, which are to be of use to the interpreter in approaching concrete cases:

> The penis is like a man's parents since it contains the generative code (*spermatikos logos*), but also like his children since it is their cause. It is like his wife and girlfriend since it is useful for sex. It is like his brothers and all blood relations since the meaning of the entire household depends on the penis. It signifies strength and the body's manhood, since it actually causes these: for this reason some people call it their "manhood" (*andreia*). It resembles reason and education since, like reason (*logos*), it is the most generative thing of all.... It further suggests surplus and possession since it sometimes opens out and sometimes is relaxed and it can produce and eject. It is like hidden plans since both plans and the penis are called *mêdea*; and it is analogous to poverty, slavery, and imprisonment since it is called "necessity" and is a symbol of constraint. It is like the respect of being held in honor, since it is called "reverence" (*aidôs*) and "respect." (1.45, see Winkler 1990, 41)

The selection of which association to follow up will depend, here as elsewhere, on the totality of the dream content and on the role of these associations in the dreamer's particular history. But this catalogue should suffice to show that Greek beliefs do not understand the penis as signifying itself—at least, not very often. More often, its presence in a dream points elsewhere, to the network of external and public relations that constitute the focus of a male citizen's anxieties. Freud expressed the view that the excessive preoccupation with money and success that he encountered in America showed that Americans were overly given to sublimation, and indeed had become, as a result, sexual nonentities.[18] What is for him sublimation is for an ancient Greek the core and deepest point of desire and anxiety.

The account of mother–son incest occurs as part of the analysis of dreams of sexual intercourse, which itself falls into three sections: dreams about intercourse "according to convention," about intercourse "contrary to convention," and about intercourse "contrary to nature" (see Winkler 1990, 33–40). In the first category are dreams of all kinds of nonincestuous and nonoral intercourse, both active and passive, with partners of either gender (the one exception being "a woman penetrating a woman," which, as we shall see, falls in the third category). Although the goodness or badness of the events predicted by the dream is often connected with the generally approved or nonapproved nature of its content—thus the dream of penetrating someone is usually, though not always, more auspicious than the dream of being penetrated—the whole group is called "according to convention," regardless of the genders and positions of the actors. "Against convention" are two sorts of dream contents: dreams of incest, and dreams of oral sex. "Against nature" are contents that simply seem to Artemidoros too weird to have any ordinary social signification at all, things that are just off the ordinary map—having sex with a god, having sex with an animal, having sex with oneself (this not in the sense of masturbation, but in the sense of self-penetration and self-fellatio); and, finally, "a woman penetrating a woman."[19] It is important to note that the dream of something "against nature" need not be ill-omened; everything depends on the further analysis of the content, the postures of the actors, etc. (Thus, as we have seen, it can be very good to dream of mounting an animal.)

Artemidoros' account of mother–son incest is longer than any other discussion in the incest section—on account of the fact, he says, that "the analysis of the mother is intricate and elaborate, and susceptible of many discriminations. It has eluded many dream analysts" (1.79). Here is the main part of Artemidoros' account—the ancient analogue, or disanalogue, of Freud's oedipal wishing:

> The intercourse in itself is not sufficient to show the intended significance of the dream, but the postures and positions of the bodies, being different, make the outcome different. First we should speak of frontal penetration with a living mother—for it also makes a difference in the meaning whether she is alive or dead (in the dream). So if one penetrates his own mother frontally—which some say is according to nature—and she is alive, if his father is in good health, he will have a falling out with him, because of the element of jealousy which would occur no matter who was involved. If his father happens to be sick, he will die, for the man who has the dream will assume authority over his mother as both son and husband. It is a good dream for all craftsmen and laborers, for it is usual to refer to one's craft as "mother," and what else could sexual intimacy with one's craft signify except having no leisure and being productive from it? It is good too for all office-holders and politicians, for the mother signifies the fatherland. So just as he who has sex according to the

conventions of Aphrodite controls the entire body of the woman who is obedient and willing, so too the dreamer will have authority over all the business of the city.

And he who is on bad terms with his mother will resume friendly relations with her, because of the intercourse, for it is called "friendship" (*philotês*). And often this dream has brought together to the same place those who were dwelling apart and has made them be together (*suneinai*). Therefore it brings the traveler too back to his native land, provided his mother happens to be living in the fatherland; otherwise, wherever the mother is living, that is where the dream is telling the traveler to proceed.

And if a poor man who lacks the essentials has a rich mother he will receive what he wants from her, or else he will inherit it from her when she dies not long after, and thus he will take pleasure in his mother. Many too have undertaken to care and provide for their mothers, who in turn take pleasure in their sons.

The dream sets right the sick man, signifying that he will return to the natural state, for the common mother of all is nature, and we say that healthy people are in a natural state and sick people are not. Apollodoros of Telmessos, a learned man, also remarks on this. The significance is not the same for sick people if the mother (in the dream) is dead, for the dreamer will die very shortly. For the constitution of the dream woman dissolves into the matter of which it is composed and constituted and most of it being earth-like reverts to its proper material. And "mother" is no less a name for the earth. What else could having sex with a dead mother signify for the sick man but having sex with the earth?

For one who is involved in a suit over land or who wants to buy some land or who desires to farm, it is good to have sex with a dead mother. Some say that it is bad for the farmer alone, saying that he will scatter his seeds on dead land, that is, he will have no yield. But in my opinion this is not at all correct, unless however one repents of the intercourse or feels upset.

Further, he who is in a dispute over his mother's property will win his case after this dream, rejoicing not in his mother's body but in her property.

If one sees this dream in one's native country he will leave the country, for it is not possible after so great an error (*hamartêma*) to remain at the maternal hearths. If he is upset or repents the intercourse he will be exiled from the fatherland, otherwise he will leave voluntarily.

To penetrate one's mother from the rear is not good. For either the mother herself will turn her back on the dreamer or his fatherland or his craft or whatever might be his immediate business. It is also bad if both are standing upright during intercourse, for people adopt such a posture through lack of a bed or blankets. Therefore it signifies pressures and desperate straits. To have sex with one's mother on her knees is bad: it signifies a great lack because of the mother's immobility.

If the mother is on top and "riding cavalry," some say this means death for the dreamer, since the mother is like earth, earth being the nurturer and progenetrix of all, and it lies on top of corpses and not on top of the living. But I have observed that sick men who have this dream always die, but the healthy men live out the remainder of their lives in great ease and just as they choose— a correct and logical outcome, for in the other positions the hard work and heavy breathing are for the most part the male's share and the female role is relatively effortless; but in this posture it is just the opposite—the man takes pleasure without laboring. But it also allows him who is not in the light to be hidden from his neighbors, because most of the telltale heavy breathing is absent. (1.79)

There follows a brief digression on the naturalness of the frontal position; and then, in a transition to the following section on oral sex, Artemidoros analyzes the dream of oral sex with one's mother. To that dream we shall turn later; first, however, some comments on the material just cited. The strikingly non-Freudian nature of the analysis is evident; but a few concrete observations will help to pin it down. First, there is nothing special about mother–son incest in Artemidoros' account of the soul's inner language. It is just one more signifier, and it is not singled out as playing an especially fundamental role. It is ranked along with other cases of incest, and all incest along with oral sex; and, as we have already said, the entire account of sexual dreaming is a very brief portion of the longer analysis.

Second, the dream of mother–son incest, like other sexual dreams, is significant, not in terms of underlying sexual wishes, but in terms of things like getting control over an estate, having authority in the city, getting on well with one's family and friends, getting or losing one's health, and so forth. The mother's body frequently signifies country or property. Even when, in the opening paragraph, a dispute with one's father is mentioned as one possible significance of such a dream, it is made just one possibility among many, and is not basic to what follows in any sense. Furthermore, the father's jealousy is just ordinary sexual jealousy, "the element of jealousy which would occur no matter who was involved." The dream signifies a rupture in one's fortunes, since good relations with one's family are conventionally taken to be a central part of one's fortunes. But neither its specifically sexual significance nor the identity of the parties is dwelt upon. And we must take note of the fact that very many of the dreams in this section are auspicious— again impossible if they were read as in every case denoting a hostile wish.

Third, the significance of these dreams is to be understood not by focusing exclusively on the fact of incest—to which, of course, the Freudian account single-mindedly directs us—but rather in terms of the specific sexual positions and activities employed. Artemidoros is very insistent about this. Thus, to penetrate one's mother from the front is usually good, to penetrate her from behind usually bad. Standing intercourse, in characteristic fashion, is immediately taken to have an economic significance, in terms of the lack of bedclothes and furniture. The position with the mother on top—in Artemidoros' novel interpretation, of whose cleverness he is evidently proud—is auspicious (for a healthy man) because it is associated with ease and an absence of heavy breathing.

Fourth and finally, there is not the slightest hint here that the dream should be connected to any deep and extended narrative pattern of sexual wishing going far back into one's childhood and repressed in adulthood. Such dreams are read matter-of-factly, like others, in terms of the dreamer's current profession, fortune, and so forth; the mother's significance in the dream frequently comes from his current professional activities. And far from expressing disturbing repressed sexual material, the dream's sexual content is not taken to be especially disturbing. Consider the case of the farmer, whose dream of incest with the *corpse* of his mother is auspicious, "unless one repents of the intercourse or feels upset"—apparently not the usual case! We might add that the range and variety of dreams of this type that were reported to Artemidoros may itself give evidence of an absence of repression of such ideas in Greek culture. For many contemporary people who read this section, what seems oddest is that all these dreams should have occurred at all, in this undisguised form. To the Greeks it seems, apparently, perfectly normal and natural, just as natural as the fact that one's especially deep anxieties about money, health, and citizenship should assume, in a dream, a disguised form. In short, if anything is, here, so disturbing that it invites repression, it is the soul's anxiety about external goods.[20]

Now we must turn to one further dream in the sequence, "the most awful (*deinotaton*) dream of all," says our author. For this dream might seem initially to cast doubt on some of our claims—although more closely inspected, I believe, it supports them. This dream, as I have said, forms the transition between the section on incest dreams and the section on dreams of oral sex. Its analysis goes as follows:

> The most awful dream of all, I have observed, is to be fellated by one's mother. For it signifies the death of children and loss of property and serious illness for the dreamer. I know someone who had this dream and lost his penis; it makes sense that he should be punished in the part of his body which erred. (1.79)

A Freudian interpreter might suppose that Artemidoros here at last betrays the Freudian nature of his, and his patients' concerns. For the "most awful dream," after all, is a dream of intercourse with the mother. And having the dream is linked to the idea of a merited sexual punishment for a transgression that is, apparently, specifically sexual. Sexual error signifies a sexual loss. Don't we have here, after all, the proof that the deepest and most fearful things in the ancient unconscious are, after all, sexual things, and that a repressed thought of incest is, after all, connected in this culture with a fear of the loss of virility?

Things are not so simple. First of all, there is an obvious and striking departure from Freudian concerns in the fact that the dream is terrible not on account of its incestuous content—many incest-dreams, we recall, are auspicious—but on account of the mode of copulation. Here, as elsewhere in the discussion, Artemidoros expresses his culture's view that to perform oral sex is unclean and base; to be made to perform it on someone else is a humiliation. The discussion that ensues makes it plain that the uncleanness of the performer's mouth is thought to make it impossible to share kisses or food with this person any more. (In general, any dream of oral sex with a known person signifies a separation from that person.) Thus the dream of the fellating mother is understood as a dream of the humiliation of the mother by the son, a humiliation that is bound to destroy the household. It is for this reason, and not on account of its specifically incestuous content, that it is so inauspicious. And the son's error, for which he is punished, is not to engage in intercourse with his mother; it is to cause his mother to perform an unclean act after which the household can never be the same. Well might such a dream signify "the death of children and loss of property and serious illness."

Second, what the dream does in fact signify is, as we just said, "the death of children and loss of property and serious illness." The man who loses his penis is just one case of "serious illness," a case picked out by

Artemidoros because of its ironically apposite nature. But, as elsewhere, the "real" significance of the dream is in the dreamer's relation to "external goods." And the punishment of the dreamer is the loss, not only of a bodily part, but of the chance to have, in the future, a family of his own. Because he did something destructive and antifamily, he loses the chance to have a family, and to enjoy the position of status and control signified by the penis.

In short: the dream of incest is, at bottom, a code, through which the soul speaks to itself about what it most deeply hopes and fears. Not sex, but control over external goods, are the content of those most basic hopes and fears.

Epicurus and Lucretius: Unconscious Fears and Waking Actions

With Epicurus we return to the fourth–third centuries B.C.E.—although most of the material I shall discuss is actually preserved only in Lucretius' *De rerum natura* of the first century B.C.E. It is not clear which elements in Lucretius' account of unconscious fear can be traced back to the thought of Epicurus, but for now I shall proceed as if there is a single coherent shared view here.[21] It will become evident, I think, that, whatever the date of this view's origin, it reflects many of the cultural preoccupations that still animate Artemidoros' account somewhat later; and it seems possible to treat it as a source—however theoretically distinctive—for many similar points about what the mind represses and how it speaks to itself.

The Epicurean view of the unconscious differs from Artemidoros' view in two crucial ways. First, it abjures the popular connection between the life of the sleeping or otherwise unconscious mind and future events. Dreams and other voices in the breast have significance as the record of habits and practices, as the signs of a bodily condition, or as the rehearsal of pervasive anxieties. These categories are connected in that the pervasive anxieties of the soul frequently record the habits of a religious society. Anxieties are not innate, but learned, and habits of discourse and thought form patterns of fear and longing. This focus on the present and the past of the soul might seem to make Epicurus' view incomparable with that of Artemidoros; for he might seem to be denying the existence of what Artemidoros calls *oneiroi*, and giving us an account merely of *enhupnia* and related phenomena, all of which Artemidoros found rather uninteresting. But a closer look shows, I think, that things are not this simple. For Epicurus' theory, like Artemidoros', concerns itself with a secret language of the soul, a complex internalized symbolism in which the mind discourses to itself about what profoundly matters to it. Epicurus, like Artemidoros, is not concerned merely with transient states of little depth. And, like Artemidoros, he is interested in that which is still at work powerfully within—so, once again, he is not focusing, any more than Artemidoros, on obvious repetitions of the day's activities and wishes.

The first major difference, then, is less major than it at first appears. The second is more substantial. This is that Epicurus uses his account of unconscious wishing and fearing to explain behavior in waking life. The Epicurean unconscious is active in sleep, but not in sleep alone. As people live their daily lives, the theory claims, they are influenced in a variety of ways by wishes of which they are not aware. These wishes can be brought to light by philosophical examination—and when they are, they will turn out to have broad explanatory significance. This extension of the unconscious' explanatory role, together with the complex Epicurean account of how such desires are properly unearthed and confronted, gives Epicurus a claim to be called the primary ancient forerunner of modern psychoanalysis. But his account, as we shall see, is most unpsychoanalytic in its concrete content.[22]

According to Epicurus, then, the mind speaks to itself about what it most deeply wants and fears. And its deepest wants and fears concern its own finitude. The longing for immortality and the fear of death are at the heart of its discourse to itself (Nussbaum 1990d). This fear or longing is, as we shall shortly see, in the first place a response to the human child's perception of itself as powerless in a situation of great danger, as it emerges naked, hungry, needy, into the world. As the infant becomes increasingly aware, on the one hand, of its great weakness, and, on the other hand, of the delight of living, it develops, progressively, a desire to secure itself in life by protecting its fragile boundaries. This idea is pursued through various stratagems of aggression and self-fortification, described by Lucretius in convincing detail. Money-making, for example, is an attempt to fortify oneself against death, since poverty feels like a condition very vulnerable to death (Nussbaum 1990d). Warlike aggression is, once again, an attempt to make oneself invulnerable (Nussbaum 1990d, 1990b). The pursuit of honor and fame is a pursuit of one's own deathlessness, through securing power over one's society (Nussbaum 1990b). And finally, erotic love is, among its other features, a stratagem to solidify and secure oneself, by achieving a fusion with a person who is seen as an embodied divinity (Nussbaum 1989, 1990b). All of these stratagems are nourished by religious cult, which holds out the idea of an afterlife, further feeding both desire and fear. But in their basic form, such anxieties seem to belong to the condition of human life itself.

Lucretius makes it clear that most of the time people are unaware of the fears that are motivating their behavior. The "true voices" are buried "deep in the breast," beneath a "mask" of confidence (Nussbaum 1990d).

They say that they do not fear death—and yet their behavior betrays them. "Thus each person flees himself" (Lucretius III.1068)—and is aware, at most, of a sensation of great weight in the region of the breast. In moments of abrupt confrontation with the facts of one's condition, however, rationalization becomes no longer possible, and the true voices emerge. It is this possibility of a confrontation which brings confirmation of the fear from the patient herself that gives the hypothesis of unconscious fear—otherwise supported primarily through the linking of behavior patterns—such conviction and power (Nussbaum 1990d).

A central task of the Epicurean philosophical community is to diagnose and then to cure such anxieties, and the "boundless" longing that is linked with them. There is evidence that the community encouraged pupils to divulge their hidden thoughts and feelings to the teacher, in order to receive his philosophical criticism and therapy (Nussbaum 1986b, and 1994, ch. 4). The importance of this sort of "frank speech" is repeatedly stressed as an essential tool of therapy; and one's friends participate in the process, helping the teacher to know as much as possible about the structure of the pupil's illness. We know little about how the Epicurean teacher went about bringing repressed unconscious fears to the surface—but the many analogies between philosophical teaching and medical diagnosis show that they were well aware of this as a problem and investigated the resources of personal narrative with this in mind (Nussbaum 19866, 1994, ch. 4). Meanwhile, the school placed great emphasis on memorization and repetition, in order to drive the healthful teachings of Epicurus deep down into the soul, to a level at which they may even, as Lucretius reports, fill one's dreams (Nussbaum 19866, 1989). Memory and repetition are the student's ways of taking Epicurus into her unconscious, so that his teaching will "become powerful" (*Letter to Herodotus* 85) in her inner world, and can help her in her confrontation with error, even when she is not consciously focusing on the problem. Like Menoeceus, she "will never be disturbed either awake or asleep" (*Letter to Menoeceus* 132)—for the wise person, and that person alone, "will be the same when asleep" (Diogenes Laertius X 120), undisturbed by any flood of pent-up anxieties, such as those that occur in most people's lives. Memory makes philosophical discourse active and effective in the pupil's soul.

It should by now be apparent that, despite the differences in temporal orientation and normative structure, the Epicurean view has much in common with the popular beliefs summarized by Artemidoros. This should be no surprise, since Epicurus' therapeutic target is just such popular beliefs, and their deleterious effect on the mental life. What Artemidoros takes for granted and makes the subject of his trade, Epicurus wishes to cure by philosophical therapy. But the content is very much the same. In both cases, the human mind is seen as structured around a very general set of anxieties about one's limited control over one's worldly position. These anxieties are seen as to some extent very hard to avoid; for even Lucretius stresses that every living thing longs for the continuation of its life, and consequently shrinks from death (Nussbaum 1990d). But they are powerfully fed by cultural teaching in which great importance is attached to "external goods" that the pupil does not control. The mind obsessively broods about command over these goods; and it cooks up elaborate symbols to meditate about its future with respect to them (in the case of Artemidoros), or its present emotional states that relate it toward an uncertain future (in the case of Epicurus). For Epicurus, the mind goes still further, moving the agent to undertake projects of self-fortification in waking life, projects of whose real significance the agent is unaware, and which will not really achieve the deep goal for which the agent pursues them.

For Epicureans, as for Artemidoros, sex is just one element in this pursuit of control. Epicurus has little to say about sex in the surviving texts; but he clearly does not think of it as a very deep or central force in human life. The desire for sexual gratification is classified as a desire that is "natural but nonnecessary": i.e., one that is not merely the product of false social teaching, but one whose gratification is inessential to the good human life (Nussbaum 1989). In a famously odd passage, he ranks sexual enjoyments along with other indulgences in unnecessary luxury items:

> The truly pleasant life is not produced by an unbroken succession of drinking bouts and revels; not by the enjoyment of boys and women and fish and the other things that a luxurious table presents. It is produced by sober reasoning that seeks out the causes of all pursuit and avoidance and drives out the beliefs that are responsible for our greatest disturbances. (*Letter to Menoeceus* 132, see Nussbaum 1990c)

This passage presents Epicurus' view, not the popular views he criticizes. But still, it is evidence for his belief that in no person does sexual desire go, so to speak, to the very core of the personality. People may think sexual desire to be deeper than it is, just as they allegedly think the need for fish and meat to be deeper than it is. But, like other desires for luxuries, sexual desire is the sort of desire that can in fact be therapeutically removed, without injuring the personality in the process. Even culture, which ranks it too high, does not make it so central to the pupil's life that she will be injured by getting rid of it.

Thus even from the point of view of the cultural material that is internalized and buried in the average person's unconscious mind, sex apparently does not play a central role. Lucretius' famous critique of erotic love does show in detail how socially learned constructs of *erôs* influence both waking and sleeping life. But he does not seem, any more than Epicurus, to think of sex as offering a clue to the essence of the personality. He shows that the construction of love out of natural bodily desire is just a peculiar chapter in the soul's quest for transcendence of its mortal limits. For the wish of erotic desire, as I have said, is to achieve fusion with a partner who is seen as a goddess (Nussbaum 1989a, 1990c). The poet shows that this wish is the vehicle of a more general wish to transcend one's own finite mortal condition; its only remedy is to learn to "yield to human life," *humanis concedere rebus* (Lucretius V.1172). Erotic desire is a form of the basic desire to transcend one's limits and insecurities, achieving control and stability (Nussbaum 1990b).

Lucretius speaks of the family and its desires. But, once again, the treatment focuses on security rather than on sexuality. First of all, the relation between mother and child gets no special treatment in the poem. Both parents are believed to be intensely concerned about the survival and safety of their offspring; and the "softening" that comes about when they begin thinking of how to protect their vulnerable children is a major ingredient, the poem shows, in the development of morality and society (Nussbaum 1990b). But when the life of the infant itself is described, it is not the mother, but rather the nurse—as one might expect in this society, at least in the social classes who would be Lucretius' primary readers—who plays the central role. And in this relationship too, the issue is need and security, not sexuality. The infant, helpless and weeping from the disturbances of birth,

> like a sailor cast forth from the fierce waves, lies naked on the ground, without speech, in need of every sort of life-sustaining help, when first nature casts it forth with birth contractions from its mother's womb into the shores of light. And it fills the whole place with mournful weeping, as is right for someone to whom such troubles remain in life. (5.222–27)

The "gentle nurse" now calms the child with rattles and baby talk, ministering to its lack of self-sufficiency; and the poet bleakly remarks that the rougher, better equipped wild beasts have no need of such soothing amusements (229–30). The drama of infancy is a drama of vulnerability and protection. The infant's desire is for freedom from pain and disturbance. The world it encounters is a world that contains countless sources of pain and disturbance. Its central perception of itself is therefore as a being very weak and very helpless. And its relation to the adults around it focuses on its passionate desire to secure to itself what nature on the whole withholds: comfort, clothing, food, protection.

I believe that the Epicurean account of the predicament of the infant, and of the fruits of this predicament in later anxieties, provides a comprehensive explanatory underpinning for the popular beliefs about "external goods" that Artemidoros records.[23] It also provides what Artemidoros, given his practical professional goals, does not try to provide, an account of the early origins of later deep anxieties. The Epicurean analysis of the anxieties of most human beings, and of their roots in infancy, really does, it appears, get at what people were really most deeply and often unconsciously worrying about. This should not surprise us, since Epicurus insists that therapy cannot proceed without correct diagnosis; and Epicurus' greatness as a psychoanalyst has been remarked before. But if we put the theory together with the rich and concrete record of ordinary belief in Artemidoros, we have at least the basic outlines of a non-Freudian theory of infancy, and of later unconscious anxieties, fears, and hopes. This theory focuses on the human being's lack of natural security and on its consequently urgent needs for various external goods. Relations to parents and other close adults are understood as mediated by this general need. Adults are providers of what is needed, bulwarks against danger, sources of support.[24] In another connection Lucretius remarks that when protection fails on account or some act or nonact of another, the natural consequence will be anger and aggressive behavior. Although he does not apply this observation to the case of the infant, it would not be hard to do so.[25] Thus we would also have the basis for a complex and interesting account of aggressive wishes toward parents and other caretakers, when pain and disturbance are not warded off. But this aggression would have little to do with specifically sexual longing and jealousy, everything to do with the desire for security and control.[26] It would be a fascinating task to work out further the details of such a theory.[27]

OEDIPUS AND HIS FORTUNE

But now instead, all too briefly, I want to make some suggestions about ways in which this set of concerns might illuminate our approach to the *Oedipus Rex*. I have spoken elsewhere (Nussbaum 1986a, 1992) of the central role of tragedy in providing Greek citizens with a map of human possibilities, showing, as Aristotle says, "things such as might happen" (*Poetics* 9) in a human life. I have also said that tragedies frequently seem to do this by exploring extreme cases, nightmares, so to speak of the human attempt to live well in an insecure world (Nussbaum 1986a, ch. 13). I would now like to suggest that we might fruitfully approach the *Oedipus* as, so to speak, a dream issuing from the unconscious of its citizen watchers, but an unconscious of the ancient, rather than the Freudian, kind. What I mean is that if we ask ourselves how an ancient audience might actually see in the play a kind of possibility for themselves, connecting themselves to the characters through the emotions of pity and fear, which (as Aristotle persuasively says) require, both of them, the belief that one's own possibilities are the same as those of the protagonists—if one asks this question, one is bound to focus, not on the literal events of the play, but on what one might call their Artemidoran symbolism. In the world whose preoccupations I have tried to depict, an average member of the audience is very unlikely to believe it a salient possibility for himself that he would actually do what Oedipus does here, killing his father and marrying his mother. For one thing, the net of circumstances that brought this about in Oedipus' life is too strange and complex to be very likely to be replicated. But if, on the other hand, we see the literal events as representing, as in an Artemidoran dream, possibilities for the rise and fall of human fortunes, we can far more easily see what a citizen would find terrifying here. If someone who enjoys the extreme of control, prosperity, and in general good fortune can be so brought low by events and circumstances beyond his control, then no human life seems safe from this possibility. For most lives start out more vulnerable and less prosperous than his was. Such was, in fact, the understanding of the play put forward as the obvious one by a very perceptive ancient critic, namely, the Stoic philosopher Epictetus. Tragedies in general, he wrote, show "what happens when chance events befall fools"—by "fools" meaning human beings who attach value to items beyond their control (Nussbaum 1992, 1993). And seeing the fall of Oedipus should, he argues, remind us just how uncontrolled items like power, wealth, and family connections really are, giving us a motivation to sever our concern from such things and to adopt the austere values of Stoicism.

If one turns to the play with these ideas in mind, one is struck by the fact that while, on the one hand, *erôs* seems to be absent from it, *tuchê* is omnipresent.[28] Oedipus is introduced as *kratiston*, most powerful (40); and yet the city itself has been afflicted by forces beyond its control, so that the citizens can already be addressed as "pitiable children," *paides oiktroi*. At line 145, beginning on his fateful search for the causes of the pollution, Oedipus announces, "We shall either emerge fortunate (*eutucheis*), with the god's help, or as fallen (*peptôkotes*)." Immediately the Chorus, entering, begins to speak of its anxious fear and tension (151ff.). And of course, from the first, Oedipus is present to the audience (through his name alone) as a cripple, someone cast out naked into the world and maimed by its dangers, a Lucretian, rather than a Freudian, infant.

The detailed working-out of this reading must wait for another time. Its direction and outlines should already be clear. But I can end this adumbration of such a reading by mentioning that, whether the final lines are genuine or not, they suit admirably the focus of the play as a whole, and of this account: for they portray Oedipus as, on the one hand, successful and "most powerful," on the other, as one who "came into such a great tidal wave of misfortune." And their famous moral is the moral of so much of the ancient Greek ethical tradition, insofar as it does not reject the importance traditionally attached to external goods: "Call no mortal prosperous ... before he passes the end of his life having suffered nothing terrible" (1529–30).

What relationship might such a reading of the play—and, in general, such an account of the stresses of infancy and of unconscious fears, longings, and aggressions—have to psychoanalysis? I have spent most of this chapter showing how much ancient "psychoanalysis"—for I think we may call it that—diverges from a single-minded and possibly reductive concern with sexuality that we find in some parts of the Freudian tradition. Indeed, it seems to show the Freudian emphasis on sexuality as time-bound, the local feature of a society unusually anxious about this particular aspect of human life, and therefore in need of repression on that topic.

But there are other psychoanalytic approaches that seem far more in tune with the emphases and concerns of ancient psychology.[29] I plan in future work to compare the ideas I have just investigated with some of Melanie Klein's ideas about infancy and the genesis of fear and aggression—and with other related work in the object relations school. For while the Kleinian theory is still in some respects Freudian, her account of infancy endows it with complex relationships to objects, seen as providers or hinderers of support.[30] And usually the issue of the infant's great neediness and its inevitable pain and frustration is stressed in her writings far more than that of sexual desire *per se*. Her infant's relation to the breast that either feeds or fails to feed it could usefully be compared, I believe, to the Lucretian account of the genesis of aggressive wishes, particularly if we expand his account as I have suggested. And since the Kleinian picture of the infant's life endows it, early on, with the possibility of complex emotions such as fear, anger, and envy, once again this seems to invite comparison with the Epicurean account of similar material, and of its eventual repression. Even though Klein does pay homage to Freud concerning the primacy of sexual desire, it seems plain that most of the time her concern is with a broad range of needs and longings, most of them connected around the issue of self-sufficiency and incompleteness. Pursuing the comparison would be of interest, if only for comparison's sake.

But my real interest in it is a deeper one. For I believe that the ancient views I have discussed are profound and highly plausible in a way that goes beyond strict cultural boundaries; and yet, equally clearly, that they are culture-bound in certain ways, and lack, in some areas, a richness of development that would be required if they were ever to become powerful and plausible for a contemporary understanding. It might emerge, however, that the confrontation between these views and the modern views of thinkers such as Klein, Fairbairn, and Winnicott, and of both with the best of recent cognitively oriented work in experimental psychology, for example the work of Lazarus (1991) and Seligman (1975), might generate a philosophical theory of the human longing for control and self-sufficiency that would preserve the best features of both sources, and link them in a new account of fear, aggression, pity, and love.[31]

NOTES

1. For an excellent study of Artemidoros, to which I shall refer frequently in what follows, see Winkler (1990).

2. It is clear that both the dreamer and the dreamer's sexual partner may be either male or female: in this case as in many others, that does not affect the dream's significance. Here as elsewhere, the Greek uses but a single word for what we distinguish as fellatio and cunnilingus: *arrhêtopoiêsai*, "do the unmentionable." The operative distinction in Artemidoros' account is between its active and passive voices, as the dreamer either performs such activity or has it performed upon him/her.

3. This chapter was originally written for a conference on Sophocles' play and modern psychoanalysis; in this version I have chosen to retain the focus on this particular tragedy on account of the great influence of Freud's reading, although numerous texts could have done as well for my purposes.

4. It is paradigmatic of the type of action Aristotle calls involuntary out of excusable ignorance—*Nicomachean Ethics*, III.1. I discuss this case, with other references, in Nussbaum 1986a, ch. 9 and interlude 2. See also Sophocles' *Oedipus at Colonus*, where Oedipus describes his acts as involuntary: lines 1.70–74, 5211–49, 960–87, and cf. 1565.

5. On the issue in tragedy, see Nussbaum (1986a); and on the German critics, especially ch. 13.

6. I reviewed Volume 2 critically in Nussbaum (1985); the relevant point to emphasize here is that, by concentrating on philosophical writers such as Plato and Xenophon, and neglecting other more popular sources, such as the orators and Aristophanes, Foucault could only reach partial conclusions.

7. See also Price (1986).

8. For 1.78–80, I follow Winkler's translation (1990, 210–26); elsewhere the translations are my own where Winkler does not translate the passage, his when he does. This case is discussed (though not translated in full) in Winkler (1990, 29).

9. Freud is mistaken about this aspect of Artemidoros' theory, charging him with reading dreams according to a fixed universal key; see Winkler (1990, 29–30), referring to *Interpretation of Dreams* (Freud 1900, 98–99).

10. This shows the unfairness of Freud's critique of Artemidoros for neglecting interconnections among dream images.

11. Here we find confirmation of the cultural view in accordance with which the young males who are the objects of (older) male desire—the *erômenoi*—are not thought to feel sexual desire themselves (or at least, this is the cultural norm—Dover 1978; Halperin 1990). This is why sexual dreams belong to a later time of life. Of course a young person might still use sexual imagery to signify some underlying anxiety; but I think that it is Artemidoros' point that the signifiers have to be familiar from experience, in order to establish their connections with the deeper signified.

12. On the study of children and their inclinations in ancient thought, see Brunschwig (1986). On the appeal to the nature of the child as part of Epicurean ethical argument, see Nussbaum (1994, chs. 4, 12) and the earlier version of the argument in Nussbaum (1986b).

13. See also Winkler (1990, 26–27, 33ff.).

14. Friendships are, for Aristotle, constituents of *eudaimonia*, not just external instruments. Money, property, etc. are instrumentally valuable. Virtuous action, the primary constituent(s) of *eudaimonia*, is not called an "external good," since it is caused by virtuous traits of character, which are within the agent's own control. Strictly speaking, however, it can be impeded by fortune—by the absence of some of the usual "external goods."

15. Central in such projects is usually the claim that virtue is sufficient for *eudaimonia*—this idea is defended, it seems, by Socrates, Plato, and the Greek and Roman Stoics.

16. On this see "The Democratic Body," in Halperin (1990). On sex as an aspect of the public sphere, see also Winkler (1990, 27).

17. Of course, strictly speaking, anxiety is what is signified by a dream, not the signifier in a dream. But Artemidoros seems to suggest that experiences that are themselves sources of anxiety (baldness for example) will naturally serve a signifiers for other deeper fears.

18. See Abelove (1993) for references to Freud's correspondence on this point.

19. Penetration is the fundamental sex act for the Greeks—see Winkler (1990, passim); Halperin (1990). So fundamental is it that a sex act between two women can only be imagined as (per impossibile) a form of penetration; and it is for this reason that the act seems to require an alteration in the laws of nature.

20. It is noteworthy here that Artemidoros does not dwell often on the anti-conventional or illicit status of incestuous intercourse, which might have been a way of linking incest with external fortunes without focusing centrally on its sexual wish-content. This, I think, is the direction Plato takes in the passage on dreaming in *Republic* IX, where he speaks of the incest dream as something that appetite will contrive, unfettered by reason: in other words, unfettered by reason, appetite is altogether lawless.

21. For further discussion of this point, see Nussbaum (1990), and Nussbaum (1994, ch. 4).

22. Fuller development of the account presented here is found in Nussbaum (1989 1990d, 1990b, 1990c, and 1994, chs. 4–7). (Ch. 5 is a later version of 1989a, ch. 6 of 1990d, ch. 7 of 1990b.) All of these articles contain full references to the relevant ancient texts, and to the secondary literature.

23. We arrive here at a complex issue in Epicurus' thought. For to the extent that he presents the concern for externals as motivated by an appropriate and more or less inevitable concern for one's own safety, he would appear to endorse these concerns, or at

least some of them, as rational. On the other hand, he is determined to reject most of the concerns society actually has for these goods—including all anxious concern about death—as irrational. The difficulties this creates for his project are analyzed in Nussbaum (1990d, 1990b).

24. Compare the view of animals and infants in Lazarus (1991) and the related observations in Bowlby (1982, 1973, 1980).

25. See especially Bowlby (1973), Klein (1984, 1985). On Lucretius, see Nussbaum (1990b).

26. On the enormous importance of control for the emotional life of both animals and humans, see the remarkable analysis in Seligman (1975).

27. This is what I am trying to do in *Need and Recognition: A Theory of the Emotions*, The Gifford Lectures for 1993.

28. *Tuchê* designates those aspects of life that human beings do not control: it means "luck" in that sense, not in the sense of "randomness."

29. Indeed, cognitive psychology is now to a great extent converging with psychoanalysis on this point—see Lazarus (1991); Seligman (1975); Oatley (1992).

30. Klein (1984, 1985), Fairbairn (1952). The same is true of the theory of emotion now most favored in cognitive psychology: see Lazarus (1991); Ortony, Clore, and Collins (1988); Oatley (1992).

31. This chapter was originally presented at Cornell University at a conference on the *Oedipus Rex* and modern psychoanalysis. I wish to thank Phillip Mitsis for the invitation, and for helpful comments. I am also grateful to Myles Burnyeat and Peter Rudnytsky for their suggestions.

BIBLIOGRAPHY

Abelove, H. (1993). "Freud, Male Homosexuality, and the Americans," in *The Lesbian and Gay Studies Center Reader*, ed. H. Abelove, M. A. Barale, D. M. Halperin. New York: Routledge, 381–93.

Artemidoros. 1963. *Artemidori Daldiani Onirocriticon Libri V*, ed. R. A. Pack. Leipzig: Teubner.

Bowlby, J. 1973 *Separation: Anxiety and Anger*. New York: Basic Books.

———. 1980. *Loss: Sadness and Depression*. New York: Basic Books.

———. 1982. *Attachment*, 2d ed. New York: Basic Books.

Brunschwig, J. 1986. The Cradle Argument in Epicureanism and Stoicism. In *The Norms of Nature*, ed. M. Schofield and G. Striker. Cambridge: Cambridge Univ. Press, 113–44!

Diogenes Laertius. *Lives of the Philosophers*, ed. and trans. R. D. Hicks, Vol. 2. Loeb Classical Library. Cambridge, MA: Harvard Univ. Press, 1979.

Dover, K. J. 1978. *Greek Homosexuality*. Cambridge, MA: Harvard Univ. Press.

Fairbairn, W.R.D. 1952. *Psychoanalytic Studies of the Personality*. London: Tavistock.

Foucault, M. 1985. *The Use of Pleasure (The History of Sexuality*, Vol. 2), trans. R. Hurley. New York: Pantheon.

———. 1986. *The Care of the Self (The History of Sexuality*, Vol. 3), trans. R. Hurley, New York: Pantheon.

Freud, S. 1990. *The Interpretation of Dreams*. In *The Standard Edition of the Complete Psychological Works*, ed. and trans. J. Strachey et al., 24 vols. London: Hogarth Press, 1953–74, Vols. 4 and 5.

Halperin, D. 1990. *One Hundred Years of Homosexuality and Other Essays on Greek Love*. New York: Routledge.

Henderson, J.J. 1975. *The Maculate Muse: Obscene Language in Attic Comedy*. New Haven: Yale Univ. Press.

Klein, M. 1984. *Envy and Gratitude and Other Works, 1946–1963*. London: Hogarth.

———. 1985. *Love, Guilt, and Reparation and Other Works, 1921–1945*. London: Hogarth.

Lazarus, R. 1991. *Emotion and Adaptation*. New York: Oxford Univ. Press.

Nussbaum, M. 1985. Review of Foucault. *New York Times Book Review*, November 10.

———. 1986a. *The Fragility of Goodness: Luck and Ethics in Greek Tragedy and Philosophy*. Cambridge: Cambridge Univ. Press.

———. 1986b. Therapeutic Arguments: Epicurus and Aristotle. *The Norms of Nature*, ed. M. Schofield and G. Striker. Cambridge: Cambridge Univ. Press, 31–74.

———. 1989. Beyond Obsession and Disgust: Lucretius' Genealogy of Love. *Apeiron* 22:1–59.

———. 1990a. Review of Halperin 1990 and Winkler 1990. *Times Literary Supplement*, June.

———. 1990b. "By Words, Not Arms": Lucretius on Anger and Aggression. In *The Poetics of Therapy*, ed. M. Nussbaum, *Apeiron* 23:41–90.

———. 1990c. Therapeutic Arguments and Structures of Desire. *Differences* 2: 46–66. (Volume on *Society and Sexuality in Ancient Greece and Rome*, ed. D. Konstan and M. Nussbaum.)

———. 1990d. Mortal Immortals: Lucretius on Death and the Voice of Nature. *Philosophy and Phenomenological Research* 50:303–51.

———. 1992. Tragedy and Self-Sufficiency: Plato and Aristotle on Fear and Pity. Long version in *Oxford Studies in Ancient Philosophy* 10. Short version in *Essays on Aristotle's Poetics*, ed. A. Rorty. Princeton: Princeton Univ. Press, pp 261–90.

———. 1993. Poetry and the Passions: Two Stoic Views. In *Passions & Perceptions*, ed. J. Brunschwig and M. Nussbaum. Cambridge: Cambridge Univ. Press.

———. 1994. *The Therapy of Desire: Theory and Practice in Hellenistic Ethics*. Princeton: Princeton Univ. Press.

Oatley, K. 1992. *Best Laid Schemes: The Psychology of Emotions*. Cambridge: Cambridge Univ. Press.

Ortony, A., Clore, G.L., and Collins, A. 1988. *The Cognitive Structure of Emotions*. Cambridge: Cambridge Univ. Press.

Price, S. 1986. "The Future of Dreams: From Freud to Artemidorus," *Past and Present*, 113:3–37. Rpt. in Halperin, D., Winkler, J., and Zeitlin, F., eds., *Before Sexuality: The Construction of Erotic Experience in the Ancient Greek World*. Princeton: Princeton Univ. Press, 1989.

Rudnytsky, P. 1987. *Freud and Oedipus*. New York: Columbia Univ. Press.

Seligman, M.E.P. 1975. *Helplessness: On Depression, Development, and Death*. New York: Freeman.

Winkler, J.J. 1990. *The Constraints of Desire: The Anthropology of Sex and Gender in Ancient Greece*. New York: Routledge.

JONATHAN LEAR

Knowingness and Abandonment:
An Oedipus for Our Time

This conference is not only about what psychoanalysis can contribute to culture, but about what culture can contribute to psychoanalysis. This is a relief. For the psychoanalytic profession has for too long clung to a defense which is, by now, outworn and boring: namely, the stance that psychoanalysis has a special secret to give to culture. For about fifty years, the profession acted out its own identification with Oedipus, pretending to have solved the riddle of the unconscious. This is ironic because this stance is an *exploitation* of the transference—analysts putting themselves forward as possessors of esoteric knowledge—whereas the whole point of analysis is to *analyze* the transference. Analysts portrayed themselves as "already knowing" the secret, whereas what makes analysis special is its unique form of not already knowing. No wonder the culture became suspicious. And analysts, for their part, fell into confusion and frustration that their "message" was not being received with awe, wonder, respect. In retrospect, one can see that this exploitation of the transference had self-defeat built right into it.

Analysis is not essentially a body of esoteric knowledge; it is a peculiar form of mental activity, a peculiar form of speaking and listening, a peculiar form of life. Above all, it involves a certain form of listening: listening to oneself, listening to another. And if we listen to the culture with an analytic ear, we can gain insight both into the culture and into our fundamental

From *Open Minded: Working Out the Logic of the Soul* by Jonathan Lear, pp. 32–55. © 1998 by the President and Fellows of Harvard College.

psychoanalytic myths. It is in listening to the culture that I have found a way to reinterpret the Oedipus myth, the archaic myth of psychoanalysis.

If one reads the newspapers, follows the news, one can quickly come to see that there is a crisis of knowingness in the culture. I shall begin with the current flap over campaign finance, not because it is fundamental in itself, but because it is happening this week. It is the cultural equivalent of what an analysand brings into a session on any given day. No matter when this conference occurred, there would be something in that week's newspapers which was symptomatic.

In the campaign-finance scandal, one can watch the culture slowly waking up. Before the election, it was virtually only William Safire who had the audacity to intimate a corrupt "Asian connection"; then other journalists joined in as ever more instances of corruption were brought to light; but political commentators are baffled, and somewhat irritated, that—to this date, at least—President Clinton's standing in the polls has not been dented. Of course, that may well change. But so far, Clinton can still stand before the nation and do his bring-us-all-together, focus-on-the-larger-issues shtick; he can even righteously call for campaign-finance reform; and, though he drives Maureen Dowd wild, he can, for the moment at least, get away with it. How come? Basically, the public feels it *already knows* that campaign finance is corrupt. The public attitude so far has been: so what's new? Here we can see how the stance of "already knowing" functions as a defense: if you already know, you do not need to find out. And Clinton is masterful in exploiting this defense. It is often thought that we have *discovered* that Clinton is a bit of a con man, but this cannot be the whole truth. Clinton *presents himself* as a bit of a con man—and this is enormously reassuring. For if *he* is willing to let us know that he's conning us, then, in an odd sort of way, he emerges as trustworthy: we can *count on him* to engage in a bit of sleaze when our backs are turned. And when some bit of sleaze does emerge, the public has a sense of "already knowing" he was up to some such thing. And I suspect the Clinton campaign thought it could get away with its dubious fundraising because it knew that the public "already knew"—and thus wouldn't care.

If this defense is going to collapse, it will be around anxious intimations that we don't "already know." Here are two places where one can see anxiety starting to break through: First, in the idea that this is an *Asian* connection. For beneath the legitimate surface concerns that a foreign country may have been trying to affect electoral outcome, there is the cultural phantasy of the inscrutable Oriental. And this image has its own *phantastic a priori*: it's built into the very idea of the Inscrutable Oriental that we couldn't possibly "already know" what they are up to. That's what it is to be inscrutable. And that's why Clinton's blanket reassurance—you know me, I'm just an honest con man, trying to get by—can't possibly extend to cover an Asian connection. A priori, we cannot possibly "already know" the inner workings of an Asian connection: this is part of the logic of the inscrutable.[1]

The second moment of anxiety comes in the revelation of an active disruption in the flow of knowledge between the FBI and the White House. FBI agents informed two lower-level members of the National Security Council of an investigation into an Asian connection, but told them not to inform anyone higher up. Here the public cannot possibly assume it "already knows" what is going on: for this is a scenario which dramatizes *not* already knowing. No one can say with any confidence who "already knows" what is going on—indeed, if there is anyone who "already knows." This has to provoke anxiety and fascination that the order of knowingness has been disrupted.

Here I am reminded of that rapidly receding moment of public fascination with Dick Morris' adultery. The moment passed quickly—Morris was able to command a two-million-dollar advance yet not able to sell any books—but, still, it is worth thinking about why there was any moment at all. On its own, the idea that a political consultant holed up in a Washington hotel suite, with his wife tucked safely away in Connecticut, should have an affair with a prostitute is hardly news. It can almost be deduced a priori from the idea of a political consultant. On its own, it is one big yawn. What fascinated press and public was that in this incident there was confusion as to who was already in the know. The prostitute was not merely a prostitute; she was a prostitute keeping a secret diary. Even before her toes dried, the incident was being recorded unbeknownst to a man whose job it is to be in the know. And, of course, the political consultant was keeping his own diary, unbeknownst to the president he was supposedly serving. And the president ... well, who knows? It seemed as though there were unplumbable depths of broken trusts. And the established order of knowingness was disturbed in countless ways.

* * *

Now when the order of knowingness is undisturbed—when the culture can rest in its phantasy of "already knowing"—there is a widespread sense of boredom and irritation. One has only to read the political columns in the newspapers leading up to the last election: columnists registered crescendos of frustration that this was a campaign designed so that there should be no surprises.[2] What bothered the commentators, I suspect, was a sense that their boredom was the product of a successful campaign.

But if journalists are bored silly by already being in the know, hell hath no fury like journalists who discover they are not. Here is one delicious symptom. In 1995 Random House published *Primary Colors*, a political novel about a southern governor's campaign for president. The novel, whose author was Anonymous, shot to the top of the best-seller list, and there was much fascinated speculation about who Anonymous might be. Anonymous even wrote an essay for the *New York Times Book Review* explaining why he or she had decided to be and to remain anonymous. In the winter of 1996, *New York Magazine* published an article by an English professor at Vassar claiming that, on the basis of linguistic analysis, Anonymous must be the political commentator Joe Klein. Klein energetically denied the charge until the summer, when the *Washington Post* ran a story saying that the handwritten corrections on a galley proof of *Primary Colors* matched Klein's handwriting. He then 'fessed up.

The immediate result was a firestorm of moralizing denunciation in the press. The *New York Times*, for example, deemed it fit to run a major editorial on the subject titled "The Color of Mendacity." Here is a selection from that editorial:

> it is shameless of Mr. Klein to excuse his falsehoods as similar to the protection of confidential sources. "There are times," he said, "when I've had to lie to protect a source, and I put that in this category."
>
> In fact, principled journalists do not lie to protect sources. They rely on constitutional and statutory guarantees of journalistic privilege. Scores of reporters have maintained silence, sometimes to the point of going to jail, and their publications have spent a lot of money to defend the confidentiality guarantee in court. But they do so without lying. To try to stretch a noble doctrine to excuse a duplicitous book-selling scheme is irresponsible and disreputable ...
>
> Mr. Klein wants his colleagues to view his actions as a diverting and highly profitable whimsy. But he has held a prominent role in his generation of political journalists. For that reason, people interested in preserving the core values of serious journalism have to view his actions and words as corrupt and—if they become an example to others—corrupting.[3]

Strong words. Strong feelings. But they don't altogether make sense. I have no interest in defending Mr. Klein, and there is no doubt that Mr. Klein did not handle the whole situation well, but I find this reaction startling. First, we may want to make it a tautology that "principled journalists do not lie to protect sources," but this pompous moralizing covers over a wealth of complex relations which journalists regularly maintain with the truth. Of course, there are a handful of cases in which a journalist went to court, and even to jail, to protect the confidentiality of a source. But in the world of political journalism, it is a commonplace that not only can politicians, advisers, lobbyists speak to journalists "off the record," but the very fact that they have had "off-the-record" conversations, "deep background" briefings, and so on is itself kept "off the record." As a result, stories regularly appear which look as though they are a general surveying of the political scene when in fact they are a reaction to and outgrowth of a few privileged conversations. This is a form of misleading the reader about sources which everyone knows about and few mind. It is an everyday form of deception which the *New York Times* tolerates, if not encourages.

But, second, when Mr. Klein lied it was not about any journalistic fact, source, or story, but as an expression of his desire to protect his anonymity as the author of a novel. Why should we expect an author who publishes a book anonymously and who writes an essay explaining his desire to protect his privacy to tell the truth when he is asked about his authorship? From what pulpit can one so *clearly* see that the public's right to know, or a journalist's right to a straight answer from a fellow journalist, always trumps the right to privacy? In normal social life, we recognize that if we don't want our friends and neighbors to lie to us, there are certain questions we just don't ask. By and large, we don't ask people how much money they earn or whether they have satisfying sex lives. And there is only one person in the country about whom we feel we have the right to ask whether he is having an affair: the president of the United States. (Incidentally, I have been told that a number of Mr. Klein's friends refrained from asking him whether he was Anonymous because they didn't want to put him in the embarrassing position of having to lie to them.)

Suppose Mr. Klein had added a prefatory remark to his book: "Because I want to protect my privacy I have decided to publish this book anonymously. This has the unfortunate consequence that should you ask me directly about it, I shall have to lie. I am sorry about that, but one solution is: don't ask!" Would *that* have made everything all right? And, implicitly, isn't that what he *did* do, by publishing the book anonymously?

I mention this example because I think that the moral outrage about Joe Klein's lie is serving as a rationalizing defense, hiding emotions that are less well understood. If boredom and irritation accompany the claim to already know, the violation of the presumption to already know is met with moralizing fury. It seems almost as though a taboo has been violated.

Of course, these examples are anecdotal and by themselves prove nothing, but if you look around for yourselves I think you will see that other examples abound.[4]

* * *

I hope enough has been said to suggest to you that there is something funny going on with "knowingness" in the culture, something we do not understand very well. With this puzzlement in mind, I think we can go back and read *Oedipus Tyrannus* as the fundamental myth of knowingness. Before offering an interpretation, I should like to make two preliminary remarks.

First, a word of warning. It is a symptom of our age that there is what one might call *the fundamental transference-trap of interpretation*. This manifests itself as a sense that, in offering an interpretation, there is no escape from making one of two choices: either one presents oneself as offering the real truth, about Oedipus, say; *or* one says that one's interpretation is one among many good-enough interpretations. On the first choice, one is forced to imitate Oedipus, and pretend to guess and reveal the secret of the text. Shrinking from that absurd fate, one feels compelled to adopt a wishy-washy relativism, and try to put a brave or playful face on it. Must life be so impoverished? Obviously, I think the answer is no. The sense that this is our only choice should show us that we are living in a constricted universe of possibilities. The interpretation which follows should be thought of as falling on neither side of this false dichotomy. The point is neither to reveal the hidden secret of Oedipus nor to add one more interpretation to the good-enough pile, but to invite one to see something which is right there in the text.

Second, it might help to open up the space of interpretation if we begin, in true oedipal fashion, by killing off Freud's Oedipus. We cannot begin to appreciate the meaning of Oedipus if we continue to think that Oedipus was oedipal.[5] According to Freud, Oedipus acts out unconscious childhood wishes which we all share—to possess one parent and get rid of the other. And the fact that we all have such wishes accounts for the deep resonance the play has for us—according to Freud.[6] The proper response to this reading is embarrassingly simple: there is no evidence for it. Oedipus does kill his father, marry his mother, and have children with her. But none of this can be used to support Freud's reading; these are the facts his account is supposed to explain. Freud needs to show that these events occur *because* Oedipus has oedipal wishes. Not only does Freud make no effort to do so— he simply points to the Oedipus myth—there are in the text no hints of oedipal wishes. Of course, if one is already convinced of the oedipal reading of the Oedipus myth, one will see the entire play as providing evidence. And it will seem satisfactory simply to point to the play. However, as soon as one takes one skeptical step backward and asks the question "How do we know that in acting this way Oedipus is acting out *oedipal* phantasies, as opposed to some other phantasy?" one comes to see that the surface evidence of the text points in another direction.

This in no way counts against the psychological reality of the oedipus complex; just the opposite. It is precisely because the oedipal configuration is so prominent in so many that it has been possible for a generation of readers to see Oedipus as oedipal. And it is a virtue of Freud's account that it attempts to explain why the drama continues to move us.

People tend to be at their most parochial when they speculate about the human condition. For it is here that they challenge themselves to wander over all of human being, and in the effort make it clear how incapable they are of doing so. Freud thought he had found something universal about the human condition, and he took it as evidence in favor that the same universal could be found back in Sophocles' play. But Freud assumes that this universal is *psychological*—a configuration of wishes *inside the psyche*—and he here shows himself to be a child of the modern world. For Sophocles, "the human condition" did not point inevitably to the human psyche, but to the objective conditions in which humans had to live. It is the human condition to have to live out a fate. And—at least, from the ancient tragic perspective—fate is part of the basic fabric of the world. It is taken to be as fundamental an aspect of the world as we take gravity to be—only, unlike gravity, fate is impossible to defy. Sophocles was wrong that fate is basic to the world, Freud was wrong that the oedipus complex is a psychological universal, and I do not intend to enter a mug's game of trying to come up with some other candidate for the human condition. Rather, there are certain themes in the Oedipus drama which reverberate with our age, and we would do well to listen to them.

Oedipus is not the king. He is *the tyrant*. This is a crucial distinction. It is reflected in Sophocles' title *Oedipus Tyrannus*, and it is flattened in the Latin translation *Oedipus Rex*, and then in the English *Oedipus the King*. For Oedipus to be king, he and the Theban citizens would have to understand that he is the son and heir of King Laius. His claim to the throne would then *run through his blood*. The actual claim he makes on the throne *runs through his mind*. It is he who solved the riddle of the Sphinx and saved Thebes from disaster. Thebes lacked a king, and they thought there was no heir, so the citizens made Oedipus tyrant by acclamation. The king is dead! Long live the tyrant! For the ancient Greeks, "tyrant" did not only have the negative meaning it has for us today; it also referred to a leader who did not inherit the throne along traditional bloodlines.[7] In the case of Oedipus, the fact that he is tyrant means that he comes as close as was possible in ancient Thebes to being its democratically elected leader. And he gains his position on the basis of his achievements—of *what he does*—rather than on the basis of any given sense of *who he is*. In the modern world, the very idea of an inherited claim to rule has fallen into disrepute—though when one observes the public fascination with JFK Jr. one can see that though the cultural superego disapproves of the *idea*, the impulse is still there. In ancient Thebes, the idea had not been challenged, but Thebes had nevertheless been thrown into a proto-modern situation: it had to devise some *other* form of legitimate rule. The riddle of political legitimacy is more puzzling than the riddle of the Sphinx, but Oedipus solves both for the Thebans at one blow: in solving the riddle of the Sphinx, Oedipus becomes Thebes's savior. There is no further question of who should rule.

Oedipus' legitimacy flows from success. Oedipus solidifies his position by marrying the queen and having children by her, but, at bottom, everyone knows that his only real claim on the Thebans is his ability to protect them. And so, when, a generation later, Thebes is struck with miasma, it is only natural that the citizens should turn to him, "the first of men, both in the incidents of life and in dealing with the higher powers" (lines 33–34).[8] Now, the only evidence of divine favor is his practical success. It is not as though prophets have come forward saying the gods have ordained that Oedipus should rule; nor have the oracles been properly consulted to determine whether it is a good idea for Oedipus to marry the queen and assume the throne. In effect, the Thebans have taken practical success to be a sign of divine favor. They *think* there are two conditions which make Oedipus first among men—worldly success and divine favor—but there is only one. Should Oedipus start to flub the incidents of life, there is no way he could say, "Well, yes, but I'm *still* first in dealing with the higher powers."

Oedipus is clearer about this than are the citizens of Thebes. When he gets into a quarrel with the prophet Tiresias, he says angrily:

> Why, come tell me, how can you be a true prophet? Why when the versifying hound was here did you not speak some word that could release the citizens? Indeed, her riddle was not one for the first comer to explain! It required prophetic skill, and you were exposed as having no knowledge from the birds or from the gods. No, it was I that came, Oedipus who knew nothing, and put a stop to her; *I hit the mark by native wit, not by what I learned from birds*. (390–398; emphasis added)

Oedipus takes his success with the Sphinx to rest entirely on his ability to think things through. He accepts the responsibility as well as the praise: for

Oedipus, his triumph has sprung full-grown from his own mind. But if his mind is the source of his legitimacy, that inevitably puts him in a delicate position, for he has nothing else to fall back on other than his own resources. So when the citizens of Thebes make this plea, "Best of living men, raise up the polis!" (49), there is an implicit "or else." Oedipus' position rests on his ability to deliver Thebans from harm. Much has been made of Oedipus' steadfast determination to solve the riddle of the miasma, as though it reveals his strength of character—and it may well do so. But it is also true that if he cannot do so, he has little other claim on them.

More than any other figure in the ancient world, Oedipus is the self-made man. At birth he is abandoned by his parents, given to a shepherd to be exposed to die on a mountain. Later he abandons what he (mistakenly) takes to be his natural family, social position, and inherited claim to the throne in Corinth, and, through solving the Sphinx's riddle, he thinks his way into a new family, new social position, new throne. The very first word of the play reveals how far Oedipus thinks his mind can go in creating the world around him. "Children!" Oedipus addresses the suppliants assembled in front of the palace. Oedipus has made them into his "children" by becoming tyrant of Thebes; he has made the polis into his family. From Sophocles' perspective, of course, this is outrageous impiety: the family is part of the natural order, a sacred unit, and it is hubristic idiocy to assume one can simply make one, like an artifact. But looking back from this perspective, Oedipus looks like an intimation of postmodernity, refusing to take any category, even the family, as simply given. The bitter irony, of course, is that, unbeknownst to him or the Thebans, these are his "children," the polis *is* his family: Oedipus ought to be recognized as the king, the blood ruler, not merely as the tyrant he and the citizens take him to be. As it is, Oedipus, with some plausibility, takes himself to have got where he is by the clever use of human reason.

Oedipus also displays a "knowingness" eerily reminiscent of contemporary culture's demand to already know. When Oedipus asks a question, he takes himself to know the answer. So, for example, when Oedipus asks his "children" why they have come, and they describe the miasma which has overcome the city, he says, "I am not ignorant of the desires with which you have come; yes, I know that you are all sick" (59–61). He expected their plea and has already sent his brother-in-law, Creon, to Delphi to consult the oracle. But there is a sickness in this "knowingness": reason is being used to jump ahead to a conclusion, as though there is too much anxiety involved in simply asking a question and waiting for the world to answer. On the few occasions when someone challenges Oedipus' claim to already know—the prophet Tiresias, Creon, and the Messenger—Oedipus explodes with anger and suspicion.

Consider the dustup with Tiresias. Creon returns with the message that the murderer of Laius is alive and well in Thebes, and that until he is found and expelled, there will be pollution in the city. A practical task has now been set. The prophet has been summoned for help, but he will not speak. "You will find it easier to bear your fate and I mine," he says to Oedipus, "if you do as I say" (320–321). A puzzling remark; but instead of following the advice or inquiring into its meaning, Oedipus explodes. There is, for Oedipus, no imaginative space to envisage the situation as anything other than a practical problem; and, as they say, if you're not part of the solution, you're part of the problem. Tiresias is blocking his way, refusing to let him "knowingly" leap to a practical conclusion. Oedipus interprets it as an aggressive act and strikes a retaliatory blow: "I am so angry that I will leave unsaid nothing of what I understand!" (345). In other words, anger breaks down Oedipus' inhibition—and what pours forth is a paranoid delusion that Tiresias himself had a hand in the murder and then conspired with Creon, for mercenary reasons, to blame Oedipus. Nothing could be more absurd than to charge this otherworldly prophet with such crass and mundane motives, but Oedipus finds his own phantastic way of leaping to this conclusion anyway. *Inside* Oedipus' phantasy, the charge looks reasonable: so not only can Oedipus feel righteous in his anger; he can also attack the challenge to his claim to already know.[9]

But whatever Oedipus *says* about his *reason* for anger, what he *puts on display* is the same movement of soul which led him to kill his father. Laius blocked his physical path to Thebes, Tiresias blocks his mental path to a conclusion, and in each case Oedipus strikes a retaliatory blow. In his attack on Tiresias, Oedipus *acts out* the murder of his father even as he inquires into it. On each of these occasions, he is under so much pressure to get to his conclusion that there is no time to grasp the full meaning of what he is doing.

Here we can see one way in which the determination to know can be used to obscure any possibility of finding out. Oedipus does not have to inquire into Tiresias' silence, because he already knows. And what he purportedly knows is that Tiresias is a fraud. There is no room within this delusion to see Tiresias as a vehicle of a meaning he doesn't yet grasp, no room for the possibility that the world is different from what he takes it to be. The delusion turns Tiresias into a "crafty beggar, who has sight only when it comes to profit" (388): it paints him not only with base, but with *mundane* motives. The space of inquiry has collapsed, it has imploded into one point: that which Oedipus, in his "knowingness," takes himself already to know. And there is no place for a challenge to Oedipus' "reasonableness" to take hold. Oedipus admits as much himself. Creon pleads with Oedipus to hear him out, and to think about how unreasonable the conspiracy charge laid against him is. Oedipus responds: "I am a poor listener to you, for I have found you to be a bitter enemy to me" (545). Because he has already "figured out" that Creon is part of the conspiracy, Oedipus doesn't have to listen to what he says.

Even when he isn't angry, there is a flatness in his reasoning. With the Sphinx, Oedipus may have "hit the mark by native wit," but he didn't understand it. He treats the Sphinx's riddle as a straightforward puzzle—though one in which the stakes are very high (as though it were set by an archvillain)—ignoring any sacred dimension or oracular meaning which would require interpretation. And he therefore fails to see that if "human" is the solution to the riddle, *he is not part of the solution.* The Sphinx had famously asked: "What walks on four legs in the morning, two legs in the afternoon, and three legs in the evening?" But Oedipus walked on three legs in the morning (because his legs were pinned together), limped in the afternoon, and walked on four legs in the evening (blind, he is led by his daughter Antigone). Oedipus is someone who can jump to the conclusion of a riddle and still not get it. If he grasped the riddle's irony, he would recognize that he is a perversion of "human."

Consider Oedipus' own account of how he got to Thebes. As he explains to his wife, Iocaste, Oedipus was brought up in Corinth, the son of King Polybus and Merope. He was "the greatest of citizens" until this chance occurrence: at a dinner party a drunk told him he was not his father's child.

> *I was riled, and for that day scarcely controlled myself;* and on the next I went to my mother and my father and questioned them; and they made the man who had let slip the word pay dearly for the insult. So far as concerned them I was comforted, but *still this continued to vex me, since it constantly recurred to me.* Without the knowledge of my mother and my father I went to Pytho, and Phoebus *sent me away cheated* of what I had come for, but came out with other things terrible and sad for my unhappy self, saying that I was destined to lie with my mother, and to show to mortals a brood they could not bear to look on, and I should be the murderer of my father who had begotten me.
>
> *When I heard this, I left the land of Corinth,* henceforth making out its position by the stars, and *went where I could never see accomplished the shameful predictions of my cruel oracles.* And I will tell you the truth, lady! When I was walking near this meeting of three roads, I was met by a herald and a man riding in a wagon, such as you describe; and the leader and the old man himself tried to drive me from the road by force. In anger I struck the driver,

the man who was trying to turn me back; and when the old man
saw it, he waited till I was passing his chariot and struck me right
on the head with his double-pointed goad. Yet he paid the penalty
with interest; in a word, this hand struck him with a stick, and he
rolled backwards right out of the wagon, and I killed them all. But
if this foreigner had any tie with Laius, who could be more
miserable, and who more hateful to the gods, than I. (779–816;
emphasis added)

In other words, Oedipus goes to Delphi because he is troubled by remarks
impugning his parentage, but as soon as he hears the oracle he treats it as a
simple fact that Polybus and Merope are his parents.

I have daydreamed about meeting Oedipus on the road from Delphi to
Thebes. Somehow I am able to avoid his blows, and I get to ask him this
question: "Given that you went to Delphi because you were troubled by a
remark that Polybus wasn't really your father, why do you respond to the
oracle by fleeing Corinth?" Oedipus can give no coherent answer. If he
wasn't troubled about who his father was, he had no reason to go to the
Delphic oracle; if he was troubled, he shouldn't simply have assumed that
Polybus was his father. Note that his acts are incoherent not only from our
point of view; they are incoherent from what would be his point of view, if
only he could focus on the problem. Oedipus is suffering *reflexive breakdown*:
he cannot give a coherent account of what he is doing. But he can't focus on
the breakdown—and thus remains unconscious of it—because he is too busy
thinking. He assumes he *already knows* what the problem is; the only issue is
how to avoid it. What he misses completely is the thought that his
"knowingness" lies at the heart of his troubles: what he doesn't know is that
he doesn't know.

When Oedipus hears the oracle, he has no reason to move in any
direction at all. But he assumes he already knows the geography of his
sorrow: where in physical space his troubles are located and where he can get
away from them. Oedipus decides to flee Corinth as a strategy for evading
the oracle. Of course, from an ancient Greek perspective, it is absurd for
Oedipus to think that if he just plays his cards right, he can avoid his fate. But
Oedipus remains a haunting figure *for us* because, for a moment at least, his
thinking propels him out of that ancient outlook. And into disaster.

What Oedipus *does* have reason to do is to avoid killing any older man
and to avoid having sexual intercourse with any older woman. Of course, the
first thing he does on hearing the oracle is to kill a man, old enough to be his
father, who looks a lot like him.[10] He then goes directly to Thebes—
"without passing go"—a state in which the king has recently and

mysteriously gone missing—it is not even known whether he is dead—and he takes in marriage the *possibly* widowed queen, a woman old enough to be his mother, a woman who does not know what happened to her previous husband, a woman who cannot give a full account of what happened to all of her children. If Oedipus wants to avoid his fate, he's certainly off to a good start! Oedipus' acts are so ridiculous that, were his fate not horrific, this would be the stuff of a hilarious comedy.[11]

*   *   *

I do not intend to second-guess Oedipus. It is fatuous to speculate what Oedipus might have done instead. Oedipus is a fictional character, and in the ancient Greek world from which he sprung, there was no such thing as escaping one's fate. Insofar as there is something Oedipus might have done, but didn't, that something wouldn't have led him out of his fate; insofar as there is something which would have blocked fate, that something was not a real option for Oedipus.[12] The point, however, is not to give Oedipus retrospective advice, but to lay out the drama of Oedipus so that we might learn something about ourselves. After all, we do not take ourselves to inhabit a world inexorably ruled by fate. So if we feel some resonances of Oedipus in ourselves, even if *Oedipus* couldn't have done other than he did, *we* may be able to.

So when we ask "Where does Oedipus' 'knowingness' come from?" we are not trying to psychoanalyze Oedipus—as though he were one of our acquaintances whose motives we were trying to figure out—but to trace a certain movement in the human soul whose outcome is a "knowing" stance with respect to the world. Sophocles is offering a diagnosis of "knowingness": both a critique of its thinness as a way of being in the world, and an account of how it comes to take over a culture. And insofar as this "knowingness" presents itself as reason, Oedipus the tyrant becomes—as Plato long ago recognized—Oedipus tyrannized—tyrannized by what *he* takes to be the reasonable movement of his own mind.

Oedipus Tyrannus is a tale of abandonment. Oedipus is abandoned by his parents, and in response he abandons himself to thinking. *He thinks with abandon*. If Descartes ushers in the modern world with the dictum "I think, therefore I am," Oedipus offers this anticipation: "I am abandoned, therefore I think." He acts as though thinking could compensate him for his loss, but since there can be no compensation, the thinking has to become so enthusiastic, and so thin, that it blinds him to any recognition of loss. Thus "knowingness" comes into the world. The powers of the human mind are glorified at just the moment when it becomes too painful to recognize that the mind cannot do all that we would wish. In this sense, Sophocles is offering a critique of *impure* reason—which is all he thought human reason could ever be.

Aside from the fact of Oedipus' abandonment, there is much evidence in the play that this is a big deal for *Oedipus*. We have already seen that one drunk's remark—which anyone else would have taken as seriously as "your mother fucks slaves"—leaves Oedipus with troubling and repetitive thoughts. His reaction is startling. It is one thing to be contemptuous of a drunk's appalling behavior; it is quite another to lose control of one's thoughts and emotions, to leave home never to return. Oedipus here *acts out* his abandonment. Just as the infant Oedipus was expelled from home and state in order to be exposed to his fate on a mountainside, Oedipus the young man expels himself from home and state and exposes himself to his fate by going to Delphi.[13] From there, as we have seen, he reasons his way into incoherence and disaster.

Of course, for Oedipus to have recognized his abandonment, all he had to do was look down. The wounds through his ankles emblazon abandonment in his every step. But the wounds are too painful—psychologically, if not physically—to think about. When, just before the dénouement, the Messenger brings them to his attention, Oedipus says, "Ah, why do you remind me of that ancient grief?" (1033). He calls it "a dreadful brand of shame that I had from my cradle" (1035). And he is indeed *branded*: as the Messenger explains to him, "it was from that occurrence that you got the name you bear" (1036). All Oedipus had to do was to think about the meaning of his name, wonder why anyone would have named him *that* and looked down at his feet. He would have been en route to discovering who he was.

Instead Oedipus displays a stunning lack of curiosity. He is able to go through life with a name which describes an all-too-suspicious wound without pursuing the thought that the meaning of the name might have something to do with him. That is, he uses the naming function of names defensively, to ignore the meaning of his name. Suppose your name were Abandoned Smith. Would you be able to get through life treating your name as just a name, without a serious wonder whether it had descriptive import for you? And when Oedipus, as a young man on the run, arrives in Thebes, he is remarkably incurious about the missing king. Oedipus marries Iocaste, assumes the throne, has four children with her, and raises them to young adulthood. Only then, when the polis is struck with miasma and the Delphic oracle says that Laius' murderer is in the state and must be expelled, does Oedipus seriously inquire into the fate of his predecessor (102–131). "How long is it now since Laius ... vanished from sight by a deadly stroke?" he asks

(558–560). Does it make sense that Oedipus should be asking this question about twenty years after the event?[14]

If there is evidence in the text of Oedipus' phantasies, they are not oedipal, but phantasies of lowly birth. Oedipus is worried that the drunk's taunt is true, that his mother *did* have sexual relations with a slave—that he is the offspring and *that* is why he was abandoned. When Iocaste begs Oedipus to cease his inquiries, he responds, "Do not worry! Even if I prove to be the offspring of three generations of slaves, you will not be shown to be lowborn!" (1062–63). And as she rushes from the stage, Oedipus interprets this as a flight from the recognition of his base origins. "Leave her to take pride in her noble family!" he says bitterly (1070)—and he defiantly concludes (1076–85):

> May whatever burst forth! Even if it is lowly, I desire to learn my origin; but she, for she is proud in woman's fashion, is perhaps ashamed of my low birth. But I regard myself as child of good fortune, and shall not be dishonored. She is my mother; and the months that are my kin have determined my smallness and my greatness. With such a parent, I could never turn out another kind of person, so as not to learn what was my birth.

In the same breath in which he vows to uncover the circumstances of his birth, he declares that, really, he is the child of fortune. On the surface, he is saying that fortune has made him into the kind of person who must find out the truth. But just below the surface is the claim that he owes his real identity to fortune—she is the true mother—so anything he might find out about his biological mother could only have secondary significance. The claim to already know pervades the search to find out.

Oedipus takes the same "knowing" stance with respect to the oracles. As soon as he hears an oracle, he assumes he already knows what it means. So, when Creon comes back from Delphi, he treats the oracle merely as information for practical reason to take into account. This is just the way he treated his own oracle: if he is fated to kill his father, he'd better steer clear of Corinth. Indeed, Oedipus takes the oracle to have "cheated" him, because it did not directly answer his question. And in response Oedipus tries to use his own practical reason to "cheat" his fate. Of course, from Sophocles' point of view, all of this is outrageous impiety: oracles are vehicles of sacred meaning, which are necessarily opaque to human reason. For Oedipus, by contrast, the sacred is treated as a simple extension of the domain of practical reason. The oracle is treated like a hot tip from a very good source.

Oedipus is living a life which denies the possibility of tragedy. He cannot recognize any dimension of meaning other than the one he already knows. It's fine, he thinks, to consult oracles and prophets if they can give useful advice; otherwise they're worse than useless. His way of life shows that he does not take seriously the idea that there may be meaning opaque to human understanding. He even says as much.

When he hears the news of Polybus' death from old age, he says to Iocaste: "Ah, ah, lady, why should one look to the prophetic hearth of Pytho, or to the birds that shriek above us, according to whose message I was to kill my father? ... Polybus lies in Hades, and with him have gone the oracles that were with us, now worth nothing" (963–972). Of course, from a religious perspective, this news could not possibly count against the oracle: it would have to signify that the oracle was somehow not understood and required further interpretation. Oedipus draws the opposite lesson: that there is no point to the activity of interpretation. No sooner does he hear the news than he already knows its significance. In short, Oedipus' confidence in his powers of practical reason shields him from recognition of another realm meaning— and, thus, Oedipus cannot recognize the possibility of tragedy until he is overwhelmed by it.

It has sometimes been claimed that Oedipus is the first philosopher: because of his determination to find out the truth, because of his reliance on human reason in his pursuit, and because he abjures mysticism and obscurantism.[15] But this misses the point. Philosophy, Aristotle says, begins in wonder, or awe. If so, Oedipus cannot get started: he is too busy figuring things out to have any such experience. He is too busy thinking to experience the terror of abandonment, the awe of fate. One may well ask: is that why Oedipus is thinking so hard? Philosophy becomes impossible because the originating act of wonder is too terrible. What takes its place is ersatz: a thin "pragmatism" which purports to offer a solution to any problem. Within this pragmatic outlook, every problem does look solvable. Even the miasma can be attacked "by careful thought" (67). The joker in this deck is that in seeing the miasma as a practical problem, Oedipus remains blind to its divine meaning. Oedipus' practical reason can solve every problem, because it cannot see the problems it cannot solve. They are so meaningless, they cannot even be formulated: thus even dismissal becomes impossible.[16] Oedipus is not the first philosopher; he is the first ersatz-philosopher.

*   *   *

For Sophocles, the point of this tragedy is to beat the audience into submission. The strategy is simple. In the Sophoclean universe there are only two possibilities: *either* one relies rigidly on human reason *or* one submits to a divine realm. In neither position is there room for philosophy, that peculiarly thoughtful response to awe. Before the catharsis, awe is impossible because, like Oedipus, one "already knows"; in the catharsis, one experiences awe, but submission is built in. The tragedy is meant to terrify us out of self-confidence and into religiosity.

It's an emotional one–two punch. First, the audience is softened up with pity. We can feel compassion for Oedipus because he is so human: we can see ourselves reflected in his puffed-up self-importance. But pity also requires a sense of distance. We can see the absurdity in Oedipus' movement of thought, in a way which he cannot. That is one reason why an audience is able to take pleasure in watching a tragedy performed onstage. On the face of it, one might wonder why anybody would want to see the portrayal of human disaster. One reason may be that humans simply enjoy watching dramas of other people being destroyed; but there is also a deeper reason. When we pity Oedipus, we can indulge the illusion that we know how things *really* are. It is *Oedipus*, not we, who is stuck with the partial and distorted perspective. Being in the audience, it is as though we are looking on the world from an absolute perspective.

Then comes the second punch. There comes a moment when we recognize that our pity rests on illusion, the illusion that we know absolutely. But we don't. On this occasion we may well be right that Oedipus is making some disastrous mistakes in his thinking and in his emotional life, but overall we are not fundamentally better off than he is. We each must rely on our own sense of what is reasonable and unreasonable. We can, of course, test our views against those of others, but, then, so can Oedipus! There is always the possibility that our "tests" are as distorted as the views we are trying to test. Of course, this does not mean that anything goes, that one test is as good or as bad as another; nor does it mean that there are no practical steps we can take to test our thoughts and emotions. But it does mean we have to give up the illusion of an absolutely independent perspective from which to check how well our reasoning is going—and this should encourage a certain humility. The luxurious sense of distance required for pity vanishes. And fear becomes real. Precisely because of our humanity, we too may bring down catastrophe.

But there is a crucial difference between the Athenian audience for whom this play was written and ourselves: catharsis has become impossible. The Athenian audience was able to experience what Aristotle called "a catharsis through pity and fear." Tragic fear purged the narcissistic temptation to make inflated claims for humanity, but *only* because the audience had a well-worn path of retreat—to religious awe. For fifth-century

Athenians, tragic consciousness consisted in the recognition that humans lived their lives in the intersection of two realms of meaning, one human, the other divine and opaque. These divine meanings had profound, sometimes catastrophic, consequences for humans, but these meanings were all but humanly incomprehensible.[17] In other words, tragic consciousness takes human life to be powerfully affected by unconscious meaning. For the Greeks those meanings were part of the basic order of the universe—the gods were on Olympus, fate was embedded in the natural order. Formally, this is the same structure as Freud's topographical model, though Freud continues a tradition which begins with Plato of placing this other realm of meaning inside the human psyche. What the Greek poets took to be the castrations and devourings of the gods, Plato took to be artistic representations of lawless, unconscious desires. But this is a difference which makes all the difference.

Catharsis was possible for the Athenian audience because there is relief in submission. Oedipus was abandoned by his parents, but he and his audience were surrounded by the gods. And there is profound comfort in being able to move almost automatically from hubristic overconfidence in human "knowingness" into humble religious submission. But for us that path is blocked. There is no obvious retreat from "knowingness," for there is nothing clear to submit to. We have been abandoned by our parents *and abandoned by the gods*. Since the Enlightenment, modernity has constituted itself around the idea that there are no categories which are simply given— that even the most basic categories like fate, family, nation must be legitimated before the tribunal of human reason, and cannot simply be handed down as part of the basic moral order of the universe. There seem to be no fixed categories which are simply handed down from beyond. There seem to be no meanings to our lives, no values, which are exempt from our critical scrutiny. This is what Nietzsche meant when he had his madman proclaim that God is dead.[18] How can there be relief when everything is up to us? We seem thus to be trapped in the Oedipal position of "knowingness," with no place to go.

That is one reason, I suspect, we hold on to "knowingness" in spite of our boredom and irritation with it: the "alternative," if there is one, is nameless. This, I think, is one of the more profound reasons that Freud-bashing has recently become so popular in our culture. Of course there are other reasons, some of them good ones: a reaction against a previous hagiography of Freud and inflated claims for psychoanalysis; the demand for cheaper and more biochemical forms of treatment; and so on. But it is striking that none of the Freud-bashers tries to give an account of the fundamental human phenomenon to which all of psychoanalysis is a response: the fact of motivated irrationality. Humans regularly behave in ways they do not well understand, which cause pain to themselves and others, which violate their best understanding of what they want and what they care about. And yet, for all of that, there is, as Shakespeare put it, method in their madness. These behavings are not simply meaningless intrusions into ordinary life: they express some motivational state, they have a "logic" of their own. Once you recognize the phenomenon of motivated irrationality, you are committed to there being some form of unconscious meaning. This is a fact which is recognized by Plato and Aristotle, by Augustine, Shakespeare, Proust, and Nietzsche. Freud's originality lies only in the systematic ways he worked out this fundamental idea.

Freud-bashers act as though once they have killed Freud, they have no further problem: as though there were no such thing as unconscious meaning which needs to be accounted for. In this way, Freud-bashers are like latter-day Oedipuses, blind to the realm of unconscious meaning, confident that any real human problem can be both posed and solved by the transparent use of practical reason. We can, as Oedipus put it, "hit the mark by native wit," not by what we learn from the birds. In short, Freud-bashing retraces Oedipus' steps, partaking of a manic, Enlightenment defense which does not even acknowledge the problem which psychoanalysis sets out to address.

But this manic defense is collapsing even as I speak. The movement from modern to postmodern consciousness can, I think, be seen as a recreation of the oedipal drama, but without any fixed denouement. Modernity constituted itself with a manic, oedipal defense: even though the gods have left, human reason can take their place. The human mind can create and legitimate all it needs or should want. That is, in response to abandonment, Enlightenment consciousness abandons itself to thinking. One might view the postmodern consciousness as originating in the collapse of this defense. No matter how strident the Freud-bashers, no matter how insistently the culture clings to its "knowingness" and its boredom, oedipal confidence is breaking up before our eyes. Of course, one response to this collapse is pathetic, not tragic: the attempted flight back to postmodern, fundamentalist forms of religious engagement. Another response is the playful, even mischievous, breaking up of traditional forms which one finds in so much postmodern literature, art, and philosophy. Tragedy begins with the recognition that neither response will work for long: that flight is not possible, that breaking up past orthodoxy is itself a defense which will eventually collapse. It is in such intimations that ancient Oedipus, Oedipus the tyrant, still has the power to reverberate deeply in our souls.

Notes

1. There is another fantasy about Asians which is significant: that they are going to engulf us. They will engulf us by sheer numbers—as Secretary of State Dean Rusk intimated in the early 1960s with his classic "a billion Chinese by ..."—or the Japanese will engulf us by taking over our economy, taking over Hollywood, taking over Rockefeller Center, and so on.

2. For example, on election day A. M. Rosenthal wrote: "Am I better off than I was four years ago? No. In a way important to me I am not only worse off than in 1992, but worse than ever before in my adult life. I have been cheated of the opportunity to make a decision satisfactory to me in the choice of President, the single most important privilege of citizenship ... For the first time in my voting life neither major party offered us a choice that pays suitable honor to our intelligence and citizenship"; "Am I Better Off?" *New York Times*, November 5, 1996.

And on the day after the election, Frank Rich wrote:

"Don't you feel better already? Or as a politician might put it: are you better off today than you were 24 hours ago? Here at last is one question the entire nation can answer in the affirmative. Had the election lasted a single moment longer, the country might have started to get nostalgic about Phil Gramm....

"Whom and what did we not get sick of? Aside from the voters, the only people worthy of sympathy in '96 are the candidates' children ...

"What could have made election year '96 more exciting? The year is littered with what-ifs. What if Lamar Alexander, the jes-folks millionaire, had switched from red plaid to silver lamé? ...

"Still those who say the year of campaigning was completely worthless are wrong. If nothing else, I discovered that the year's political rhetoric could be a better cure for insomnia than either counting sheep or playing 'Six Degrees of Kevin Bacon.' Once in bed, eyes shut, the trick is to take the empty yet incessantly repeated candidates' phrases and squeeze as many of them into a single sentence as possible." Frank Rich, *New York Times*, November 6, 1996.

3. Editorial, *New York Times*, July 19, 1996.

4. Or, to take a final example, consider the hoax which NYU professor of physics Alan Sokal played on the editors of the literary-critical journal *Social Text*. What makes this hoax a milestone in the history of academic hoaxes is not that Professor Sokal publicly declared his article to be a hoax the moment it was published, but that the hoax was right there on the surface of the article. *Anyone* who read the article with understanding would have to recognize it as a joke. (Paul Boghossian and Thomas Nagel made this point in a letter to *Lingua Franca*.) The article mentions "the axiom of choice" as though it were part of feminist set theory, when anyone who had taken even the first weeks of an introduction to axiomatic set theory would know that the axiom of choice was simply an elementary axiom concerned with forming sets by selecting members of other sets. It has everything to do with set theory, nothing to do with politics; and that is a flagrantly obvious fact. That is what made this hoax so embarrassing. For the editors, who have long taken a knowing stance with respect to the world, to be able to publish the article, they *could not have known* even the most elementary facts about the areas in which they were publishing articles. The editors were hoist on their own petard of knowingness.

5. For an extended critique of the Freudian reading of *Oedipus Tyrannus*, see Jean-Pierre Vernant and Pierre Vidal-Naquet, *Myth and Tragedy in Ancient Greece* (New York: Zone Books, 1990).

6. Sigmund Freud, *The Interpretation of Dreams*, *SE* 4: 262–263; Lecture XXI, "The Development of the Libido," *Introductory Lectures on Psychoanalysis*, *SE* 16: 331. See Letter 71 to Fliess, October 15, 1897, *SE* 1: 265.

7. See Bernard Knox, "Why Is Oedipus Called Tyrannos?" *Classical Journal* 50 (1954).

8. Sophocles, *Oedipus Tyrannus*, ed. and trans. Hugh Lloyd-Jones (Cambridge, Mass.: Harvard University Press, 1994), lines 33–34. All translations in the text are based on this source.

9. See, e.g., Aristotle, *Rhetoric* II.2.378a31 ff.

10. As Iocaste tells him at 742–743.

11. Note Socrates' demand, at the end of the *Symposium*, that poets ought to be equally good at comedy and tragedy.

12. Thus all such claims of the form "If *only* Oedipus had ____ed, he would have escaped his fate" are either false or empty. See Bernard Williams, *Shame and Necessity* (Berkeley: University of California Press, 1993).

13. He will, of course, expel himself again when he learns of his original abandonment. For Oedipus, "remembering" does not replace, but rather occasions, repetition.

14. I have heard it objected that this is just dramatic license, a device to let the audience know the passage of time. My response: Sophocles is a better poet than that. If all he wanted to do was impart that information, Oedipus could easily have said, "Yes, of course, it's twenty years now since ..."

15. J. Goux, *Oedipus, Philosopher* (Stanford: Stanford University Press, 1993).

16. To borrow Lacan's ironic reading of the second chorus in Antigone: nothing is impossible for man; what he can't deal with he ignores; Jacques Lacan, *The Seminar of Jacques Lacan*, Vol. 7: *The Ethics of Psychoanalysis, 1959–1960*, trans. Dennis Porter (London: Routledge, 1992). p. 275. Cf. the modern descendants: in verificationism, Popperianism, ordinary-language philosophy, these problems are meaningless.

17. See Vernant and Vidal-Naquet, *Myth and Tragedy*, p. 27.

18. Friedrich Nietzsche, *The Gay Science*, trans. W. Kaufmann (New York: Random House, 1974), 125.

CHARLES SEGAL

Life's Tragic Shape:
Plot, Design, and Destiny

REMOVING PRECONCEPTIONS

One of the hardest problems in approaching the *Oedipus Tyrannus* is trying to look at it freshly. To do that, one must remove a few layers of misconception; so I have to begin with a few "nots." This is *not* a play about free will versus determinism. The Greeks did not develop a notion of a universal, all-determining Fate before the Stoics in the third century B.C.E. The human characters are not mere puppets of the gods; no figure in Greek tragedy is. To be sure, the supernatural elements are important: Apollo, the plague, the oracles, Teiresias' prophetic knowledge. But the play does not label any of these as the certain *causes* of suffering. There are no gods on stage, as happens regularly in Aeschylus and Euripides, nor is there the direct confrontation of powerful god and crushed mortal victim that occurs at the end of Euripides' *Hippolytus* and *Bacchae*. For all its concern with prophecy and oracles, the *Oedipus* has a startling modernity precisely because these supernatural elements are not only kept in the background but are also hidden and mysterious.

The issues of destiny, predetermination, and foreknowledge are raised as problems, *not* as dogma. How much control do we have over the shape of our lives? How much of what happens to us is due to heredity, to accidents, to sheer luck (good and bad), to personality, to the right (or wrong) decision

From *Oedipus Tyrannus: Tragic Heroism and the Limits of Knowledge*, 2nd ed. by Charles Segal, pp. 53–70. © 2001 by Oxford University Press.

at a particular crossroads in life, or to the myriad interactions among all of the above? These are the questions that the play raises, and it raises them *as questions*. It shows us men and women who are both powerful and helpless, often at the same moment. Oedipus embodies the human condition in just this paradoxical relation to both open and closed conceptions of life. He is both free and determined, both able to choose and helpless in the face of choices that he has already made in the past or circumstances (like those of his birth) over which he had no power of choice. The play, as one interpreter remarks, shows us the issues of choice and predetermination as "a box of mirrors to bewilder each new generation; the whole tangle is here in this story.... The play offers to each spectator as much as he is capable of seeing."[1]

Although it is customary to group *Antigone*, *Oedipus Tyrannus*, and *Oedipus at Colonus* together as the three Theban plays because they deal with the royal house of Thebes, the three works were not conceived as a trilogy. *Antigone* was written more than a decade before *Oedipus Tyrannus*, and *Oedipus at Colonus* was composed some twenty years after. There are numerous verbal echoes of *Antigone* in *Oedipus Tyrannus* and of both plays in *Oedipus at Colonus*, which self-consciously looks back to these two works. It is helpful, therefore, to have the earlier works in mind when reading the later ones, but esthetically the three works are independent.

Oedipus does *not* have a tragic flaw. This view rests on a misreading of Aristotle (see Chapter 12), and is a moralizing way out of the disturbing questions that the play means to ask. Sophocles refuses to give so easy an answer to the problem of suffering. Oedipus' haste and irascibility at crucial moments (particularly in the killing of Laius) contribute to the calamity but are not sufficient reasons for it nor its main cause.

Finally, the play does *not* end with the self-blinding of Oedipus, but continues afterwards for nearly three hundred lines. These closing scenes are essential for understanding how Sophocles conceives of his hero and should not be neglected.

The tragic effect of the *Oedipus Tyrannus* lies in part in its dramatic irony, long ago observed by Aristotle: what seems to be bringing salvation in fact brings destruction. In the very first scene the Theban priest invokes Oedipus as the "savior" from the plague, when in fact he is its cause. Later, Oedipus will curse his savior, the man who saved him from death when he was exposed on the mountain in infancy (1349–54). Despite all the attempts to avoid the three oracles—the oracles given to Laius in the remote past, to Oedipus some twenty years ago at Delphi, and to Thebes in the present— they all come true. In this perverse-looking situation, every would-be savior in the play is also in some sense a destroyer: Creon with his news from

Delphi, the prophet Teiresias, Jocasta in the past, the two herdsmen, Apollo, and of course Oedipus himself.

The plot that unfolds these events may look like a diabolical trap set for Oedipus by the gods (which is the direction that Jean Cocteau follows in his re-working of the play, *The Infernal Machine*), but Sophocles lets us see these events as the natural result of an interaction between character, circumstances in the past, and mere chance combinations in the present. Nevertheless, by placing the oracles in so prominent a position in the action, Sophocles, from the first scene, makes the question of divine intervention unavoidable. The play forces us to ask where the gods are in this tale of extraordinary coincidences and extraordinary suffering. Even the supernatural element of the oracles operates in a human way.

Typically in Greek tragedy, the gods work through normal human behavior and motivation. They are, one might say, an added dimension of our reality, not an arbitrary negation of reality. What we mean by calling *Oedipus Tyrannus* a tragedy of fate might be more accurately phrased as Sophocles' sense of the existence of powers working in the world in ways alien to and hidden from human understanding. Karl Reinhardt has put the ancient view very well: "For Sophocles, as for the Greeks of an earlier age, fate is in no circumstances the same as predetermination, but is a spontaneous unfolding of daimonic power, even when the fate has been foretold."[2] The play leaves it an open question whether Laius, Jocasta, or Oedipus might have prevented the fulfillment of the prophecies if they had simply done nothing: not exposed the infant, not consulted Delphi, not avoided Thebes, not married an older woman, and so on.

Oracles, moreover, like dreams, are traditionally elusive, and even dreadful prophecies may prove innocuous. Herodotus, for example, tells how the expelled Athenian tyrant Hippias, accompanying the Persian invaders at Marathon in 490 B.C.E., had the "oedipal" dream that he would sleep with his mother. He interpreted the dream to mean that he would be restored to his ancient mother, his native land of Athens, but the vision is fulfilled in a very different way when he loses a tooth in the Athenian soil (Herodotus, *Histories* 6.107). Actual incest is never at issue.[3]

In contrast to Aeschylus, as we have seen, Sophocles' oracles to Laius and Oedipus do not give commands or advice; they simply state the way things are. How things got that way we do not know. All we can say, and all the play shows us, is that the events do work out as the god said they would and that the human figures bring about these events through a chain of actions that contains some striking coincidences but is nevertheless within the realm of possibility. The oracle to Thebes that sets the action in motion, to be sure, does have the form of a command: "Lord Apollo ordered us clearly to drive out the land's pollution," as Creon reports from Delphi (96–97). Yet even this command is not an arbitrary intervention but a statement about the disorder that has spread from the polluted royal house to the whole kingdom. The reasons behind the older oracles that resulted in this disease are left obscure. Equally obscure is the god's choice of the time to reveal the truth. Why did the plague not break out immediately after Oedipus' marriage to Jocasta or after the birth of his children? The chorus asks this question later in its own poetic terms (1211–13): "How, how could the plowed furrows of your father have been able to bear you, miserable man, in silence for such a long time?" We are given no answer other than the fact that such is the shape that Oedipus' life is to have, and in that intermingling of guilt and innocence, responsibility, chance, and character lies the quality that we (following Aristotle) have come to call "tragic."

Sophocles' plot has some faults, which must be confronted frankly. To achieve his dramatic effects he has had to pay a certain price in terms of verisimilitude. We have to accept that Jocasta never before discussed with Oedipus the child she and Laius exposed, that Oedipus never mentioned the encounter at the crossroads, that neither of them ever talked about the scars on his feet, that the sole witness to Oedipus' killing of Laius was also the Herdsman to whom the infant was given for exposure, and that the Messenger from Corinth who reports Polybus' death had received this child from the Herdsman. Critics have also been troubled by the fact that a man of Oedipus' intelligence takes so long to put two and two together to discover the truth, especially after Teiresias has told him that he was the killer early in the play. Modern playwrights, from Corneille to Cocteau, have recast the plot to answer these questions (see Chapter 12).

We also have to accept the facts that the sole survivor and witness simply lied about how many attackers there were (118–19) and that Oedipus is mistaken in thinking that he killed "all" the men escorting Laius (813).[4] And we have to admit that Sophocles has left vague the amount of time that had elapsed between the killing of Laius and this witness' return to Thebes to find Oedipus already in place as king (758–62). During this unspecified interval (see 558–61), Oedipus has managed to defeat the Sphinx, marry Jocasta, and become installed as king of Thebes.

A play is not a novel, and the *Oedipus*' rhythm of action is so gripping, the movement of human emotions so convincing, that these problems do not bother us while we watch or even read the play. If we do stop to think about them (as most viewers or readers do not), they all have plausible answers. Laius' trusted Herdsman who received the child for exposure would be a likely escort for the king on his journey to Delphi. A man who "fled in fear," as Creon says (118), at the attack on Laius would be likely to keep quiet out of fear after finding Laius' killer established as the ruler of Thebes. Being a slave, he is at Oedipus' mercy, and his timidity and vulnerability are clear when we see him interrogated by Oedipus later. Knowing that he failed in his duty to protect his king, he might well have lied about the number of assailants and have taken his time in returning to Thebes to give his report of the event. We may compare the Guard of the *Antigone* (223–36), who makes a point of his reluctance to report to an irascible King Creon the bad news that his orders have been disobeyed and the corpse of Polyneices has been buried.

Oedipus might be faulted for having neglected to investigate Laius' killing and for not even knowing where it happened (113–14). Yet the play shows that the old king's death was primarily the Thebans' concern in the period before Oedipus assumed the throne, and that they were too preoccupied with the Sphinx to carry out a full inquiry. Oedipus asks why they did not investigate more thoroughly, and he receives a satisfactory answer (128–31, 558–67). Newly installed as king of a country ravaged by a monster, involved with a new marriage and new duties, he would naturally have been far more concerned about the future than the past. By the time of the present action, Laius' murder was regarded as past history, and this is clear from the way Oedipus speaks of the event. The Sphinx is gone; orderly succession to the throne has occurred; and Thebes has been happy, so far, with its new ruler. The old king is dead; long live the king!

Teiresias' prophetic powers also raise questions. If he has such foreknowledge, why did he not intervene to stop the marriage of Oedipus and Jocasta? Why could he not answer the riddle of the Sphinx himself, and why did he wait so many years to declare Oedipus the killer of Laius? Oedipus raises these last two questions (390–98, 558–68), and they are never answered explicitly. When Oedipus asks Creon point blank why Teiresias delayed so long in naming Laius' killer, Creon merely says that he does not know (569). This is probably Sophocles' way of telling us to leave the matter there; the ways of prophets are obscure, after all, and especially the ways of prophets as awesome as Teiresias.

Teiresias' foreknowledge suggests the existence of forces and patterns in our lives beyond the limit of ordinary human knowledge. As to his failure to help Thebes earlier, we have to accept it as a given piece of background detail that the Sphinx could be defeated only by the young hero from outside, not an old prophet within. Monsters too have ways of their own, and Sophocles, in any case, is careful to keep details about this fabulous beast very vague.

Teiresias' silence, however, is a more interesting matter. Even in the play's present action, Oedipus has to force him to speak; so it is not surprising that he volunteered no information in the past, assuming that he knew the truth even then. Even if Apollo had revealed the truth to Teiresias long ago (a fact that we have no right to assume), presumably the god also revealed that he, Apollo, would bring it to light in his own sweet time.

Speculation along these lines is fruitless, and one runs the risk of disregarding the conventions of the literary form and falling into the so-called documentary fallacy, treating the events as if they occur in real life and not as part of a literary construct that creates a circumscribed, artificial world. For the artifice to work, however, it has to be plausible, and the meeting between the king and the prophet is indeed plausible, both dramatically and emotionally. They interact as two such leaders might be expected to respond in a crisis involving power and authority. They are both proud, stubborn, and hot-tempered men; both are defensive, and both are led to say more than they initially intended. Oedipus, we know from the prologue, will be energetically exploring every means available to do what Apollo has commanded, and find the killer. The unsolved murder of his predecessor makes him uneasy and suspicious about a conspiracy to overthrow his own regime. Teiresias too is not used to being contradicted, let alone accused. We may compare the irascible Teiresias of *Antigone* (1048–94) and the aged and blind Oedipus himself in *Oedipus at Colonus*.

It is part of the tragic pattern that Teiresias' very silence raises Oedipus' suspicions of his collusion with Creon, as we see when Oedipus interrogates Creon about Laius' death, the inquiry to Delphi, and Teiresias' silence in the past (555–65). Here again possible divine causation interacts naturally and plausibly with human motivation. Viewed as part of a divine plan, Teiresias' silence can be attributed to his knowledge, as a divine prophet, of what is bound to happen, regardless of whether he speaks. Viewed in terms of normal human behavior (especially in the volatile political atmosphere of a late fifth-century *polis*), Oedipus is justified in assuming that Creon and Teiresias have conspired to accuse him of the murder and seize power for themselves.

The silence of Teiresias has another and perhaps more profound meaning, and this relates not so much to character as to moral structure. His presence, like that of the oracles, implies the existence of some kind of order operating mysteriously in our world. The most general Greek term for this order is *dikê*, often translated as "justice" but actually connoting something like "path of retribution." It implies a process that undoes violence by violence. It restores a balance in the world order that has been upset by action beyond the limits of allowable human behavior, and this restoration of order may bring with it even greater suffering than the original crime. In simplest terms, the crimes of Oedipus, regardless of his moral guilt, are a source of this kind of disorder, and the violence that he has released will return to his world and his life.

The stain of blood that Oedipus carries from killing Laius, even though he acted in self-defense, is the source of a pollution that results in the plague. Sophocles' audience would naturally assume that the plague was sent by the gods, and Apollo's command, which Creon reports from Delphi in the first scene, confirms this. Sophocles, however, never actually says that the gods have sent the plague. In its mysterious and probably supernatural origin, the plague is both the causal agent of the process of purging disorder that the Greeks called *dikê* and the sign that this process is under way.

Oedipus' pollution would normally require ritual purification and exile from his city, at least for some years. As Bernard Williams has recently suggested, the Greek view of this aspect of Oedipus' situation may be compared with our law of torts rather than with criminal law.[5] According to criminal law (both ours and the Greeks') Oedipus is not a criminal, for he acted in self-defense in the one case and in ignorance in the second. Yet his actions (which would correspond to his liability under the law of torts) have caused serious damage, in the form of the pollution, from which individuals and the community have suffered, and he must make some kind of requital. In the *Oedipus at Colonus*, Oedipus will in fact successfully argue the legal basis of his innocence before the citizens of Colonus (258–74, 960–99). Unlike the later play, however, *Oedipus Tyrannus* stresses the sheer misfortune and unpredictability of Oedipus' situation rather than questions of legality.

The play clearly distinguishes between the parricide and incest that Oedipus committed in ignorance and the willed act of self-blinding when he discovers the truth (1329–46). This willed and self-chosen punishment also contrasts with his involuntary curse on himself as Laius' killer, which he pronounced early in the play (246–51). At the same time this curse becomes another of the tragic coincidences that stretch Oedipus' sufferings to their fullest possible pitch, for his own zeal to help his city dooms him even more horribly, "to wear out his wretched life wretchedly in utter doom" (248).

At a time of intense interest in issues of causality, motivation, and legality, the play explores the shadowy areas between involuntary crime, religious pollution, moral innocence, and the personal horror in feeling oneself the bearer of a terrible guilt. Oedipus is not completely innocent, but, as a court of human law might measure it, his suffering and the suffering of those around him (Jocasta, their children, and all those who have died in the plague) are far out of proportion to the degree of guilt. Like every great tragedy, the play forces us to rethink our comfortable assumptions about a just world order. Oedipus' tragic heroism consists in taking on himself, by his own hand, a punishment far greater than what the law would require.

The irreducible discrepancy here between what a man has done and what he suffers makes up the play's tragic view of life, a view that presents our control over our circumstances as precarious and our grasp on happiness as always uncertain. Teiresias, in his paradoxical vision-in-blindness, knows this truth but is reluctant to tell it, partly because we do not want to hear it. It is a characteristically tragic wisdom, and as such it must be wrested from him forcibly and received reluctantly, if at all.

In an old tale we find a mythical paradigm for this kind of knowledge and its difficult reception among men. Silenus, a satyr and companion of the god Dionysus, is captured and forced to reveal his knowledge. "Why do you force me to tell what it is better for you not to know?" he asks his captors. "For life is freest of pain when it is accompanied by ignorance of its own suffering ... For mortals, best of all is not to be born" (Plutarch, *Consolation to Apollonius*, 115D). The reluctant silence of Teiresias is akin to the reluctance of this wise demigod of nature; Sophocles echoes the sentiments in a choral ode in his last play: "Not to be born wins every accounting; and by far second best is when born to return there whence one has come as quickly as possible" (*Oedipus at Colonus* 1224–28).

What is at stake in Oedipus' inquiry, then, is not just his personal situation—it is also the makeup of the world and its bearing on the possibility of happiness in human life. Through Teiresias, the oracles, and the puzzlement of the chorus, questions about the orderliness, justice, or chaos of our world will be framed not in the small, petty circumstances of daily life, but in the large civic arena and against the background of the vast natural world. The mountains—especially Cithaeron, which reappears throughout the play, and also Parnassus and Olympus—are in the background, part of the outer frame, as are the places beyond the limits of the mortal world mentioned in the odes, especially the far western realm of death in the first ode (the parodos) and the eternal realm of the gods and their laws in the third (the second stasimon).

STORY AND PLOT

In looking at the remarkable design of the *Oedipus Tyrannus*, we must distinguish not only between the play and the myth but also between the *story* (the totality of the events as they might be told in chronological order) and the *plot* (the events as they appear in the order shown in the play). This play does not tell the whole myth of Oedipus, nor even the whole story of his life; it unfolds as a *plot*, a carefully chosen and constructed sequence of events at one brief, though decisive, crisis in the hero's life. From that point, the play moves both backward and forward to other parts of the myth as a whole. The plot does not give us all the details at once, nor does it present them in a continuous order or as a single, linear development. It reveals fragments, and we, like Oedipus, have to piece these together to make up a coherent narrative.

It is characteristic of Sophocles' selective narration that he reserves his most focused, continuous account of events for the few tense moments surrounding Jocasta's death and Oedipus' self–blinding (1237–85). There is no connected story of Oedipus' life, from his birth to his rule at Thebes, such as Euripides provides in the prologue of his *Phoenician Women*. Instead, the past of Oedipus is a shadowy area of elusive facts submerged in what seems to be remote, mythic time.

The plot structure has two other related effects. First, the events of the past are surrounded by mystery, both because they are so remote and so horrible and because they are recovered so gradually and so painfully. Second, the *process* of the discovery is as important as the *content* of what is discovered. This is a play about how we uncover a hidden, frightful, and frightening past. The rhythm of this process of discovery gives the play its unique power and fascination.

The play's most powerful moments come when the search for knowledge takes two different directions simultaneously. This happens first near the exact center of the play. Jocasta, intending to turn Oedipus away from further pursuit of Teiresias' prophecy, gives him the clue about the triple road that in fact intensifies his search. Later the pattern is repeated when the Corinthian Messenger inadvertently deflects Oedipus from the search for Laius' killer to the search for his own parents. At the end of this scene, Jocasta urges him not to carry his investigation any further (1056–68), but Oedipus is determined to press on, ignorant that the answer to both searches is the same. The following scene closes that gap between the two searches, but to reach that moment of "terrible hearing" (1169) Oedipus again has to wrest knowledge forcibly from one who refuses to tell. It is part of the play's irony that the same action that led to triumph in the past—namely overcoming the resistance of one who knows but won't tell (the Sphinx)—now leads to total disaster.

Telling the Story Backward: Reversible Time

The *Oedipus* is almost unique among Greek tragedies in telling its story in reverse. Nearly every crucial event in the action has already happened. The action is therefore almost all retrospective action—that is, it depicts how the characters (and the spectators too) see and understand in the present events that took place far in the past. It is part of the same effect that the play uses and scrutinizes the different ways in which stories unfold, the different ways in which one may tell one's life story, and the different ways in which such stories are heard and understood. Akira Kurosawa's film *Rashomon* offers a modern analogy. The chief events of Oedipus' life history—his birth, exposure, victories over Laius and the Sphinx, and marriage—emerge piecemeal, from different points of view and in partial, fragmented perspective. Like Oedipus, we as spectators have to reconstruct a hidden past from hints, memories, glimpses.

The play's dislocation of the chronological order of the events makes it hard, if not impossible, for Oedipus to disentangle the riddles of his past.[6] This situation helps explain why a man of his intelligence cannot see the truth and at the same time supports his claims of moral innocence later. It is a subtle but important feature of Oedipus' innocent ignorance that, whenever he tells the oracle that has darkened his life, he reports its two parts in the order incest and parricide; and only after the revelation of the truth does he report the order in which these events actually occurred, parricide and incest.[7] A third conclusion also follows, namely that we have at least to consider the possibility that something in the structure of reality itself lies behind this innocent suffering. This mysterious agent Oedipus calls "Apollo" and modern interpreters call "fate." The play, however, leaves the matter as a question, unresolved but important. Rather than giving a final answer, it shows us the hypotheses of the various characters, including the chorus, to try to account for the suffering.

Because of this way of telling its story, the play is also about narrative. It uses the special privilege of literary texts to reflect on their own artifice and to remind us of the ways in which they can suspend reality to offer an enhanced vision of reality. One of Sophocles' contemporaries, the philosopher and rhetorician Gorgias, wrote, apropos of the effect of tragedy, "He who deceives is more just than he who does not deceive, and the one deceived is wiser than the one who is not deceived."[8] In the case of *Oedipus*, the "wisdom" that we (the "deceived" audience) get comes from accepting the dramatic illusion (the "deception" of the plot) and participating in the special vision of the world that we thus receive. At the same time we know that this vision is real only in a particular sense, as a model of a problem or a hypothesis about our world that we rarely see so sharply focused in our everyday reality.

As part of its wise deception the play also exploits its freedom to tell its story in fragments, in scenes taken out of chronological order, with omissions that are filled in later, and in flashbacks. Art has the power to reverse time and so to let us see, and question, modes of causality that are invisible in "real" life. We are forced to think about the role of the gods and, especially, about the mixture of free choice and necessity in the oracles. If Laius, Jocasta, and Oedipus, for example, had done nothing to avoid the oracles, would they have come true anyway? Or by taking their evasive action did they in fact play into the hands of the gods and bring about the very events that they were trying to prevent? The literary device of telling events out of their chronological order also creates much of Sophocles' celebrated irony: the discrepancy between the larger picture that we, the spectators, see and the small piece visible to the participants who are immersed in the stream of events.

It is revealing to compare Oedipus' story with that of Odysseus, another hero whose myth embraces the whole of a life cycle. The dominant feature of Odysseus' story, as we see it in Homer's *Odyssey*, is commitment to his return from the Trojan War, a successful and ultimately happy journey home, with a clear goal and strong emphasis on the motifs of recovery and rebirth. The dominant feature of Oedipus' story is the tragic shape of a life that is always turning back on itself instead of going forward. He can realize his identity only by losing it, and then gaining it back under the sign of tragic truth.

The continuity of life-movement in the *Odyssey* corresponds to the clarity and forward movement of narrative in the epic form, in contrast to the halting, unpredictable, blocked movements of narrative in tragedy.[9] In the expansive epic frame, narrative is relatively unproblematic because time is unproblematic. Although the *Odyssey* uses retrospective narration (in the flashback of books 9–12), the hero's movement in time is steadily forward, toward his goal. In tragedy, and especially in *Oedipus*, time is constantly bending backward and forward with mysterious gaps and discontinuities. The dangers and limits that surround human life in tragedy make both generational time and narrative time uncertain, unreliable, and complicated. Even though the recognition of the limits of mortality is a major theme in the tale of Odysseus, he is always able to see, and ultimately achieve, his goal of returning to the full life that he left behind. For Oedipus past and future are always getting entangled with each other. In the terrible circularity of his life pattern, he can never pull free of the maimed life in the past.

The almost simultaneous return of the Corinthian Messenger and the Herdsman, who together saved the baby Oedipus many years ago, seems like pure coincidence, but, on reflection, it reveals a coincidence of another kind. Such returns are appropriate to a life story that cannot break free of its past. The past is always returning, in the wrong place. The child returns to the bed and to the "furrows" of his mother, "sowing" where he was "plowed," as Oedipus cries out in his agony near the end (1403–5). The son cast out by the father comes back to meet the father in just the wrong place, and so to kill him. The oracle originally given to Laius keeps returning, different yet always the same, to mark the different stages of Oedipus' life: in infancy, at the end of his adolescence, and in his maturity, when he is king of Thebes. Even a slave at the periphery of a famed king's' life turns out to be a part of a mysterious rhythm of fatally overlapping returns. The Herdsman who saved the infant Oedipus reappears at his passage between adolescence and adulthood to witness his killing of Laius, and then again at his tragic passage from full maturity to the blindness and debility of his remaining years. Sophocles does not use these coincidences as proof of a deterministic universe, but rather as the facts of an uncanny pattern of a life that is thus marked as tragic.

TIME, ORACLE, AND RIDDLE

The riddle has had the opposite role from the oracle in Oedipus' life: it is a source of pride and confidence, whereas the oracle is a source of anxiety and helplessness. Oedipus can resolve the simultaneity of the various stages of life intellectually, in the *verbal* play of the riddle; but he acts out the horror of that fusion of separate generational stages in living a *life* that fulfills the oracle.

While the answer to the riddle implies the complete span of a full life, from infancy to extreme old age, the oracle would prevent this life from getting started at all. In the form in which the oracle is given to Laius, it would first prevent a child's begetting and then prevent his growing up. Oedipus solved the riddle by seeing through its metaphor of feet for motion through life. But of course his own feet hold the secret or riddle of his life, and that is partly because of the oracle, which led his parents to bind his two feet together into one so that he, unlike the creeping, walking, and cane-using generic human being of the riddle, would never walk at all, never move through any of the stages of life.

The circular movement of time in the play itself is governed by the oracles. The first oracle is in the present: the command from Apollo at Delphi to drive out the land's pollution, the cause of the plague. It is a command and thus is directed to the future, but of course it points us back to the past, the killing of Laius nearly twenty years ago. The second oracle, given to Laius and Jocasta, referred to future events: the father will die at the hands of his son. But at the point when Jocasta tells Oedipus about this oracle, it belongs to the remote past (711–23). And Oedipus fears that his own oracle, the third, which he received at Delphi many years before, will point to his future, but when he relates it to Jocasta (787–93) it is in fact already part of his past: he has already fulfilled it in his journey from Delphi to Thebes.

Measuring and counting time is one of Oedipus' major actions onstage. But his attempts to organize time into logical patterns collapse in the terrible uncertainty of time in his own life. Rather than serving as something he can find out and know with certainty, time becomes an active force that finally has "found him out" as the one who "long ago" made that "no-marriage marriage" in which "birth and begetting," origins and maturity, were fused together (1213–15). Rather than becoming an aid to human understanding, time seems to have a kind of independent power that blocks knowledge. It blocks future knowledge because its course has been hidden from the actors. It blocks past knowledge because memory selects and filters. Both the Messenger of the blinding scene and the Old Herdsman attribute this failure of knowledge to erroneous or partial memory. Even Oedipus cannot accurately remember the details of his fatal encounter with Laius. As we now know, he did not kill all of the travelers.

Time in the play expands and contracts, producing effects of vagueness or density by turns. It is both the indefinite and inert passing of years and the single moment of crisis in decision and action, the irreversible turning point of a mans life. When he can still hope that the truth will leave his present view of himself intact, Oedipus describes himself as defined by his "kindred months" in a slow rhythm of waxing and waning, becoming small and great (1082–83). But in fact he is defined by the abrupt catastrophe of a single day (351, 478) which makes him both "great and small," king and beggar, in one instant.

Time can have an unexpected fullness, as in Creon's account of past events in the prologue. Here there seems to be an indefinite interval between the death of Laius and the arrival of Oedipus to vanquish the Sphinx, an interval in which the Thebans cannot investigate the death of their king because the Sphinx compels them to consider only the immediate present, "to regard the things at our feet, letting go the things unclear" (130–31). It is as if this major crisis in the present life of the city retreats to the obscurity of remote happenings, far beyond living memory. But Oedipus, in his confident belief that he can overcome time, announces, "But I shall bring these things to light *from their beginning*" (132).

When Oedipus thinks that he has in fact reached through time to reveal this hidden truth, the time surrounding Laius' death again has the same vagueness and fullness. Interrogating Creon, whom he now takes to be the agent of the murder, Oedipus asks, "How much time before did Laius [die]?" and Creon replies, "Times [or, years] great and old would be measured" (561). As in the prologue, that critical event, the death of the king and the father, becomes surrounded by an aura of remote, almost mythical time, as if it were an act belonging to primordial beginnings (as in one sense it did) and not to a specific historical moment in the life of an individual and a city.

Oedipus is confident that he will uncover these "beginnings" (132), but origins are more mysterious and harder to fathom than he knows. At the climactic moment of discovery this vague temporal duration is suddenly ripped open by the electrifying flash of the single moment of "terrible hearing" (1169). In the relaxed seasonal tempo of the Herdsman's life on Cithaeron, before Oedipus' birth, only the changes of summer and winter, without events, mark the passage of time (1132–39). But tragic time has a wholly different aspect: it is the single instant of decision and recognition that suddenly overturns an entire life.

It is a gift of prophetic knowledge to see time past, present, and future in a single vision. Calchas, the prophet of the *Iliad*, "knew what is and what will be and what is before" (*Iliad*, 1.70), and the prophetess Theonoe in Euripides' *Helen* "understood the divine things, those now and all those to come" (*Helen*, 13–14). In *Oedipus*, we the audience first see Oedipus in the present as king and ruler, supplicated by his people because they hope he will save them. But Teiresias, a little later, sees the Oedipus of the future, a blind man tapping his way with his stick. Jocasta and the Herdsman see Oedipus as a helpless newborn, his feet pierced so that no one will take him up. Jocasta, again, in her last words on stage, sees the whole course of Oedipus' life as one of utter misery, which she marks in her final words for him, "ill-fated" and "ill-starred" (1068, 1071). The spectator at the play enjoys the omniscient perspective of the gods; like the gods, he or she can see Oedipus in all three roles at once: the powerful king, the accursed and helpless infant, and the blinded sufferer.

TRACKING THE PAST: THE RETURN OF THE REPRESSED

Knowledge in the play results from bringing separate, individual past events together into a single moment in the present. The major action of the play gets under way with Oedipus' inquiry about Laius' murder: "Where will be found this trace, hard to track, of the ancient crime?" (108–09). The investigation is like a hunt, and Oedipus assumes that he can follow a set of tracks that will lead smoothly from the present to the past, Laius' past. But the road into the past proves not to be single but manifold, just as Oedipus himself proves to be not one but many. Thus instead of the "track" leading to only one object of inquiry, Laius' killer, it in fact diverges into several different paths—triple roads, one could say: Oedipus' origins, his exposure by his parents, his marriage with Jocasta.

This collocation of the past with the present receives vivid dramatic enactment in nearly every scene of the play. Indeed, the very first line of the play, Oedipus' address to the suppliant citizens, juxtaposes old and new: "O children, of Cadmus old the newest brood." Visually too this scene displays a combination of ages in the onstage presence of youths, mature men, and elders, as the priest explains a few lines later (15–19). Oedipus is himself an anomalous composite of "young" and "old," since the incest makes him the member of two generations simultaneously.

This combination of past and present again becomes ominously vivid in Teiresias, the old man who belongs to the past and sees the "truth" that threads the past together with the future. "The future events will come of themselves," he says at the beginning of his interview with Oedipus, "even if I conceal them in silence" (341). Instead of thus "concealing" the future, he brings it visually before our eyes in his dreadful prophecies. Although he is not understood by Oedipus in the present, Teiresias warns him that he does not see "where he is" (367, 413–15) or the future sufferings that await him (427–29, 453–60). Those sufferings consist precisely in the fact that the incest makes the father "equal" to his children (424) and removes the boundaries that should separate those stages and activities of life. Oedipus, Teiresias reveals, unknowingly inhabits this fearful simultaneity of different generations (456–60).

Oedipus' intelligence, Jocasta suggests later, lies in "inferring the new by means of the old" (916). When Oedipus does in fact bring together the "old things" of his remote infancy and early manhood with the "new things" of his present life and circumstances, he knows himself as both king and pollution, both the savior and the destroyer of Thebes.

As Oedipus begins his "tracking" of Laius' killer (109), he needs, as he says, a *symbolon* (221), a word usually translated as "clue." But the word also means a "tally," one of two parts of a token that fit together to prove one's rightful place. In Sophocles' day Athenians used such "tokens" for admission to the law courts. The investigative skill that Oedipus will demonstrate, then, consists in fitting pieces together. The word *symbolon* also has another meaning, namely the "token" left with a child exposed at birth to establish later proof of his identity. The word carries this sense in the tale of Ion, another foundling, dramatized in Euripides' *Ion*, a kind of Oedipus story in reverse. Presented with an old basket that contains the secret of his origins, Ion hesitates to open it and examine the "tokens from his mother" (*Ion*, 1386) lest he turn out to be the child of a slave (1382–83: see *Oedipus* 1063, 1168). He finally decides to take the risk ("I must dare," *Ion* 1387), just as Oedipus does ("I must hear," *Oedipus* 1170), although with very different results. Oedipus' initial objective, the public task of "tracking down" a killer by a "clue" (*symbolon* in the juridical sense), turns into the personal and intimate task of finding the "birth token" (*symbolon* in the personal sense) that proves his identity.

As the forward rhythm of the push for knowledge begins to accelerate, there is a retarding movement that pulls back toward not knowing, toward leaving origins veiled in darkness. It is appropriately the mother who takes on this retarding role. She who stood at the first beginning of his life and (as we learn) was involved in a contradictory pull between the birth and the death of her new child (1173–75), would still keep him from the terrible knowledge and thus save his life. Like all great plots, the play combines forward movement to the end with the pleasure of delaying and complicating that end.[10]

This simultaneity of past and present belongs to the uncanny or the inexplicable, which is represented onstage in the blind prophet, behind whom stands the remote and mysterious Apollo. Although Oedipus' first act is to consult Apollo at Delphi, he never integrates what Apollo and Teiresias know into what he knows. Not until it is too late does he put the oracles together by means of that intelligence whose special property is to join past and present, to connect disparate events, facts, experiences, and stages of life. Oedipus' failure in logical deduction was one of Voltaire's objections to the structure of the play.[11] But what an Enlightenment rationalist would consider a fault the ancient dramatist would consider the very essence of the tragic element. Oedipus uses his human knowledge primarily in conflict with the divine, to block, deny, contradict, or evade it.

Knowledge veers not only between human and divine, but also between active and passive. Human knowledge is actively sought and willed as the achievement of man's intellectual power. The divine knowledge comes, it seems, by chance, on precarious and unpredictable paths. The mysterious divine knowledge is conveyed through the blind prophet, but its truth is confirmed only by sheer coincidence, through the arrival of the Corinthian Messenger and then the Old Herdsman, and it is the latter who provides the clinching piece of knowledge, Oedipus' identity as the exposed child of Laius and Jocasta.

This first mention of the one person who "knows" anything is as vague as possible: the man is only "some one man" (118). Oedipus makes no attempt to refine this description. Instead he shifts attention from "some one *man*" to "some one *thing*" in his next line: "What sort of thing [did he say]? For one thing would find out many things for learning" (120). The grammatical categories of language itself—the ease of shifting from masculine to neuter (one man, one thing) and from singular to plural (robber, robbers)—lead the investigators astray from what will finally solve the mystery. Language itself encourages their deception and leads them to pursue what will prove to be, in one sense, misinformation.

Forgotten for some six hundred lines, more than a third of the play, this individual resurfaces when Jocasta's reference to the triple roads (another numerical problem) arouses Oedipus' anxiety (see 730). "Alas, these things are now clear," he says. "Who was it who spoke these words to you, my wife?" (754–55). "A house-servant," Jocasta replies, "who arrived as the only one saved" (756). This last phrase is the other, objective side of Creon's more subjectively oriented description of the man as "having fled in fear" in the prologue (118).

"Did he then happen to be present in the house?" Oedipus presses on. "No," answers Jocasta, and she explains how the servant came to Thebes, found Oedipus already in possession of the royal power and Laius dead. Touching Jocasta's hand, he asked to be sent to the fields (761) and to the pastures of the flocks, so that "he might be as far as possible out of sight of the town" (755–82). The contrast between "house" and "field" (756–61) recalls Oedipus' first specific point of investigation of Laius' death: "Was it in the house or in the fields?" (112). The sole witness there was "some one man" (118); and Creon's phrase calls attention to his unitary identity.[12] His initial "oneness," like that of Oedipus, bifurcates ominously into two. He is both the house-servant (756) and the herdsman in the "pastures of the flocks" (761). He is both the man described by Jocasta and the man described by Creon, both the man who survived the attack on Laius and the killer/rescuer of the infant Oedipus on Cithaeron. Like Oedipus, he is both an insider ("reared in the house," as he describes himself later [1123]) and an outsider, one who was sent from the house to the fields or the mountains.

This figure of the Herdsman/escort plays an increasingly important role in giving different perspectives on what really happened in the past. He possesses "knowing" (*eidôs*) from a crucial "seeing" (*eide*, 119), a play on the similarity be tween the Greek words that is not easily translated into English. But here, as throughout the drama, this wordplay is charged with meaning. At this early point in the work, when Creon mentions this lone survivor for the first time, his reported story introduces the identification of knowing with seeing that is central to the play's concern with ignorance and perception. Later, Jocasta tells Oedipus that it was after the Herdsman "saw" Oedipus on the throne that he requested from her a kind of absence of vision, to be "out of sight of the house" (762). Like Oedipus in the future, he seeks a combination of negated vision ("out of the sight of the house") and exile from his place in house and city (see 1384–94, 1451–54).

Still confident as the king searching for the killer of Laius, Oedipus then sends for this only survivor of the attack on the former king (765–770).

It is sheer coincidence that this man should also be the one whom Laius
entrusted with killing the infant Oedipus. And yet that coincidence points to
a deep necessity. Oedipus cannot progress in his role as ruler of the city,
whose task it is to discover and expel Laius' killer, until he has solved the
mystery of his own origins. He cannot solve the mystery of the plague until
he solves the mystery of himself. To do that, he has to force the figure who
holds the missing piece to recapitulate earlier stages of his life as well: when
he changed from house-servant (756) to herdsman (761) and when, in that
earlier role, he had brought Oedipus to both doom and salvation on Mount
Cithaeron (see 1349–52). The philosopher George Santayana remarked that
those who do not know history are compelled to repeat it. The Oedipus
works out the truth of this statement on the level of personal history: not to
know who you are is to be compelled to search ceaselessly for your origins.

The Herdsman's life also parallels Oedipus' in the spatial shift that he
undergoes in the course of the play, from house to mountain, from a figure
at the center of the palace life (756) to a figure at the margins of the city, in
the mountains. The Herdsman's life, governed by such different rhythms of
space and time,: proves to be causally related to Oedipus' life and also similar
to it in form, parallel in its course but also more vaguely outlined and set into
a larger and remoter frame. The condensation of Oedipus' life into the hour
or two acted out in the "real" time of the performance has behind it, like a
larger shadow, the more expansive movement of the Old Herdsman's passage
through time.

The Herdsman recurs as a figure dimly parallel to Oedipus in his life's
movements and spontaneous impulse of pity and fear, but he is also in one
essential point the opposite of Oedipus. The first specific detail given about
him is his "flight in fear" in order to be "the only one saved" (118, 756). His
characteristic mode of action in the play is evasion through running away.
This is what he did when Oedipus attacked Laius at the crossroads and what
he did again when he returned from that episode to find Oedipus ruling in
Thebes. It is also what the young Oedipus did when he heard his destiny
foretold him at Delphi (788–97). The Herdsman repeats the pattern a third
and last time on the stage when Oedipus interrogates him. He tries to escape
by evasion or denial (see 1129–31, 1146–59, 1165), but now Oedipus
compels him to face and speak the "terrible" that is contained in the truth
(1169–70).

This last scene brings Oedipus and his shadowy double together,
finally, on the stage. Now neither of them can run away. Yet this coming
together shows us their characteristic divergence. The Herdsman is a slave
(see 1123; also 764, 1168), and he seeks survival by denying the truth. The
king goes to meet his destiny head-on, confronting the "necessity" that

comes from his oracles, even if that confrontation means his death. The Herdsman/slave at the crossroads was "the only one to be saved" (756). King Oedipus is ready to become the communal victim, the *pharmakos* or scapegoat, whose single death saves the whole city (see 1409–12), although his submission to Creon in the final scene prevents that pattern from being completely realized.[13]

NOTES

1. Philip Vellacott, *Sophocles and Oedipus* (Ann Arbor: University of Michigan Press, 1971), 108.

2. Karl Reinhardt, *Sophocles*, trans. H. and D. Harvey (Oxford: Basil Blackwell, 1979), 98.

3. In the *Dream Analysis* (*Oneirokritika*) of Artemidorus (second century C.E.) even intensely sexual incest dreams have nonsexual meanings: see John J. Winkler, *Constraints of Desire* (New York: Routledge, 1990), 37–44, with his translation of Artemidorus 1.79 on pp. 213–15.

4. The contradictions and problems of the plot have been observed as early as Voltaire's *Letters on Oedipus* (see Chapter 12). For a convenient list see John J. Peradotto, "Disauthorizing Prophecy: The Ideological Mapping of *Oedipus Tyrannus*," *Transactions of the American Philological Association* 122 (1992), 7–8, 13–14. The Old Herdsman's lie is rather unusual because when Sophocles lets his characters lie, he generally provides some hint in their manner of speech or some warning to the audience that a lie is being told. Presumably in this case he could assume that the story was sufficiently familiar so that the audience would know the truth and realize the falsehood of the Herdsman's statement. The reference to his "fear" here, as well as his frightened request of Jocasta of which we are told later (758–64), also helps us to recognize that he must be lying.

5. Bernard Williams, *Shame and Necessity* (Berkeley and Los Angeles: University of California Press, 1993), 62–67. R. Drew Griffith, *The Theatre of Apollo: Divine Justice and Sophocles' Oedipus the King* (Montreal and Kingston: McGill-Queen's University Press, 1996), especially 45–69, argues, unconvincingly, that Oedipus is justly punished by Apollo for killing Laius. No one would suggest that Oedipus is innocent, and he himself immediately recognizes his polluted state as Laius' possible killer (*Oedipus* 813–23). Yet an approach, like Griffith's, which focuses on this single act, leaves out all the overdeterminations and complications that the play interweaves as essential parts of Oedipus' life story (the oracles, the plague, the coincidences, the rhythm of discovery, the character of all the figures in the story, and so on). The fragmented reading of the type that Griffith proposes reduces the richness of the tragedy to a banal moralization. For the range of interpretation in this question of Oedipus' guilt, it is worth noting that Griffith's thesis is just the reverse of the theory of Frederick Ahl, *Sophocles' Oedipus: Evidence and Self-Conviction* (Ithaca, N.Y.: Cornell University Press, 1991), that Oedipus did not kill Laius at all.

6. See Brian Vickers, *Towards Greek Tragedy* (London: Longmans, 1979), 500–13; also Adrian Poole, *Tragedy: Shakespeare and the Greek Example* (Oxford: Blackwell, 1987), 100–104.

7. Incest and parricide: 791–93, 825–27, 994–96; parricide and incest: 1184–85, 1288–89, 1357–59, 1398–1408.

8. Gorgias, fragment 82 B23 in Hermann Diels and Walther Kranz, eds., *Die Fragmente der Vorsokratiker*, vol. 2, 6th ed. (Berlin: Weidmann, 1952), pp. 305–6. The fragment is quoted by Plutarch, *On the Glory of the Athenians*, chap. 5, 348C.

9. For some suggestive remarks on the differences between time and life patterns in epic and tragedy see Bennett Simon, *The Family in Tragedy* (New Haven: Yale University Press, 1988), 13–21, 59–60.

10. See Peter Brooks, "Freud's Masterplot: A Model for Narrative," in his *Reading for the Plot* (New York: Vintage Books, 1985), 90–112, especially 101–9.

11. Voltaire, *Letter on Oedipus*, Letter 3.

12. The phrase "Laius dead" (in the same metrical position) occurs in both Creon's account of the Herdsman/escort (in 126) and in Jocasta's tale of how this man came to her after he saw Oedipus on the throne (in 759). The verbal echo is an other link between the two passages and perhaps also serves to remind us of the causal connection, still hidden from all but this herdsman, between Laius' death and Oedipus' "power" or kingship (*kratê*, 758).

13. On the scapegoat pattern, see below, Chapter 9, with note 11, and Chapter 12; also my *Dionysiac Poetics and Euripides' Bacchae*, 2nd ed. (Princeton, N.J.: Princeton University Press, 1997), 42–45.

Chronology

496–497 B.C.E.	Sophocles born.
468	With *Triptolemus*, beats out Aeschylus in first triumph at the dramatic competition.
460-450	Sometime during these years, presents *Ajax*.
443-442	Serves in government office; duties include the supervision of tributes paid to Athens by its allies.
442-441	Presents *Antigone* in Athens, winning first prize at the City Dionysia.
441-440	Elected one of ten generals to put down a revolt on the island of Samos.
440-430	Presents *Trachinian Women*. In 430 the plague breaks out in Athens.
429-425	*Oedipus Rex* performed sometime during this period.
419-410	*Elektra* presented.
409	Presents *Philoctetes*, which wins first prize.
407/406	Sophocles dies.
401	*Oedipus at Colonus* presented posthumously by Sophocles' grandson.

Contributors

HAROLD BLOOM is Sterling Professor of the Humanities at Yale University. He is the author of 30 books, including *Shelley's Mythmaking* (1959), *The Visionary Company* (1961), *Blake's Apocalypse* (1963), *Yeats* (1970), *A Map of Misreading* (1975), *Kabbalah and Criticism* (1975), *Agon: Toward a Theory of Revisionism* (1982), *The American Religion* (1992), *The Western Canon* (1994), and *Omens of Millennium: The Gnosis of Angels, Dreams, and Resurrection* (1996). *The Anxiety of Influence* (1973) sets forth Professor Bloom's provocative theory of the literary relationships between the great writers and their predecessors. His most recent books include *Shakespeare: The Invention of the Human* (1998), a 1998 National Book Award finalist, *How to Read and Why* (2000), *Genius: A Mosaic of One Hundred Exemplary Creative Minds* (2002), *Hamlet: Poem Unlimited* (2003), *Where Shall Wisdom Be Found?* (2004), and *Jesus and Yahweh: The Names Divine* (2005). In 1999, Professor Bloom received the prestigious American Academy of Arts and Letters Gold Medal for Criticism. He has also received the International Prize of Catalonia, the Alfonso Reyes Prize of Mexico, and the Hans Christian Andersen Bicentennial Prize of Denmark.

FRANCIS FERGUSSON was a leading theorist of drama. A member of the National Institute of Arts and Letters, Fergusson taught at Bennington College, Princeton University, and Rutgers University. His books include *The Idea of a Theatre* and *Dante's Drama of the Mind*.

E. R. DODDS was Regius Professor of Greek at Oxford University. An editor of many classical texts, Professor Dodds's own books include *The Greeks and the Irrational, Pagan and Christian in an Age of Anxiety*, and an autobiography, *Missing Persons*. Dodds maintained a life-long interest in mysticism, serving as president of the council of the Society for Psychical Research in the early 1960s.

THOMAS GOULD taught Greek literature and philosophy at Yale University. In addition to his translations, Professor Gould wrote the books *Platonic Love* and *The Ancient Quarrel Between Poetry and Philosophy*.

BERNARD KNOX taught classics at Yale University for many years before becoming the director of Harvard's Center for Hellenic Studies in Washington, DC. Now emeritus, Professor Knox is the author of numerous published articles and books, including *The Oldest Dead White European Males* and *The Heroic Temper: Studies in Sophoclean Tragedy*. He edited *The Norton Book of Classical Literature*.

REBECCA W. BUSHNELL is dean of the School of Arts and Sciences and professor of English at the University of Pennsylvania, where she teaches courses on tragedy and early modern English culture. Her most recent book is *Green Desire: Imagining Early Modern English Gardens*.

FREDERICK AHL is professor of classics at Cornell University and a Stephen H. Weiss Presidential Fellow. His books include *Metaformations: Soundplay and Wordplay in Ovid and Other Classical Poets* and *Sophocles' Oedipus: Evidence and Self-Conviction*.

PIETRO PUCCI is Goldwin Smith Professor of Classics at Cornell University. His most recent books are *The Song of the Sirens and Other Essays* and *Odysseus Polutropos: Intertextual Readings in the Odyssey and the Iliad*.

MARTHA C. NUSSBAUM is Ernst Freund Distinguished Professor of Law and Ethics at the University of Chicago Law School. A prolific scholar, Professor Nussbaum has published award-winning books in a range of disciplines, most recently, *Frontiers of Justice: Disability, Nationality, Species Membership* and *Hiding From Humanity: Disgust, Shame, and the Law*.

JONATHAN LEAR is John U. Nef Distinguished Service Professor at the Committee on Social Thought and in the Department of Philosophy at the University of Chicago. Trained in both philosophy and psychoanalysis,

Professor Lear is the author of numerous books, most recently, *Therapeutic Action: An Earnest Plea for Irony* and *Freud*.

CHARLES SEGAL was Walter C. Klein Professor of the Classics at Harvard University. The author of many books on Greek tragedy and Greek and Roman poetry, he received the Prix de Rome at the American Academy in Rome. Professor Segal was a senior fellow at the Center for Hellenic Studies and served as president of the American Philological Association.

Bibliography

Ahl, Frederick. *Sophocles' Oedipus: Evidence and Self-Conviction.* Ithaca, NY: Cornell University Press, 1991.

Bowra, Sir Maurice. *Sophoclean Tragedy.* Oxford: Clarendon Press, 1944.

Burkert, Walter. *Oedipus, Oracles, and Meaning: From Sophocles to Umberto Eco.* Toronto: University of Toronto Press, 1991.

Bushnell, Rebecca W. "Speech and Silence: *Oedipus the King.*" In *Prophesying Tragedy: Sign and Voice in Sophocles' Theban Plays.* Ithaca, NY: Cornell University Press, 1988.

Cameron, Alister. *The Identity of Oedipus the King: Five Essays on the Oedipus Tyrannus.* New York: New York University Press, 1968.

Dawe, R. D., ed. *Sophocles: The Classical Heritage.* New York: Garland, 1996.

Dodds, E. R. "On Misunderstanding the *Oedipus Rex.*" *Greece & Rome,* 2nd ser., 13, no. 1 (April 1966): 37-49.

Eagleton, Terry. *Sweet Violence: The Idea of the Tragic.* London: Blackwell, 2002.

Easterling, Patricia E., ed. *Cambridge Companion to Greek Tragedy.* Cambridge: Cambridge University Press, 1997.

Fergusson, Francis. *The Idea of a Theater.* Princeton: Princeton University Press, 1949.

Gellie, George. *Sophocles: A Reading.* Melbourne: University of Melbourne Press, 1972.

Girard, René. *The Violence and the Sacred.* Trans. P. Gregory. Baltimore, MD: Johns Hopkins University Press, 1979.

Gould, Thomas. "The Innocence of Oedipus: The Philosophers on *Oedipus the King*." Pt 3. *Arion* 5, no. 4 (Winter 1966): 478-525.

Griffith, R. Drew. *Theater of Apollo: Divine Justice and Sophocles' "Oedipus the King."* Montreal: McGill-Queen's University Press, 1996.

Jebb, Richard C. *Sophocles: The Plays and Fragments.* Third Edition. Cambridge: Cambridge University Press, 1893.

Jones, John. *On Aristotle and Greek Tragedy.* London: Chatto and Windus, 1962.

Kaufman, Walter. *Tragedy and Philosophy.* New York: Doubleday, 1968.

Kirkwood, G. M. *A Study of Sophoclean Drama.* Ithaca, NY: Cornell University Press, 1958.

Kitto, H. D. F. *Poiesis: Structure and Thought.* Berkeley and Los Angeles: University of California Press, 1966.

———. *Sophocles: Dramatist and Philosopher.* London: Oxford University Press, 1958.

Knox, Bernard M. W. *The Heroic Temper: Studies in Sophoclean Tragedy.* Sather Classical Lectures, Vol. 35. Berkeley and Los Angeles: University of California Press, 1964.

———. *Oedipus at Thebes: Sophocles' Tragic Hero and His Time.* New Haven, CT: Yale University Press, 1957.

———. "Introduction." In *Sophocles: The Three Theban Plays*, translated by Robert Fagles, 115-135. New York: Viking, 1982.

Lattimore, Richmond. *The Poetry of Greek Tragedy.* Baltimore, MD: Johns Hopkins University Press, 1958.

Lear, Jonathan. "Knowingness and Abandonment: An Oedipus for Our Time." In *Open Minded: Working Out the Logic of the Soul.* Cambridge, MA: Harvard University Press, 1998.

Nussbaum, Martha C. "Sophocles' *Oedipus Tyrannus*: Freud, Language, and the Unconscious." In *Freud and Forbidden Knowledge*, edited by Peter L. Rudnytsky and Ellen Handler Spitz, 42-71. New York: New York University Press, 1994.

O'Brien, Michael J., ed. *Twentieth-Century Interpretations of "Oedipus Rex."* Englewood Cliffs, NJ: Prentice-Hall, 1968.

Paolucci, Anne. "The Oracles Are Dumb or Cheat: A Study of the Meaning of *Oedipus Rex*." *Classical Journal* 58 (1963): 241-47.

Pucci, Pietro. *Oedipus and the Fabrication of the Father.* Baltimore, MD: Johns Hopkins University Press, 1992.

Reinhardt, Karl. *Sophocles.* Trans. D. and H. Harvey, New York: Barnes and Noble, 1978.

Rudnytsky, Peter L. *Freud and Oedipus.* New York: Columbia University Press, 1987.

Rudnytsky, Peter L. and Ellen Handler Spitz, eds. *Freud and Forbidden Knowledge.* New York: New York University Press, 1994.

Segal, Charles. *Oedipus Tyrannus: Tragic Heroism and the Limits of Knowledge.* 2nd ed. New York: Oxford University Press, 2001.

———. *Tragedy and Civilization: An Interpretation of Sophocles.* Cambridge, MA: Harvard University Press, 1981.

Stinton, T. C. W., "*Hamartia* in Aristotle and Greek Tragedy" (1975). In *Collected Papers on Greek Tragedy*, 143-185. Oxford: Clarendon Press, 1990.

Van Nortwick, Thomas. *Oedipus: The Meaning of a Masculine Life.* Norman: University of Oklahoma Press, 1998.

Vernant, Jean-Pierre and Pierre Vidal-Naquet. *Myth and Tragedy in Ancient Greece.* Trans. J. Lloyd. New York: Zone Books, 1990.

Waldock, A. J. A. *Sophocles the Dramatist.* Cambridge: Cambridge University Press, 1951.

Webster, T. B. L. *An Introduction to Sophocles.* Oxford: Oxford University Press, 1936.

Whitman, C. H. *Sophocles: A Study of Heroic Humanism.* Cambridge, MA: Harvard University Press, 1951.

Wilamowitz, Tycho von. *Die dramatische Technik des Sophokles. Philologische Untersuchungen*, 22. Berlin: Weidmann, 1917.

Williams, Bernard. *Shame and Necessity.* Berkeley and Los Angeles: California University Press, 1993.

Winnington-Ingram, R. P. *Sophocles: An Interpretation.* Cambridge: Cambridge University Press, 1980.

Woloch, Alex. "The Prehistory of the Protagonist." Afterword in *The One vs. the Many: Minor Characters and the Space of the Protagonist in the Novel.* Princeton, NJ: Princeton University Press, 2003.

Woodard, T. M., ed. *Sophocles: A Collection of Critical Essays.* Englewood Cliffs, NJ: Prentice-Hall, 1966.

Acknowledgments

Fergusson, Frances; *The Idea of a Theater*. © 1949 Princeton University Press, 1977 renewed PUP. Reprinted by permission of Princeton University Press.

"On Misunderstanding the *Oedipus Rex*" by E.R. Dodds. From *Greece and Rome*, 2nd Series, vol. 13, no. 1 (April 1966), pp. 37–49. © 1966 by Cambridge University Press. Reprinted with the permission of Cambridge University Press.

"The Innocence of Oedipus: The Philosophers on *Oedipus the King*" by Thomas Gould. From *Arion* 5, no. 4 (Winter 1966), pp. 478–525. © 1966 by *Arion*. Reprinted by permission.

"Introduction to *Oedipus the King*" by Bernard Knox. From *The Three Theban Plays*, trans. Robert Fagles, pp. 115–135. © 1982 Viking Press. Reprinted by permission.

"Speech and Silence: *Oedipus the King*" by Rebecca W. Bushnell. From *Prophesying Tragedy: Sign and Voice in Sophocles' Theban Plays*, pp. 67–85. © 1990 by Cornell University Press. Used by permission of the Publisher, Cornell University Press.

"Oedipus and Teiresias" by Frederick M. Ahl. From *Sophocles' Oedipus: Evidence and Self-Conviction*, pp. 67–102. © 1991 by Frederick Ahl. Used by permission of the Publisher, Cornell University Press.

"Introduction: What Is a Father" by Pietro Pucci. From *Oedipus and the Fabrication of the Father*: Oedipus Tyrannus *in Modern Criticism and Philosophy*, pp. 1–15. © 1992 by The Johns Hopkins University Press. Reprinted with permission of The Johns Hopkins University Press.

"The *Oedipus Rex* and the Ancient Unconcious" by Martha C. Nussbaum. From *Freud and Forbidden Knowledge* edited by Peter L. Rudnytsky and Ellen Handler Spitz, pp. 72–95. © 1994 by New York University. Reprinted by permission.

"Knowingness and Abandonment" reprinted by permission of the publisher from *Open Minded: Working Out the Logic of the Soul* by Jonathan Lear, pp. 32–55, Cambridge, Mass.: Harvard University Press, Copyright © 1998 by the President and Fellows of Harvard College.

"Life's Tragic Shape: Plot Design, and Destiny" by Charles Segal. From Oedipus Tyrannus: *Tragic Herosim and the Limits of Knowledge*, pp. 53–70. © 2001 by Oxford University Press, Inc. Reprinted by permission of Oxford University Press, Inc.

Every effort has been made to contact the owners of copyrighted material and secure copyright permission. Articles appearing in this volume generally appear much as they did in their original publication with few or no editorial changes. In some cases foreign language text has been removed from the original essay. Those interested in locating the original source will find bibliographic information in the bibliography and acknowledgments sections of this volume.

Index

Abandonment theme
  in *Oedipus Rex*, 195–196, 200,
    206
Aeschylus
  and the divine, 36–37
  Oresteia, 25, 80
  plays, 57–58
  Prometheus, 2
  Septem, 21
  Seven Against Thebes, 39
  Supplicants, 130
  and tragedy, 63, 205, 207
Ahl, Frederick, 228
  on Teiresias' assistance to
    Oedipus, 105–140
Ajax, 225
Anger of God, The (Lactantius), 41
Antigone
  Creon in, 19, 51, 91–92,
    101–102, 113, 122, 209
  creation of city-state in, 79
  hereditary curse in, 21, 40
  Tiresias in, 96, 99, 210
  tragedy in, 27, 60, 65, 87, 206
Archidamian War
  period of, 26
Aristophanes
  choruses, 26
  Frogs, 25, 131
  Knights, 133

Peace, 129
Wasps, 132
Aristotle
  and the divine, 34
  on freedom, 55
  Nicomachean Ethics, 19, 65
  and philosophy, 198
  Poetics, 10, 18, 59–61, 64–65,
    156
  Rhetoric, 19, 113, 115–116, 119,
    130–131
  De Sophisticis Elenchis, 113
  on Sophocles' chorus, 7
  on the tragic poet, 13–14,
    17–20, 32, 49, 59–67, 69, 71,
    80–81, 85, 175–176, 199,
    201, 206, 208
Artemidoros
  on dreams, 155, 158–173, 175
  incest and fortune, 158–165,
    167–170
  studies of, 158–159
Assoun, P.L., 142
Athens
  citizens of, 7–8, 13, 22, 25–26,
    92–94, 106, 129–133,
    199–200
  law, 23, 44–46, 80, 109
  plague in, 57–58, 77
  slaughter of Melians, 46

symbolism, 26
tributes to, 12, 73, 78–79, 207
Augustine, St., 201
De libero arbitrio, 42, 82–83

Bacchae (Euripides), 205
Beckett, Samuel
plays of, 28
vision of, 17–29
Bergson, Henri, 83
Blake, William
humanism, 1
Bloom, Harold, 227
introduction, 1–4
on the guiltlessness of Oedipus,
1–4
Bowra, C. Maurice
on the Gods, 22, 97
Burke, Kenneth, 9
on language as symbolic action,
12, 14–15
Bushnell, Rebecca W., 228
on Oedipus' failure to tell own
story, 91–104

Characters of *Oedipus Rex*
speeches, 15
and the tragic action, 13–14
Chorus in *Oedipus Rex*
function of, 7–9, 15, 26, 49, 105,
111–115, 135, 176, 212
praise of Teiresias, 122–123
questions of, 8–9
songs of, 15, 100–101, 105–107,
113
view of Oedipus, 19, 26, 42, 76,
87–88, 92, 95, 97, 101–102,
106–113, 116, 208
Christian
philosophers, 55–57, 82–84
theory of decision, 51
tragedy, 22–23, 26, 42

Cicero
On Fate, 83
Cleon
Creon compared to, 132–133
death, 132
leadership, 131–133
Clinton, William, 184–185
Cocteau, Jean, 11, 86, 208
Machine Infernale, 73–74, 207
Coleridge, Samuel Taylor
on the unity of action, 12
*Constraints of Desire: The
Anthropology of Sex and Gender in
Ancient Greece, The* (Winkler),
158–159
Cratylus (Plato), 124
Creon (*Oedipus Rex*), 4
as champion, 129–132
and Cleon, 131–133
interpretation of the oracle, 105,
107–108, 112, 114, 123,
125–126, 191–193, 197,
206–11, 217, 221
Oedipus' treatment of, 17, 19,
26, 74, 78, 98, 105, 130–131,
134, 191–92, 223
politic advice, 86, 91, 94–98,
100, 105, 112–113
rhetoric, 133, 138
taunts, 39, 101, 119
violence of, 51, 88
Croce, Benedetto, 83

Dacier, André
influence on French dramatists,
20
Dawe, R.D.
on *Oedipus Rex*, 113, 122,
129
Delphi in *Oedipus Rex*
and Apollo's sanction, 91, 108,
196

and Creon, 112, 133, 191, 197,
    206–211, 216–217
and Laius, 39, 74
and the oracle, 95, 99, 125, 194,
    196–197, 206–211, 220
silence, 92–93
Descartes, René, 195
Dodds, E.R., 148, 228
on the nihilism in *Oedipus Rex*,
    1, 17–29, 31–32, 50
Dowd, Maureen, 184

Edipe (Voltaire), 73
Ehrenberg, Victor
on *Oedipus Rex*, 21, 26, 129, 130
Elektra, 225
Emile (Rousseau), 161
Engels, Friedrich, 83
Epicurean theory
of unconscious fears, 158,
    170–173, 175–176
Euripides, 75
    Bacchae, 205
    Hippolytus, 205
    ironies, 11
    Orestes, 129, 131
    Phoenician Woman, 39, 213
    plays of, 7, 58, 219
    Trojan Women, 36
    use of tragic theater and ritual
        forms, 10–12, 26, 63, 135,
        205

Fairbairn, W.R.D., 178
Fergusson, Francis, 227
    The Idea of a Theater, 73
    on Oedipus as ritualistic scape-
        goat, 5–16
Festival of Dionysos in *Oedipus Rex*
    and the chorus, 9
    tragic theater of, 10, 12
    vegetation ceremonies, 6, 12

Fontenrose, Joseph, 133
Foucault, Michel
    History of Sexuality, 158
France, Anatole
    Penguin Island, 84
Frazer, James George, 73
Freud, Sigmund
    on dreams, 156, 159–162,
        168–169
    The Interpretation of Dreams, 47,
        72–73
    Oedipal complex, 1–2, 4, 22, 24,
        27, 50, 88, 142, 148–149,
        156–158, 165–167, 176–177,
        188–189, 201
    psychoanalysis, 142, 200–201
Frogs (Aristophanes), 25, 131

Girard, René, 96
    Violence and the Sacred, 74
Gods in *Oedipus Rex*
    greatness of, 2, 8, 151
    jealousy of, 6
    oracles, 21, 23, 39–40, 74, 76,
        81–83, 91–92, 94–95,
        98–101–102, 105–106, 108,
        111, 114, 123, 125–126, 129,
        141, 144–147, 149–151, 191,
        194, 196–198, 205–212,
        214–216, 220
    protests of, 4
    respect of, 26, 95, 97
    silence of, 92
    tragedy of, 1, 5
    and the treatment of man,
        17–18, 21–25, 32–33, 37–39,
        43, 48–53, 58–59, 74, 87
    truth and answer, 9, 11, 57
Goethe, Johann Wolfgang, 67
Gomme, A.W.
    on the Gods, 22
Gorgias, 214

Gould, Thomas, 228
　on the innocence of Oedipus,
　　31–70
Greek
　dramatists, 20, 25, 72, 85
　and dreams, 155–158, 161–162,
　　164, 168
　imagination, 11
　literature, 26, 78, 80–81, 88,
　　122, 132, 138, 142–143, 149
　moralists, 35, 82–83
　notions of pollution, 43, 45–47,
　　49, 211
　tragedy, 9–12, 14, 22–24, 26, 31,
　　33–37, 39, 59, 63, 67–69,
　　71–75, 95, 116–117, 130,
　　148, 175, 177, 189, 194–195,
　　200, 205, 207, 210, 213
Grene, David
　version of *Oedipus Rex*, 2

Hamlet (Shakespeare), 1
　and prayer, 9
Hebrew Bible
　Gospels of, 1, 26–27
Hegel, Georg Wilhelm Friedrich
　view of tragedy, 2
Hellenistic thought
　creation of, 22
　philosophers, 55
Herodotus, 81, 93
　Histories, 207
　oracles, 110
Hippocrates of Cos, 80
Hippolytus (Euripides), 205
Histories (Herodotus), 207
History of Sexuality (Foucault), 158
Homer, 2
　and the divine, 34–39, 71, 138
　heroes, 22
　Iliad, 1, 26, 35–39, 81–82
　Odyssey, 215

Hoover, J. Edgar, 86
Human nature and destiny mystery
　in *Oedipus Rex*, 6–7, 21–22,
　　27–28, 38, 50–53, 71–75,
　　81–83, 86–89, 95, 141–142,
　　145–49, 192, 194–197,
　　205–206

Idea of a Theater, The (Fergusson),
　73
Iliad (Homer), 1
　Achilles in, 26
　power of divinity in, 34–39,
　　81–82
Imagery in *Oedipus Rex*
　of Oedipus as a physician, 80
　sensuous, 15
Instructing the Orator (Quintilian),
　132
Interpretation of Dreams, The
　(Freud), 47
　destiny of Oedipus the King,
　　72–73

Jocasta (*Oedipus Rex*), 3, 23, 39, 138
　child, 21, 77, 99, 114, 162, 208,
　　211, 218, 220
　comfort of Oedipus, 47, 50, 197,
　　213
　dismissal of the prophecy,
　　76–77, 83, 86, 88, 99–100,
　　120, 123, 207, 216, 219, 221
　impiety, 9
　marriage, 40, 91, 156, 193, 196,
　　207–209, 218
　motives, 108, 110, 112
　pleas, 52, 98
　suicide, 4, 42, 49, 53, 213
Johnson, Samuel, 25

Kant, Immanuel
　thought, 23, 157

King Lear (Shakespeare), 1
Kirkwood, G.M.
  on *Oedipus Rex*, 21, 24, 40
Klein, Joe
  Primary Colors, 186–187
Klein, Melanie, 177–177
Knights (Aristophanes), 133
Knox, Bernard, 228
  on fatalism in *Oedipus Rex*,
    21–22, 26, 40–41, 48
  on Oedipus' freedom to choose
    truth, 50–51, 71–89, 148
Kurosawa, Akira, 214

Lactantius
  The Anger of God, 41
Laius (*Oedipus Rex*), 2
  crimes of, 40
  description of, 107, 110, 133,
    144, 162
  oracle, 21, 23, 39–40, 74, 76–77,
    81–83, 94, 215, 216
  quest for slayer, 13
  slaying of, 13, 22–23, 39–45,
    49–53, 58–59, 74, 78, 86,
    91–92, 94, 96, 98, 106–115,
    120–121, 123, 126–127, 143,
    145–146, 150–51, 156, 192,
    194, 196–197, 206–211,
    213–214, 216–222
Language of *Oedipus Rex*, 3
  and silence, 92, 97–98
  and the tragic action, 13–14, 42,
    77, 80, 150, 220–221
Laws (Plato), 61, 65
Lazarus, R., 178
Lear, Jonathan, 228–229
  on Oedipus' fantasies, 183–203
Lévi-Strauss, Claude, 81
Lewis, R.G., 109
Libero arbitrio, De (Augustine), 42
  human will in, 82–83

Lucretius
  of unconscious fears, 170–172,
    174–176

Macbeth (Shakespeare), 85
Machine Infernale (Cocteau), 73–74,
  207
Malraux, André, 2
Marx, Karl, 83
Miller, Gilbert
  on tragic form and ritual form,
    10–11
Milton, John
  Paradise Lost, 82
Modern detective story
  compared to *Oedipus Rex*, 21
Moralia (Plutarch)
  God's silence in, 92–94
Morris, Dick, 185

Nicomachean Ethics (Aristotle), 19,
  65
Nietzche, Friedrich, 1
  cosmic void of night, 9
  limitation of art, 4, 7, 15
  unconscious meaning, 200–201
Nihilism
  in *Oedipus Rex*, 17–29
Nussbaum, Martha C., 228
  on the ancient unconsciousness
    in *Oedipus Rex*, 155–181

Odyssey (Homer), 215
Oedipus (*Oedipus Rex*)
  accusations of, 120–122,
    126–129, 134–135, 191–193,
    210, 221
  agon between Tiresias, 9,
    14–15, 80, 96–98, 105–140,
    190
  anger of, 118–122, 124,
    126–128, 190–193

birth, 40, 48, 99, 213–214, 216, 218–220, 222
consciousness, 148, 188
curse, 106–113, 121
death, 205–224
destiny of, 20–23, 27, 32–33, 37–45, 48–53, 63, 66–67, 71–76, 81–83, 86–89, 95, 101, 141–142, 145–146, 149, 192, 194–201, 205–206
failure to tell own story, 91–104
fantasies, 27, 183–203
fear of lowly birth, 72–73, 126, 138, 183–203
freedom to choose truth, 18, 21, 23, 41, 51–53, 71–89, 100–101, 122, 124–125, 148–149, 188, 205–224
Gods' plan for, 17–20, 22–25, 32, 37–39, 43, 48–51, 58–59
guiltlessness of, 1–4, 24, 124, 137–138
human love of, 9
and incest, 11, 19–22, 40, 42, 47, 49–53, 59, 71, 74, 91, 124, 126, 134, 141–143, 145–146, 156–157, 176, 190, 210–211, 214, 218
innocence of, 21, 23, 31–70, 99, 123, 208, 211, 214
interventions, 32–33
moral faults of, 19–21, 23, 79, 87, 109, 210
and patricide, 19–24, 39–45, 47, 49–53, 58–59, 71, 74, 78, 91, 96, 98–99, 114–15, 118, 123, 126, 134, 141–143, 145–146, 150–151, 156, 176, 196–197, 206–211, 214, 216–217, 221–222
protests, 4

religious authority, 110, 120, 198
ritualistic scapegoat, 5–16, 223
self-blinding, 2, 4, 8, 11, 13, 14, 22–23, 27, 42, 44, 49, 87–88, 96, 102, 124–26, 128, 133, 144, 146, 206, 210–211, 213, 217–218
speeches, 15, 28, 77, 80, 92, 100, 103, 106–111, 122, 219
Oedipus at Colonus
Creon in, 43
hereditary curse in, 21
human condition in, 28, 87, 103, 206, 210–211
innocence in, 39–40, 42–43
notions of pollution, 44–45
Oedipus's death in, 49, 82
On Fate (Cicero), 83
Oresteia (Aeschylus), 25
crime and punishment in, 21, 80
Orestes (Euripides), 129, 131

Paradise Lost (Milton), 82
Paradox
in Oedipus Rex, 205–224
Parsons, F.J.
on Rhetoric, 130–131
Peace (Aristophanes), 129
Peloponnesian War, 75, 106
Penguin Island (France), 84
Pericles (Oedipus Rex)
death, 131
Funeral speech, 78
Persian War, 75
Philoctetes, 225
Phoenician Woman (Euripides)
the Gods' will in, 39, 213
Plato, 2, 26
Cratylus, 124
and the divine, 34, 38, 82, 84, 200–201

on freedom, 55–57
Laws, 61, 65
notions of pollution, 44, 46–47, 68
on patricides, 24, 50
Protagoras, 79
on tragedy, 52, 63–69, 95, 116, 132, 195
Plot of *Oedipus Rex*
and incest, 156
and reversible time, 213–216, 220
structure, 213
and the tragic action, 13–14, 18, 39, 49–50, 71, 80, 85–86, 126, 207–208, 212–213
Plutarch, 212
Moralia, 92–94
Poetics (Aristotle), 10, 18
concept of peripeteia, 156
and tragedy, 59–61, 64–65
Primary Colors (Klein), 186–187
Prometheus Vinctus (Aeschylus)
tragedy in, 27
Protagoras
The State of Things in the Beginning, 79
Protagoras (Plato), 79
Proust, Marcel, 201
Psychoanalysis
identification with Oedipus, 183–184, 195
myths, 184
theories of, 142, 200–201
Pucci, Pietro, 228
on the possibility of truth in *Oedipus Rex*, 141–154

Quintilian, 137
Instructing the Orator, 132

Reinhardt, Karl

on *Oedipus Rex*, 148–149, 207
Republic (Socrates)
tragedy in, 55, 57, 65–66
truth in, 124
Rhetoric (Aristotle), 19, 113
and decisions, 115–116, 119
reviews of, 130–131
Rousseau, Jean-Jacques
Emile, 161
Rudnytsky, Peter, 157

Safire, William, 184
Santayana, George, 222
Sartre, Jean Paul, 11
Schelling, Friedrich, 148
Segal, Charles, 102, 149, 229
on the paradox of *Oedipus Rex*, 205–224
Seligman, M.E.P., 181
Septem (Aeschylus), 21
Seven Against Thebes (Aeschylus)
the Gods' will in, 39
Shakespeare, William, 201
Hamlet, 1
King Lear, 1
Macbeth, 85
plays of, 20
religion in, 25
Socrates, 138
on freedom, 54–55, 57–59, 84
on evil, 46–47, 52
Republic, 55, 57, 65–66, 124
and tragedy, 63–67, 113, 115–116
Sophisticis Elenchis, De (Aristotle), 113
Sophocles
audience, 6–7, 94, 198–200
childhood, 75
chronology, 225
death, 25
fatalism, 31–70

and immoral themes, 21
irony, 4, 48, 111, 120, 215
precursor to psychoanalysis, 2
use of tragic theater and ritual
    forms, 10, 12–13, 17–18, 22,
    24, 26
State of Things in the Beginning,
    The (Protagoras), 79
Stravinsky, Igor, 73
Suppliants (Aeschylus),
    130
Symbolism
    and the action, 12, 15, 141
    of Athens, 26
    of human intelligence, 27

Teiresias (Oedipus Rex), 8
    agon between Oedipus, 9,
        14–15, 80, 96–98, 105–140,
        190–191
    anax, 113–115
    assistance to Oedipus, 23,
        77–78, 95
    Oedipus' suspicions against, 19,
        119–120, 122–23, 127–128,
        134–135, 191–192, 210
    reluctance of, 86–88, 91, 102
    rhetoric, 116–19, 121, 133, 138,
        205, 207–209, 213, 219–20
    silence of, 92–94, 96–97, 129,
        209–210, 212
    and the truth, 122–25, 128, 135,
        155–145, 147, 149–150, 210
Thebes in Oedipus Rex, 206
    citizens, 105–106, 111, 113, 123,
        126, 138, 144–146, 190–191,
        219, 221
    founder, 144–145
    interest in, 9
    Oedipus' palace in, 6–7, 87, 94,
        106, 110, 196, 208–209, 213,
        216, 222

peril of, 6, 8, 14, 117–18, 121,
    219
plague in, 74, 91, 106, 108, 114,
    205, 211, 222
savior of, 19, 23–24, 50–51, 78,
    88, 95–96, 99, 129, 189–190,
    192–194, 207, 219
War in, 106
Themistocles, 93–94, 97
Thucydides, 26, 75, 131
Thyestes
    tragic hero, 18–20, 62–63,
        65–66
Trachiniae, 225
    closing lines of, 25
Trachinian Women, 225
Tragedy in Oedipus Rex
    of destiny, 21–22, 27–28, 32,
        50–53, 63, 66–67, 71–75,
        81–83, 86–89, 141–142,
        145–149, 192, 194–201,
        205–206, 214–216
    of heroic humanism, 1, 6, 8,
        18–20, 52
    of honored Gods, 1, 5
    and human action, 9–10, 12–15,
        17–18, 21–22, 26, 42
Triptolemus, 225
Trojan Women (Euripides), 36
Truth in Oedipus Rex
    and the Gods, 9
    and Oedipus, 18, 21, 23, 50–51,
        71–89, 124–125, 148–149,
        205–224
    possibility of, 141–154
    and Teiresias, 122–125, 128,
        135, 144–145, 147, 149–150,
        210

Vernant, Jean-Pierre, 149–150
Violence and the Sacred (Girard),
    74

Voltaire, 4, 220
  Edipe, 73

Waldock, A.J.A.
  on *Oedipus Rex*, 21, 24
Wasps (Aristophanes), 132
Whitman, Cedric, 1
  on *Oedipus Rex*, 21, 26, 40
Whitman, Walt, 3
Wilamowitz, Theodor, 18, 31
Williams, Bernard, 211

Winkler, John J,
  *The Constraints of Desire: The
  Anthropology of Sex and Gender in
  Ancient Greece*, 158–159
Winnicott, Donald, 178
Women of Trachis, The, 45, 225
  chorus in, 48

Yeats, William Butler
  translation of *Oedipus Rex*,
  73–74